HITCHCOCK'S BLONDE

Hemlock Books

England

PICTURE CREDITS: *Alison Hamilton, Warner Brothers, Paramount Pictures, Universal, Metro-Goldwyn-Mayer, United Artists. Any omissions will be corrected in future editions.*

Visit our website:
www.hemlockbooks.co.uk

First published in 2009 by
Hemlock Books Limited,
The Bristol Office,
2 Southfield Road,
Westbury-on-Trym,
Bristol
BS9 3BH

A CIP catalogue record for this book is available from the British Library.

ISBN 978-0-9557774-0-0

Design by Hemlock Books Limited.

Printed in Great Britain by the MPG Books Group, Bodmin and King's Lynn.

The real story behind a macabre and secret obsession..

Grace Kelly and Alfred Hitchcock

John Hamilton

Acknowledgements

There is a myth that writing is a solitary pursuit but in this case, nothing could be further from the truth. I owe an enormous debt to the writers, critics, journalists and film students who blazed a trail before me and whose work has been identified in the Bibliography. Singling out the most significant of these is an impossible task but if I were pushed to make recommendations for further reading, I would point to Patrick McGilligan's *A Life in Darkness and Light* and Donald Spoto's *The Dark Side of Genius* in relation to Alfred Hitchcock and, for Grace Kelly, James Spada's *The Secret Lives of a Princess* and Robert Lacey's *Grace*.

I would also like to acknowledge the contribution made by the staff and facilities of the British Film Library, and my publishers at Hemlock Books—in particular Denis Meikle, who brought to the manuscript a raft of skills and experience I fear I will never acquire. Thanks go to Jane, whose efforts did not go unnoticed, to my lovely wife for working so diligently on the photos and for her unflinching commitment and belief, and to Patrick Allen, Euan Lloyd, Gil Taylor and Gordon Hessler for sharing their enthusiasm and knowledge of the subject-matter. I could not let this opportunity slip by without a word of thanks to the staff of the Intercontinental, who made the months in Düsseldorf glide past, and Gerard Gallagher and Simon Harvey, 'silent partners' in the best possible way.

CONTENTS

This one is for Alison, it matters because she does.

'Pygmalion at once fell in love with his creation—he thought it was so beautiful, and he clothed the figure, gave it jewels, and named it Galatea!'

(Thomas Bulfinch: The Age of Fable or Beauties of Mythology)

Prologue: It's Only a Movie..

'Blondes make the best victims. They're like virgin snow that shows up the bloody footprints.'

—Alfred Hitchcock to *The Sunday Times* (1973)

On March 19, 1962, the telegraph wires of the Associated Press Agency began to buzz with a news story that was quickly hailed as the 'entertainment scoop of the year'. Within hours, newspapers, radio and television stations around the world had picked up the story and were running with their own versions of the release. But this announcement had not come from the press agent of a major Hollywood star or a powerful Los Angeles producer; it was delivered by a sombre, grey-suited public servant in a small, crowded office in the South of France. Emile Comet, spokesman for the Royal Palace in Monaco, read the official press release proclaiming that Her Serene Highness Princess Grace, formerly Grace Kelly the movie actress, was returning to Hollywood...

> *'...to appear during her summer vacation in a motion picture for Mr Alfred Hitchcock, to be made in the United States. The Princess has previously starred in three films for Mr Hitchcock. The film to start in late summer is based on a suspense novel by the English writer Winston Graham. It is understood that Prince Rainier will most likely be present during part of the filmmaking depending on his schedule and that Princess Grace will return to Monaco with her family in November.'*

M. Comet gave no further details, but he concluded with the solemn thought: 'We are certain she won't make another film after this one.'

Etiquette had required the Palace to make the news public first but Hitchcock's office on the Universal Studio back lot soon released its own version, adding little more in the way of detail but confirming that the film in question was titled *Marnie*. The understated simplicity of the official press releases belied the effort that had gone into the project already. Months of careful negotiations between the Princess's representatives and Hitchcock had been preceded by years of careful plotting and planning as the director schemed to get her back in front of the cameras and re-establish a relationship which had been severed by her marriage to Prince Rainier in 1956.

Reaction from the media was overwhelming; newspapers, periodicals, television and radio stations all led with the story, and in Monaco, the press office was flooded with queries about how much Kelly would be paid and whether or not Hitchcock would show her in the nude. The frenzy continued unabated in the weeks and months following the announcement; in Monaco, Prince Rainier struggled to keep his frustration in check as he faced down a rugby-scrum of reporters from around the world, each with a more personal and intrusive question than the last. In the Bodega Bay location in California where he was filming *The Birds* (1963), a more affable and confident Alfred Hitchcock engaged in light-hearted banter with a press corps that showed up on a regular basis for its updates on *Marnie*'s progress.

Grace Kelly's return to acting meant much more than just a former movie star picking up a film career again after a few years of marriage. Hollywood's principle trade paper, *Variety*, had featured only two women in its list of the 'top box-office stars' for the years 1951–1955: Marilyn Monroe and Grace Kelly. Despite a screen career which had lasted less than five years and consisted of a mere eleven films, Kelly could count four of those among the most successful of 1954 to 1955—both in the US and UK. By 1956, at the age of only 27, she had reached the pinnacle of her craft; every male star in Hollywood wanted her for their leading lady and studios were queuing up to offer her westerns, thrillers, comedies, even musicals. Kelly's last film before her wedding, the musical *High Society*, was a massive hit, grossing $5.8m in the US alone. To put that into perspective, *High Society* outgrossed the

Grace Kelly

combined total for Elvis Presley's film debut *Love Me Tender* and the iconic *Rock Around the Clock*, both released the same year.

At the height of her fame, Grace Kelly had a mantelpiece weighted down with awards, including a Best Actress Oscar and a gold disc for the single *True Love*. While cinema-goers turned out in droves to admire her beauty, her romantic liaisons with the most eligible bachelors in Hollywood had put her face on magazine covers and and her name in gossip columns throughout the world. She was rich, sexy and sophisticated—men wanted her; women wanted to *be* her. When Kelly left Hollywood, she simply swapped one stage for another. In her new life, she displayed the same confidence and aplomb and achieved the same spectacular success. In the years following her wedding, she helped to turn Monaco from a sleepy backwater, which few outside of Europe had heard of or could find on a map, into a byword for glamour and extravagance.

Alfred Hitchcock, the man whom every newspaper lauded as the 'Master of Suspense', was arguably the most famous and influential producer-director from Hollywood's 'Golden Age', and four of his films feature in the American Film Institute's list of '100 Greatest American Movies' (a feat that only Billy Wilder can match). Prominent among the four is *Rear Window* (1954), the second of his collaborations with Kelly. Even before he arrived in Hollywood, Hitchcock had been a huge success in his native Britain after fashioning a series of thrillers that included *The 39 Steps* (1935) and *The Lady Vanishes* (1938), both widely regarded as classics of the genre. He was never awarded a Best Director Oscar, something which irked him throughout his life, but he had the satisfaction of being fêted by cinéastes and critics alike. Equally important for a man who checked the returns from his pictures before he read the reviews, Hitchcock was fabulously wealthy; a number of shrewd business deals, masterminded by agent Lew Wasserman, had given him control (and later ownership) of many of his best-known films, while his subsequent ventures into television with both *Alfred Hitchcock Presents* and *The Alfred Hitchcock Hour* had taken his face and distinctive (and carefully cultivated) brand of dry humour into the living rooms of millions. By the early 1960s, Hitchcock had created a formidable brand name for himself—one that he exploited across film, television and publishing—and with some justification, he could claim to be better known to the public at large than many of the top stars of the day.

The undoubted box-office appeal of the names of Hitchcock and Kelly on a movie marquee might have sparked excitement in the media but there was another side to the story—one that the same reporters may well have suspected but were not in a position even to hint at in their columns. Kelly and 'Hitch' had masterfully manufactured their respective public images, but each was aware of just how fragile was the façade.

Behind his droll screen persona, the real Alfred Joseph Hitchcock was a mass of contradictions, something which he himself recognised but could never quite resolve. The director who was so terrified of being accosted that he would refuse to walk across the studio lot for fear of being spoken to by a stranger was the same man who would stoop to any level for attention. Throughout his career, Hitch would treat the public not only to his celebrated cameos but to a slew of publicity appearances promoting his television shows, ranging from Hitch in drag to Hitch garbed as Little Lord Fauntleroy; later, Londoners were treated to the sight of a Hitch mannequin floating in the Thames (face-up, of course) to promote *Frenzy*.

Hitchcock spent much of his professional and personal life in the company of the most beautiful women in the world, and yet in 1978, he made the astonishingly

Alfred Hitchcock

frank admission to biographer John Russell Taylor that he had been celibate for forty years. It was a confession that certainly did not signal a disinterest in sex—quite the opposite; even the most casual observer of Hitchcock's movies could see that they were created by a man fascinated and excited by the politics of desire. Hitchcock shared this fascination with the viewing public and over the course of his cinematic career, treated himself and his audiences to on-screen depictions of heterosexual and homosexual love, as well as scenes of intercourse, bondage, domination, sado-masochism, necrophilia, rape and strangulation.

Hitchcock's penchant for glacial blondes is well known and he often spoke about the 'fire beneath the ice'. Alma Reville, his wife and lifelong romantic partner, may have represented the motherly qualities that he had looked for in a spouse but, on screen, he was always searching for what he described as the 'drawing room type, the real ladies, who become whores once they're in the bedroom'. This was the template that he had in mind when he cast Grace Kelly in *Dial M for Murder* (1954), a film where the female protagonist has a passionate affair (mostly off-screen) which leads ultimately to brutal murder but whose sense of manners requires her to introduce her lover to her husband and then sit quietly at home while they set off on a boys' night out together.

Kelly came to Hitchcock having played prim and proper in her two previous pictures and movie-goers, if they considered her at all, would have thought of her as demure and aloof, but the screen image was a long way from the reality..

Grace Kelly was ambitious and determined, and she had the *savoir-faire* to use whatever advantages nature had given her to get ahead. Away from the screen, she flirted, teased and, if the studio gossip is even halfway true, slept with a string of men who were in a position to influence her career. Zsa Zsa Gabor, Kelly's contemporary in Hollywood and no stranger to romantic liaisons herself, claimed in her autobiography that, 'Grace had more boyfriends in a month than I had in a lifetime!' To the wives and girlfriends in Hollywood, she was viewed as a threat to domestic bliss. Kelly biographer Jane Ellen Wayne records the actress saying, 'I was thought to be a danger.. The worst was when Hollywood columnist Hedda Hopper started to persecute me with her hatred. She warned all the producers, directors and actors against me. Hedda called me a nymphomaniac.' In short, Grace Kelly was seen by many who knew her as the embodiment of Hitchcock's drawing room ladies with whorish attitudes...

Of the three films that Alfred Hitchcock made with Grace Kelly prior to their projected reunion for *Marnie,* two—*Rear Window* (1954) and *To Catch a Thief* (1955)—were specifically rewritten and reshaped to suit the actress's personality and the qualities that Hitchcock saw in her. These two movies were more than a director utilising a favourite performer; they were lovingly and carefully crafted to emphasise her beauty and her sexuality—they were visual love letters, with the director inviting his audience to gaze in awe at the wonder that was Grace Kelly. She became Hitchcock's *idée fixe*, and he would have continued to make films with her had the little matter of a Royal Wedding not got in his way.

When Kelly abandoned Hollywood for the South of France, she left behind a director who determined that if he were no longer to have her, he could at least recreate her image. Over the years that followed, Hitchcock hired a series of actresses and bound them to him by exclusive contracts while he remodelled their hair, their looks and their personae in an attempt to turn them into *his* Grace. Even as he toiled with his surrogates, Hitch never gave up on the hope that he would be able to lure her in front if his cameras once more; he was confident that if the timing was right and he could find the right property, she would come back to him..

In 1962, Alfred Hitchcock had the timing down to perfection and he was convinced that he had the right project. *Marnie* was to be his late masterpiece; it was the perfect Hitchcock film and it had been designed to feature the ultimate Hitchcock blonde...

Chapter 1

The Naughty Boy

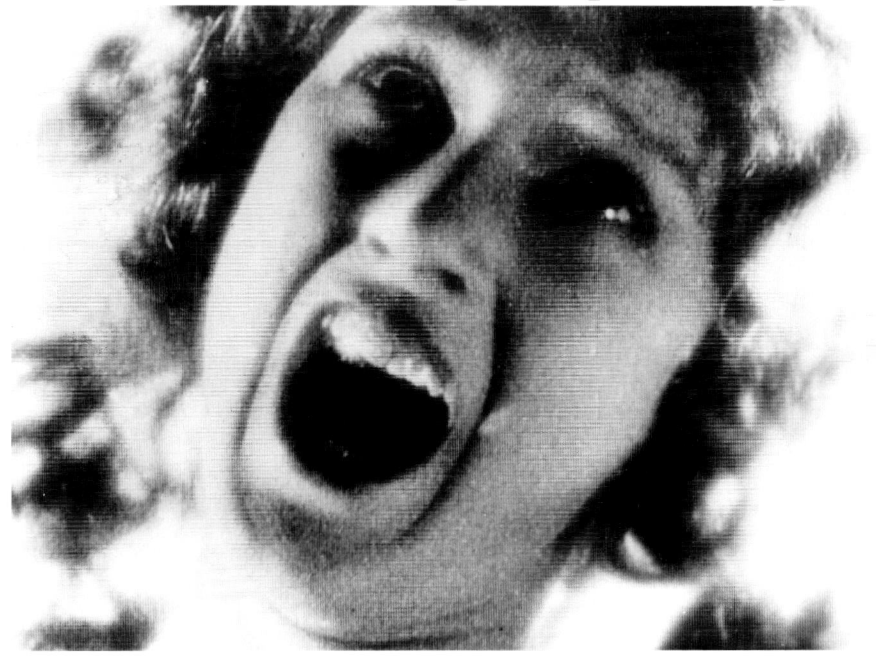

The Lodger

'I think my mother must have frightened me when I was a little boy.'

–Alfred Hitchcock

Surely it was inconceivable that this gentle, mild-mannered gentleman could be the monster of cruelty and cunning that Bunting had now for the terrible space of four days believed him to be!

–*The Lodger*, Marie Belloc Lowndes (1913)

Always acutely aware of his public image, Alfred Hitchcock took great care to present himself as a droll, intelligent and thoughtful Edwardian English 'gentleman', with slightly more than a passing interest in the macabre.

Partly to protect his privacy and partly to maintain this assiduously-crafted façade, Hitchcock seldom discussed the details of his childhood or his relationship with his parents—particularly his relationship with his doting mother Emma, which would become a source of endless fascination for interviewers. Whenever he was pinned down on the subject, he resorted to a series of well-worn anecdotes, geared more to maintaining his 'master of the macabre' image than to providing insight. These stories, which nearly always carried an air of the apocryphal, would appear throughout his career with subtle variations; one of his favourites seemed to offer some explanation of the director's fear of incarceration. 'I was four or five years old,' Hitchcock recalled, 'when my father gave me a note and, without saying a word, sent me off to the local police station to deliver it. I handed it to the sergeant behind the desk and he read it, looked at me and then put it away in his pocket. He led me round behind the desk and into the cells; he then locked the door behind me and left me there alone in the darkness for five or ten minutes. After he let me out he said: "That is what we do to naughty boys."'

The youngster's misdemeanour, if there was one, has been lost in the mists of time and even Hitchcock claimed to have forgotten what it was that had warranted such punishment. However, like most of his stories, it was designed to draw attention not to himself but to his work: an innocent wrongly imprisoned, false accusations, and a respect, bordering on fear, of the police, are all themes that would recur in his canon. That Hitchcock inadvertently throws some light onto his father—after all, what sort of man has his child tossed in a police cell to prove a point?—is purely coincidental.

Hitchcock's father William was born into the Church of England, but he had embraced Catholicism in order to marry Emma Jane Whelan and from their nuptials in 1886, this branch of the family became staunchly Catholic. Soon afterwards, the couple moved to Stratford in East London where William ran a small but successful grocery business. The couple's first child, also christened William, was born in 1890, and daughter Ellen followed in 1892 as the business started to prosper. By the time Alfred, the last of the Hitchcock children, was born in 1899, the family's financial position could be considered comfortable, if still far from wealthy.

As a couple, William and Emma Hitchcock seem to typify Victorian conventions and standards; she stayed at home, attending to the household and raising the children, while he worked long hours, six days a week, to ensure that the family was provided for. William expected the children to show proper obedience to their parents and an unwavering respect and devotion to his belatedly-acquired Catholic principles. While her husband was instilling into them a strong work ethic and thriftiness with money that bordered on the miserly, Emma would indulge her children as only mothers can. As the baby of the family, Alfred (or 'Hitch', as he dubbed himself from an early age) was his mother's favourite, and a close bond and mutual dependency developed between the pair that lasted well into the youngster's adulthood. When he was persuaded to talk about his background, Hitch would speak fondly of his mother while his father remained an aloof and distant figure.

Never comfortable with games or sport, Hitch was a bookish child, happier observing the neighbourhood children at play than participating himself; in consequence, he was not a popular child and he developed few close friends. Alfred Hitchcock never really deviated from this solitary path and, throughout his life, he would be ill at ease in group situations or with people whom he did not know or trust—more often than not, he preferred his own company or that of his immediate family.

At the age of eleven, Hitch was enrolled at St Ignatius College, a Jesuit grammar school in Stamford Hill, Middlesex, where he was educated in the rigours of Latin, mathematics, French, English and, of course, religious knowledge. Frivolities like the theatre or cinema were not so much shunned by his tutors as openly attacked as 'ungodly'. This was one value that the Hitchcocks did not share with the Jesuits and family outings to a stage play or vaudeville show were the highlight of the young Hitchcock's early years; the fact that this entertainment was 'forbidden' made it all the more enticing and exciting. The theatre offered Hitch an escape from the drabness of his daily life and when Emma or William could not take him, he would go on his own, sit in the cheap seats, and soak up the ambiance.

At St Ignatius, Hitchcock, a dumpy, moon-faced child, thrived in an environment where books rather than physical pursuits were the order of the day. But there were still signs of quiet rebellion against authority. Hitch developed a taste for practical jokes—always, he maintained, with the intention of humour—but many of his japes, even from his schooldays, bordered on cruelty. Hitchcock biographer Donald Spoto records how a younger boy found himself manhandled by Hitchcock and an unnamed accomplice into a forbidden area of the school: the basement. There he was stripped to his underwear, to which his assailants pinned firecrackers, and bound hand and foot; as Hitchcock and his co-conspirator ran off, the firecrackers exploded. Fortunately, the boy was unhurt.

The young Alfred Hitchcock was hardly the stuff of a school bully; he was acutely self-conscious about his weight and appearance, and he lived in mortal dread of being ridiculed. If anything, the practical jokes were a defence mechanism intended to draw attention from himself and onto something less personal. Even when he was pushing his pranks to a sadistic extreme, Hitchcock would shun any form of confrontation. He never lost this inability to deal with conflict; later in life, he would refuse to deliver criticism or bad news to colleagues, and he was more likely to brood in his trailer than to express personally any disappointment that he might have felt with regard to their behaviour.

As he matured, Hitchcock developed a peculiar hobby which set him further apart from children his own age; he enjoyed visiting the Old Bailey, London's Central Criminal Court, and he became fascinated by the machinations of the English legal system, as well as the indissoluble relationship between crime and punishment. Hitch also made a number of visits to Scotland Yard's infamous 'Black Museum', with its collection of exhibits from the Yard's greatest crime scenes. An adolescent fascination with the more salacious side of crime never left Hitchcock and nearly sixty years later, the excited schoolboy bubbled to the surface when he described the experience to Rex Reed of the *Chicago Sun-Times*: 'They've got all the shoes of prostitutes from the gaslight era. Did you know that the colour of every scarlet woman's shoes determined what her speciality was? If a man saw a prostitute walking along Waterloo Bridge at night he knew she did one thing in red heels, another thing in blue heels..'

Hitchcock later extended his researches to the Vice Museum in Paris, where he was particularly taken with bondage and its use in sexual gratification, recalling, 'It is somewhere in the area of fetishism, and it has a sexual connotation.. I noticed there was considerable evidence of sexual aberrations through restraint.' The use of restraint—in particular, that of handcuffs—would surface throughout his film career, perhaps most famously when Robert Donat's hero-on-the-run is inconveniently shackled to the beautiful Madeleine Carroll in *The 39 Steps*. Hitchcock emphasised the sexual undercurrent to their plight when he allowed his hero's careless hand to brush against Ms Carroll's leg as she removes her stockings.

As he grew older, the precocious Hitch expanded his world beyond that of the theatre and developed a fascination with the flickering black and white images offered by cinema. At an age when most adolescent boys were using the movies as a venue to pursue their romantic aspirations with the opposite sex, Alfred Hitchcock sat alone, studying the techniques of film. Within a very few years, he was able to develop an encyclopaedic knowledge of what then was still a relatively new medium.

On December 12, 1914, William Hitchcock died at the age of 52. Having ignored repeated warnings from family and friends, he had refused to cut back on his punishing work routine and although the end had been in sight for some time, it still came as a devastating blow to his wife Emma—over the next few years, she would come to depend more and more on her youngest son for comfort.

By that time, Hitch was out of formal education and drifting through a series of dead-end jobs, with little interest or enthusiasm. His father's death had been a coming-of-age moment; elder brother William took over the business, which meant that Hitch had to knuckle down and find himself a trade. He enrolled at the London County Council School of Engineering and Navigation, where he studied mechanics, electricity, acoustics and navigation with the vague notion of becoming an engineer. It was a practical choice rather than an emotional one and to escape the dry world of engineering, Hitch also attended courses on art at London University.

Hitchcock's first 'proper job' was as a technical estimator at the London firm of W T Henley Telegraph and Cable Company and, almost as soon as he started, Hitch persuaded his new boss to allow him to design the company's advertising slogans. The cinema had now overtaken almost everything else in the young man's imagination and he was spending all his spare time and money watching examples of the rapidly developing art-form. Hitchcock went far beyond a mere movie fan; he devoured all the film magazines and trade papers that he could find and he pored over every detail of how films were made and of the people who made them. Hitchcock's heroes were not the screen idols of the time, like Douglas Fairbanks and Charlie Chaplin, but the creators of the films—directors like Fritz Lang, F W Murnau and D W Griffith.

Moving into full-time employment did little to expand Hitchcock's circle of friends and he had little, if any, social contact with his work-mates. He was still too self-conscious about his physique and appearance to make any approaches to the opposite sex. 'I have always been uncommonly unattractive,' he told Dorothy Chandler. 'Worse yet, I have known it. The feeling has been with me so long, I cannot imagine what it would be like not to feel that way.'

Hitch retreated so far from social interaction with the opposite sex that the only women he came into direct contact with were his mother and sister. That is not to say that the boy was not interested in sex—he just lacked the confidence or skills to do anything about it. Cinema, long since established as a solitary experience for Hitchcock, became his only outlet, and he took whatever vicarious pleasures he could from the silver screen, confessing years later, 'I learned everything I knew about sex from films.'

W T Henley may have been paying his wages but Hitchcock spent most of his time at the company looking for ways to break into the fledgling British film industry. Opportunity finally presented itself when he read that Famous Players-Lasky Corporation, the American film company, were to open an office and sound stage at Islington, in central London. Hitchcock seized the initiative to send them some examples of his artwork, formatted to suggest title cards from movies. It was pretty basic stuff, as he revealed to François Truffaut: 'If a line read "George was leading a very fast life by this time," I would draw a candle, with a flame at each end, just below the sentence. Very naïve.' Naïve or not, it was enough to convince the studio, and Hitchcock was hired on a part-time basis.

Hitchcock's unbridled enthusiasm soon took him beyond that limited role and, while still working for Henley's during the day, he would spend all his spare time, evenings and weekends, at the studio. No job was too menial so long as it allowed him to observe the director and technicians at work, and he soaked up everything that he could learn about the art and craft of film-making. When Famous Players-Lasky came through with a permanent job offer, Hitchcock quit Henley's and established himself at the Islington studio with the grand designation of Head of Titles Department; from there, he graduated to editorial and work on scripts.

After a series of box-office failures, the company called an end to its British

The Mountain Eagle (Alfred Hitchcock, Alma Reville)

experiment and the Islington studio space was thrown open to independent film-makers on an ad hoc basis. Hitchcock stayed on, and from 1923–25, he worked for producer Michael Balcon and what subsequently would become Gainsborough Pictures. By now, Hitchcock not only was designing his title cards but also writing scripts, designing sets, and supervising casts and costumes; it was the young man's energy and enthusiasm as much as any talent he displayed that endeared him to Balcon and ultimately led to his directorial debut—the producer simply felt that his young protégé had earned his chance.

Hitchcock's debut as a director was *The Pleasure Garden* (1925), produced through Gainsborough and shot on location in Germany. A torrid melodrama set partly in the tropics and partly in a London music hall, *The Pleasure Garden* was not well received by Gainsborough's financial backers in London who, despite Balcon's strong support, felt it unreleasable and insisted it be placed out of harm's way in the studio vaults. That decision was made by C M Woolf, a close collaborator of Balcon's, who shared his colleague's passion for cinema but not his judgement and who was singularly opposed to the idea of giving Hitch a second chance behind the camera. By the time Woolf had voiced that opinion, however, he was too late and the young director had already helmed his second feature, *The Mountain Eagle* (1926), also shot in Germany. After complaining vociferously, Woolf extracted his revenge by ensuring that it, too, was held back from distribution.

Balcon put up a spirited defence of Hitchcock, but the young man was not universally popular within the company. Many of the older hands at the studio, who regarded themselves as craftsmen, resented the way that Hitchcock had mastered their skills in just a few months. The fledgling director, in his youthful exuberance, had made the situation worse by constantly lecturing his elders on better and more exciting ways of making pictures. Woolf, a businessman rather than a filmmaker, put his faith in the company's longstanding employees and assured them that despite Gainsborough's perilous financial situation, Hitchcock's films would not see the light of day.

While Hitchcock fretted over the cavalier treatment of his first two films, Balcon demonstrated unstinting support by handing him a third, and it was this one—shot in London—that was to provide a foretaste of the director's future career. *The Lodger: A Story of the London Fog* (1927), often called simply *The Lodger*, was a mystery thriller modelled on the Jack the Ripper murders. The film starred Ivor Novello as the title character, believed—wrongly—to be a serial killer. The 'Is he?/Isn't he?' gimmick undermined the story's shaky narrative structure but clever editing (by Ivor Montagu) and stylistic flourishes by Hitchcock ensured the film was a remarkable exercise in tension and technique. Many of the features later identified as Hitchcock trademarks also came into play, including a cameo appearance by himself and, more significantly, the use of an imperilled heroine—blonde, of course—to elicit audience empathy.

Appropriately for a tale based on Britain's most notorious sex-killer, *The Lodger* also marked the first time that Hitchcock explicitly linked sexual gratification with

The Lodger (Ivor Novello)

brutalisation and murder, a salacious juxtaposition that sent a frisson of excitement through the audiences of the 1920s. Even Woolf had to concede that there was no question of holding *The Lodger* back and almost as soon as it opened, queues of willing customers formed. Not only was *The Lodger* a massive commercial hit but it was hailed by reviewers as that rarest of beasts, a British film that could compete on equal terms with its Hollywood counterparts. Hitchcock always regarded *The Lodger* as his first 'proper film', and it was certainly the first time that the critics spoke of him as an emerging talent.

Hitchcock's apprenticeship at Gainsborough also gave him the one thing that his life had lacked so far: a strong female influence, beyond that offered by his family unit. Nottingham-born Alma Lucy Reville was working at the studio as a freelance editor—one of the very few women in that position in England at that time—and she was highly regarded in her field. Alma had encountered Hitch when he was designing the title cards at Famous Players-Lasky and had been struck by his serious, almost single-minded approach to his work. Hitchcock, although attracted to Alma, felt duty-bound by the standards of the time; it was simply not the done thing to approach a woman who, technically at least, was his superior. It was not until he had graduated to assistant director that Hitch even dared to strike up a conversation with the quiet redhead. Over the next few years, their paths crossed more and more frequently and a mutual admiration developed out of their common love of film. 'We wrote letters to each other,' Alma told Dorothy Chandler, 'but they weren't love letters. They were letters about filmmaking.'

Alma was the same age as Hitch and she shared his quiet, introspective nature; as far as close companionship was concerned, she lived only for her work and seemed destined for spinsterhood. Their courtship was so inconspicuous that when the couple announced their engagement, few of their work-mates had even realised they were seeing each other. Most considered Alma and Hitch to be an odd match; Hitch stood at 5' 8" and weighed nearly two hundred pounds, while the petite, mousy Alma weighed only a fraction of that and barely reached to Hitchcock's shoulders. Quite apart from their odd physical appearance, the couple had markedly different outlooks: Alma seldom drank alcohol and preferred to pick away at modest portions of food; Hitchcock, on the other hand, while conventional in his tastes in food and drink, took great pleasure in indulging—frequently over-indulging!—in both.

Hitchcock and his future bride continued to work together at Gainsborough, most notably *The Pleasure Garden,* after the debutant director had nervously asked her to join his crew. Thereafter Alma would be the one constant in Hitchcock's life, whether it was taking a formal credit (editor, continuity, script) on his pictures or reading scripts, viewing footage and whispering suggestions. Marriage could almost be seen as the natural extension of their professional collaboration and, even at the height of his fame, Hitchcock would refer to Alma as 'my severest critic'. As many of his screenwriters were to find out, the highest praise that the director could offer was, 'Alma liked that scene you wrote..'

Throughout their engagement, Hitch and Alma observed the strict proprieties required by Edwardian society; Hitch continued to live with his mother and Alma with her parents in Twickenham. Their courtship largely consisted of meeting up at the studio and afterwards having dinner and taking in a film. Hitchcock never made any bones about the fact that he was a virgin when he married and, apart from the insights that he had gleaned from the screen, would admit that he was totally ignorant of the workings of the human—particularly female—body. Hitch and Alma married in December 1926 and Alma, who might have had ambitions of her own as a director, immediately subordinated her career to that of her new husband. Following on from the pattern adopted by his own parents, Hitchcock adopted the role of breadwinner and, as soon as practicable, Alma assumed the position of homemaker; the new Mrs Hitchcock would continue to work in films, but increasingly intermittently and soon exclusively on Hitch's own features.

Spurred by the success of *The Lodger*, Gainsborough rushed to put Hitchcock's previous films into cinemas (though Woolf took little satisfaction from the return on his investment). But its newly-christened 'star director', barely established, was becoming frustrated by the hand-to-mouth nature of the Islington setup. Hitchcock

Alfred Hitchcock and Alma Reville on their wedding day

already felt that he had outgrown Balcon's operation; when his next two projects, both unimpressive adaptations of established plays, flopped, he decided that the time had come to try to build on his success elsewhere.

Over at Elstree, in Hertfordshire, British International Pictures (BIP) had built one of the best-equipped studios in Europe and, if the facilities alone were not enough, an additional carrot for Hitch came in the shape of a three-fold increase in his salary. In 1927, he quit his comfortingly-familiar Islington base and signed a three-year, twelve-film contract for the princely sum of £13,000 per year—the highest salary paid to a British director at the time.

The move was not the roaring success that Hitchcock had hoped for. His first projects for his new studio received respectable notices but suffered lacklustre box-office performances. A fretful Hitchcock was convinced that he had made the wrong move. Then, in 1929, he was set to work on a routine thriller called *Blackmail,* adapted from a play by Charles Bennett. The picture featured blonde Austrian actress Anny Ondra as a shopkeeper's daughter named Alice, who is lured to the lodgings of a local artist. The intentions of the artist are made all too obvious to the audience, but the naïve girl manages to miss them until the last minute; the ensuing struggle to preserve her honour ends only when she takes a bread knife to her attacker. Alice flees the scene of the crime but finds that there was a witness who decides to exploit the situation to his own advantage..

Blackmail started out its life as a rather conventional silent melodrama—albeit with a rather risqué premise—until BIP's enterprising founder John Maxwell hit on a better idea. Maxwell had acquired sound recording equipment from the US and decided that *Blackmail* would be the perfect vehicle on which to try out the new apparatus. Hitchcock, his cast and crew, were sent back to the studio floor to re-shoot as much of the film as BIP could afford—which was not a great deal—using sound equipment. Hitchcock's masterly contribution was in selecting just the right scenes to re-shoot and, uniquely for such an early feature, in determining how the concept of sound 'effects' could be used to increase the tension. The finished film, though crude and rather clumsy in execution, was touted as the first British 'talkie' and resulted in a box-office bonanza that outstripped even *The Lodger*.

Blackmail (Alfred Hitchcock, Anny Ondra)

The film itself is largely consigned to footnotes now, but Hitchcock ensured his leading lady of something approaching immortality when he recorded a sound test on set. A youthful Hitchcock flirts outrageously with a giggling Ondra. 'Have you been a good girl?' he asks. 'Oh, no!' Ondra exclaims, and bursts out laughing. 'Have you slept with men?' 'No!' The director then continues, 'Now come right over here, Miss Ondra, and stand still in your place, or it won't come out right—as the actress said to the soldier.' Preserved in the archives of the British Film Institute, this has to rate as one of the more unusual legacies from early cinema and it gives a rare insight into Hitchcock's easy humour when he was working with people whom he liked and trusted, particularly women. Ondra, who also starred for Hitchcock in the far less interesting *The Manxman* (1929), made an attractive leading lady, and the fact that she spends most of *Blackmail* in a state of nervous agitation in the face of imminent danger made her even more appealing to the director. Her accent limited her career in British films, but Ondra has the honour of being one of the more distinctive of Hitchcock's blondes.

Hitchcock, who was now a family man—Patricia Alma Hitchcock (often called Pat) had been born the previous year—was an ebullient character and he would warble excitedly to any member of the press who approached him for an interview. Realising how fickle public attention could be, he took the unusual step of forming his own management company for the express purpose of ensuring that his name stayed in the forefront of people's minds—the marketing of 'Hitchcock' as a commodity had begun. The director had no intention of joining the ranks of worthy but uncelebrated craftsmen whose names are only known to film-buffs; he was the first British film-maker to recognise the importance of name and image, and for the rest of his career, he would be a shrewd and calculated promoter of his own brand.

Hitch and Alma soon settled into a pattern of comfortable if modest domesticity; when they returned from honeymoon, they moved into an unexceptional two-bedroom apartment on the Cromwell Road in West London and when Pat came along, they transformed the spare bedroom into a nursery. Later, to give them a break from the hustle and bustle of London, they bought a quaint little cottage in Shamley Green in rural Surrey, but even then the couple never embarked on a lifestyle that could be described as being in any way lavish. Hitchcock, who had learned frugality from his father, was loathe to spend money on such things as furniture and decorations and preferred the functional to the elaborate; visitors often commented on how shabby his carpets and curtains looked. But there were some things that the Hitchcocks never skimped on and one of these was travel. Foreign adventures and exotic locations were not uncommon for the family; in December 1931, for example, Hitch, his wife and daughter departed Cromwell Road for a three-month extended vacation that took them to Africa and the Caribbean.

The Lodger and *Blackmail* were Hitchcock's most successful films of the period by far, both critically and financially, but despite his own interest in the macabre and the obvious appetite for same among cinemagoers, the director still had no thought of specialising in thrillers. His work for British International focused mainly on melodrama, including *Juno and the Paycock* (1930), an uninspired version of the Sean O'Casey play set during the Irish troubles. Later attempts to extend his range, such as a romantic musical called *Waltzes from Vienna* (1934), sank without a trace. Hitchcock did not completely abandon the world of thrillers but his BIP effort *Murder!* (1930), which fused an Agatha Christie style 'whodunit' with thinly-veiled transvestism and homosexuality, failed to find an audience.

Homosexuality, or at least oblique references to it, had already cropped up in several of Hitchcock's films, notably *The Pleasure Garden*, and the director was to

Mr and Mrs Alfred Hitchcock

use the same subtext in many of his later movies, in particular, *Rope* (1948), where the killers are two affluent students implicitly in love with each other. Perhaps the most famous example would come in *Strangers on a Train* (1951), where Hitchcock manipulates a repressed love/envy subtext into his tale of two would-be killers swapping murders. The idea that sexual deviancy could be linked to certain criminal activities also featured in many of his more successful films.

Many years later, the director made the outrageous statement that 'marrying Alma saved me from becoming a poof'. The remark was designed to shock rather than convey any hidden truth, but it is noteworthy that Hitchcock the teenager shared many of the traits commonly associated with homosexuality, including a close dependence on a mother to almost the total exclusion of other women. Like most of those who work in the arts, Hitchcock was open-minded about homosexuality, male and female, and if anything was more curious than repelled.

Many in the worlds of the theatre and film industry flouted the law and lived more or less openly with partners of the same sex, and although homosexuality would remain illegal for another forty years, the authorities—provided that a degree of discretion was observed—usually turned a blind eye. Matinee idol Ivor Novello, who starred for Hitchcock in both *The Lodger* and *Easy Virtue* (1928), hid his own sexual preference from his legions of female fans and while working together, he and Hitchcock often engaged in conversations on the subject. It was an education for Hitch, but it was not his first encounter with what Oscar Wilde had termed, 'the love that dare not speak its name': he would tell François Truffaut a story of how, as a bright-eyed young innocent working in Berlin, he, a German film director, and the daughter of the studio boss had befriended two German girls who had accompanied them back to their hotel. After trying unsuccessfully to lure the men into bed, the girls decided to cut their losses and go to bed with each other! Hitch records how his companion 'put on her glasses to make sure she wouldn't miss anything.'

In 1931, by the time he came to film *Rich and Strange*, an odd black comedy co-written by Alma, Hitchcock had become disillusioned with British International Pictures; this was, he said, his 'lowest ebb'. For its part, the studio had found the director's output difficult to market and the expected box-office returns had never materialised. The decision to terminate the agreement was made by mutual consent. Hitchcock, without a permanent home for the first time since becoming a director, entered a period of drift.

Hitchcock's worst nightmare was failure and throughout his life, at moments of stress or depression, he took refuge in uncontrolled eating; his weight ballooned and the press began sarcastically to refer to him as the 'Buddha of British films'. When Michael Balcon, recently moved to Gaumont-British Picture Corporation, threw him a lifeline, Hitchcock seized it with both hands. With no specific project in mind, Balcon invited Hitch to submit any ideas that he might have and picked the best of the choices on offer. The result was *The Man Who Knew Too Much* (1934), a spy thriller which provided Hitchcock with a template for much of his later work and gave the director his first bona fide hit since *Blackmail.*

The Man Who Knew Too Much centres on a holidaying couple who stumble into an assassination plot and are caught between the authorities and the ruthless terrorists who will stop at nothing, including the kidnapping of a child, to achieve their nefarious ends. The film marked the first appearance of Hitchcock's famous 'MacGuffin', a plot device that serves no real purpose in the narrative other than to propel the action forward—in this case, the notional attempt at 'assassination'.

Hitchcock's attitude to money was again in evidence during the setting-up of the film. The rights to the project were in the hands of BIP, but Hitch assured Balcon that he could use his powers of persuasion to secure them for £500. He then completed the purchase for £250 and proceeded to charge Gaumont-British the full amount, while Balcon remained unaware of the true price. Hitchcock liked to tell this story as an example of how he had put one over on the studios; however, given that he was already on a comfortable salary, and that Balcon had been a staunch supporter of his during the director's early years, it also showed pettiness and a curious disregard for professional loyalties. (Hitchcock, so the story goes, felt so guilty over the subterfuge that he used the money to have a bust of Balcon made, which he then presented to his employer as a gift—Balcon flatly refutes this version.)

The Man Who Knew Too Much was to launch Hitchcock into his most successful and productive period since becoming a full-time director and, instead of trying to diversify, as he had after *Blackmail*, he took what he saw as the fundamental ingredients in the success of the film and set out to recreate them in a more ambitious project culled from the pages of John Buchan's unwieldy novel, *The 39 Steps*.

Hitchcock and writer Charles Bennett took Buchan's basic premise and spun it into a breathless chase movie, mixing in Nazis, secret formulas and an innocent man framed, and adding for good measure a comically-romantic subplot. Robert Donat starred as the film's intrepid hero Richard Hannay, while Madeleine Carroll was the blonde inadvertently caught up in the mayhem who spends most of her screen time handcuffed to Hannay. Carroll was one of the biggest stars in British cinema at the time and she epitomised the cool, elegant image that would become associated with Hitchcock heroines for the next three decades.

The actress, who would go on to star in his next film, *Secret Agent* (1936), was also the victim of one of the director's most infamous practical jokes. On the first day of shooting, Hitchcock introduced his leading players to each other for the first time and, after explaining the setup, handcuffed them together to start rehearsals. Before he could proceed any further, Hitchcock was 'called away' to attend to another

The 39 Steps (Robert Donat, Madeleine Carroll)

matter and he claimed to Donat and Carroll that he had mislaid the key to the lock on the cuffs. The actors remained shackled together until he returned some hours later, by which time they had experienced the frustrations and embarrassments of their screen counterparts. Speaking about the ploy in the film, Hitchcock said, 'The handcuffs brought out all kinds of thoughts in the audience's minds. For example, how do they go to the toilet was one obvious question. And the linking together is a kind of—I think it refers more to sex than anything else.'

Hitchcock's treatment of his stars would vary from person to person but overall, he stuck to his oft-quoted view that 'actors are cattle' and treated them accordingly. (He frequently denied that he had actually made the remark, stating that the correct quote was: 'Actors should be treated like cattle.') Those who arrived on his set, knowing their lines, understanding their contribution and ready to listen to and enact instructions, would be treated with respect and occasionally even affection. Others such as John Gielgud, star of *Secret Agent*, who needed constant reassurance and praise, would be crushed by what they saw as Hitch's indifference. His reluctance to become involved with his actors was a constant throughout his life, and his most successful partnerships were with the likes of Cary Grant, who by his own admission was a master at creating 'Cary Grant' and thus required no input from his directors, or James Stewart, the consummate professional, who likewise never thought to question character motivation. However, Hitchcock's treatment of his leading ladies was more inconsistent.

Meeting Madeleine Carroll before filming began, the director was clearly taken with her and he offered the advice, 'Don't act—just be yourself.' Onscreen and off, Hitchcock delighted in subjecting his glamorous star to one ordeal after another: 'Nothing gives me more pleasure than to knock the lady-likeness out,' he quipped. At the same time, he was prepared to sit with Carroll between setups and discuss her performance, as well as explaining in detail how he planned to photograph her and how she would look. In contrast, the far more down-to-earth and homely Peggy Ashcroft, who featured in *The 39 Steps*, was barely acknowledged. By the time he came to make *Secret Agent*, Hitchcock was photographing Carroll as though she were the brightest light in the firmament, in radiant and loving close-up. Indeed, many critics consider that it was the attention paid to Carroll that undermined the overly-sensitive John Gielgud; the actor certainly thought so and was distressed that he could not win more demonstrative support from his director.

On the whole, Hitchcock's attitude to his crew was similar to the one that he adopted towards actors; he liked to work with people whom he could trust and rely upon and while he was never generous with either money or praise, he would take it as a personal slight if any of his regular technicians left him to work for another director. His crews generally responded to his near-encyclopaedic knowledge of filmmaking and respected his quest for perfection, but their respect did not put them beyond the butt of his practical jokes.

On at least one occasion, Hitchcock's cruelty got the better of him, and the spoiled child who was capable of pinning fireworks to a school friend re-emerged. Hitch made a wager with a cameraman that he could not spend an evening in an empty studio handcuffed to his camera; the poor man should have known better but he accepted the bet. Before everyone left for the evening, Hitchcock bound the poor fellow and left him with a cheery 'good luck' and a drink laced with laxative!

After the spectacular success of *The 39 Steps, Secret Agent* proved to be something of a disappointment. However, Hitchcock knew that he had now found his *oeuvre* and his next film, *Sabotage* (1936; confusingly adapted from Joseph Conrad's *The Secret Agent*), offered audiences another tale of sinister foreigners and dogged British policemen. It marked the end of his association with Gaumont-British; after a long, slow decline, the company closed its production unit and parted company with Balcon and his team.

But Hitchcock, the inveterate worrier, was for once relaxed about his immediate future. He was in negotiations with Gainsborough over a two-film deal and had verbally committed to work with the volatile Charles Laughton, as soon as they could settle on a suitable project. By 1937, Hitchcock was the most successful director working in Britain and, thanks to his publicity manager, far and away the best known. But despite his personal success, he was frustrated by what he saw as the constant boom/bust nature of the indigenous industry, the constant scrambling for finance, and the studio bosses who ran things like a gentleman's club. He was outspoken on the lack of imagination shown by filmmakers and the primitive facilities which they had to endure, and he felt that his status was not reflected in either his salary or in the recognition that he received. Perhaps inevitably, Hitchcock gazed enviously to California and Hollywood, where giant studios offered limitless opportunities and rewards, in a country where film—at least in his view—was embraced equally as an art-form and as an entertainment medium.

After finishing the first of his two Gainsborough features, *Young and Innocent* (1937), Hitchcock let it be known that he was interested in making the switch to

The travelling Hitchcocks

Hollywood and, after receiving positive noises from both Metro-Goldwyn-Mayer and Selznick International, he arranged a 'family holiday' to meet his American suitors. But the meetings did not go as planned; Hitch's high opinion of his own worth scared off MGM early in the proceedings and gave David O Selznick pause for thought. By the time the Hitchcocks were ready to return to London, a contract had been agreed in principle but not in detail.

Nevertheless, Hitchcock arrived back in England with one thought in mind—fulfilling his commitment to Gainsborough so that he could free himself to move across the Atlantic. He settled on the only viable project he could find: an uninspiring script that had been intended originally for another director but abandoned. From this inauspicious start, *The Lady Vanishes* (1938) emerged, another rollicking tale of duplicitous Nazis and English stiff-upper lips, which cemented Hitchcock's reputation as one of the great story-tellers and gave him the most successful film of his British career.

Hitchcock continued to negotiate with the Americans throughout the winter of 1937, but it was not until the following summer that a deal was finally hammered out and he agreed to shoot a film for Selznick early in 1939—after he had honoured his long-standing arrangement with Charles Laughton.

Hitchcock later conceded that he had been flattered into working with Laughton and his business partner Erich Pommer, partly because the size of the advance they had offered. As a hired hand, albeit a sympathetic one, Hitch had no say in the material that they had chosen and he was disheartened to learn that his last English film for the foreseeable future was to be an adaptation of Daphne du Maurier's melodramatic pot-boiler, *Jamaica Inn* (1939), which had been published two years earlier. Hitchcock tried frantically to free himself from his contract with Laughton, even offering to sell his own house to repay the advance, but the portly actor was insistent, and it was a miserable Hitch who set out to tackle what he considered to be a poor script. To make matters worse, Laughton the producer began to extend his influence into the territory that Hitchcock felt was exclusively his; the two clashed over the casting, plot details and budget. If Hitchcock ever entertained second thoughts about leaving England, *Jamaica Inn* ended them; he hated the script and the location, but most of all he hated working with the temperamental Laughton. The flamboyant bisexual was insecure to the point of paranoia; his mood-swings ranged from effervescence to manic depression in the blink of an eye and he required constant pampering, cajoling and attention. When he received little encouragement from the director, he staged childish tantrums, went off into brooding silences and employed shameless dramatics. This was all beyond Hitchcock's limited capacity to empathise; he bit his tongue and counted the days that remained to him in Britain.

> **'If I was making Cinderella, everyone would look for the corpse.'**
>
> —Alfred Hitchcock

Having now agreed terms with Selznick, Hitchcock's arrival in New York could not have been better stage-managed to restore his confidence. *The Lady Vanishes* had taken America by storm and he was being acclaimed as a great talent; it was already the most successful British film ever and was hailed as Best Film by the prestigious New York Film Critics' Circle. Hitch and Alma suddenly felt very much at home.

Selznick was anxious to set his new director to work, but Hitch and Alma were enjoying the attention too much to rush to Hollywood and they made leisurely progress from New York, where their ship docked in March 1939. Much to Hitchcock's delight, the press seemed to be everywhere, requesting interviews, firing questions about his imminent American debut and canvassing his views on Hollywood movies. He revelled in the attention and adopted his public persona of a dry, slightly aloof but vastly amenable eccentric. As a rule, Hitch found the journalists knowledgeable about film (and in particular *his* films, which pleased him no end), respectful and genuinely interested in him. He enjoyed their company so much that he extended his meandering journey west to give as much time as possible to the media.

Upon their arrival in Los Angeles, Hitch and Alma settled into an apartment off Wilshire Boulevard and began to explore the local community. Hitchcock never felt tempted to join LA's famous 'English colony'—those ardent ex-pats who would gather round actor C Aubrey Smith's Union Flag in MacArthur Park for cricket and afternoon tea. He preferred instead to entertain small groups of selected guests, plying them with fine wines and liquor and gently shocking them with a barrage of blue jokes. These gatherings seldom included other directors who might have stolen his limelight, but writers were always good value, as well as actors and actresses who expressed the appropriate level of appreciation for his work.

Among the first to endear themselves to Hitch were Clark Gable and Carole Lombard, very much the 'in' couple and the closest that Hollywood had to its own version of royalty. Hitchcock was particularly taken with Lombard, a beautiful, sophisticated woman who could swear like a trooper. He enjoyed her bawdy sense of humour and her love of the macabre and they bonded so well that when she moved into Gable's ranch, Hitchcock took on the tenancy of her Bel Air home, which she continued to visit as often as was practical.

Apart from entertaining at home, Hitch had discovered that Los Angeles had a thriving line in restaurants, and he soon acquired a preference for Chasen's, which became a weekly treat; his favourite meal when eating out was double steak followed by champagne. Company on these occasions was generally restricted to Alma or an associate from his current project; such evenings offered Hitch a welcome respite from the studio, especially when things were not going entirely to plan—as was now the case at Selznick International Pictures.

After much debate, Hitchcock had settled on an adaptation of *Rebecca* (1940), also from the pen of Daphne du Maurier, as the first film for his new employer. However, the preparation had to be sandwiched between his other commitments, including yet more interviews—much to David Selznick's frustration.

In England, Hitchcock was used to being left to his own devices; however, he found to his annoyance in Hollywood that he had now to contend with the views of a great many others. Having purchased a hugely-respected bestseller, Selznick wanted to stay rigidly faithful to the source and made it clear that he expected Hitch to adopt the same approach. Hitchcock had a stated view that books required to be adapted to the needs of the cinema and he was keen to ensure that *Rebecca* would be seen as a 'Hitchcock' and not a 'Du Maurier' film. Selznick saw things very much the other way around and was soon bombarding Hitch with instructions on story structure and the look and the feel of the film, as well as the casting.

After a great deal of discussion, Laurence Olivier was signed for the leading role of Max de Winter, partly on the understanding that he would play opposite Vivien Leigh—the couple were in the throe of a passionate and much-publicised love affair; Leigh had already made a number of films in Britain, but Selznick claimed a proprietary interest over his 'discovery' after he cast her in *Gone with the Wind* (1939). Hitchcock, who was less keen, dismissed the idea, and a dozen or so actresses were duly tested and rejected before Selznick agreed to substitute Joan Fontaine, a British unknown who had been in Hollywood for a number of years without creating much of an impression. Hitchcock, who had preferred Anne Baxter, was impatient to start shooting and reluctantly accepted his producer's alternative choice.

Fontaine was slim and delicate and obviously nervous at finding herself cast opposite the imperious Olivier, to say nothing of working for the intimidating Alfred Hitchcock. When she arrived on set for the first time, her anxiety was so apparent that she was already well on her way to capturing the essence of du Maurier's timid and insecure heroine. But Hitchcock was determined to extract something more from her than mere anxiety. He told her that Olivier thought her performance poor, calculating correctly that the actress would go to any lengths to calm her illustrious co-star on the matter, and that her desperation to please would be plain to see on the screen. He then kept her apart from the rest of the cast to create a sense of alienation in her, which was central to the kind of performance that he felt was needed.

By controlling and manipulating the young Fontaine, Hitchcock ultimately teased out the perfect embodiment of du Maurier's heroine. However, the actress

***Rebecca* (Judith Anderson, Joan Fontaine)**

was deeply uncomfortable with a relationship where the acceptable boundaries of employer/employee were blurred. 'He seemed to want total possession of me,' she told Donald Spoto. 'He wasn't convivial, and he didn't arrange for us all to go to lunch together or to sit down for a chat. He was a Svengali. He controlled me totally.'

On the set, Hitchcock's approach to the filming was pretty much the same as it had been throughout his career. He employed storyboards—graphic representations of the camera's POV—to work out angles in advance. This technique was not common in Hollywood, which meant that he soon acquired a reputation for being inflexible when it came to suggestions on the day and it brought him into direct conflict with Selznick, as *Rebecca* was effectively being 'pre-cut'—which is to say that Hitchcock was only shooting what he needed to assemble the picture his way; there were no alternative shots. Selznick was thus deprived of the abilty to recut the film *his* way.

With a budget of nearly $1m, *Rebecca* was the most expensive film to date for Hitchcock and Selznick was anxious to ensure not only that the director was given everything he needed to complete the picture but that the finished article reflected the requirements of the studio. Hitchcock had never experienced this situation before; where Balcon had made requests and suggestions, Selznick was issuing instructions. Even so, Hitch got off lightly; his new employer was also absorbed with endless tinkering on *Gone with the Wind*, and even the inexhaustible Selznick could only work so many hours in the day. Rather than confront Hitchcock directly, Selznick kept up a constant flow of memos which the director chose either to act upon or ignore—more often than not, the latter. By the end of shooting, the relationship between the two could best be described as tense.

Although it made only a modest profit on its initial release, most critics enjoyed *Rebecca* and it has gained an enduring appeal over the years. The American Motion Picture Academy acknowledged the achievement, handing Selznick a Best Picture award and honouring Hitch with a Best Director nomination. Joan Fontaine also received a nomination as Best Actress.

The accolades may have represented a satisfactory outcome with regard to *Rebecca*, but the battle with Selznick for control of the picture took its toll on Hitchcock and he sought refuge as always in comfort eating; his weight topped the 300lb mark, as his food and alcohol consumption escalated massively.

Independent film producer Walter Wanger offered the émigré Englishman a temporary escape from the claustrophobic confines of Selznick's empire. Wanger had made his name with films like *Trade Winds* (1938) and *Stagecoach* (1939), and he was trying to launch an adaptation of Vincent Sheean's *Personal History*, a tale of spies, murder and comic mayhem in the run-up to a world war. Wanger had struggled for some time to get the project off the ground and now looked to Hitchcock as his last chance before events in Europe rendered his investment 'old news'. For the use of Hitchcock, Wanger was willing to pay Selznick $5000 a week—a handsome 100% profit for Selznick International—while the director himself, much to his chagrin, remained on his regular weekly salary.

On the more positive side, Hitchcock responded to Wanger's hands-off approach and in particular to his agreement to use Hitch's regular collaborator, Charles Bennett. Not even Selznick's refusal to loan out Joan Fontaine for the female lead spoiled the director's mood; he settled for American born Laraine Day, with Joel McCrea playing the American writer on the trail of Nazis in London. In return for his considerable investment—around $1.5m spent mainly on sets—Hitch presented Wanger with the retitled *Foreign Correspondent* (1940), a cleverly-contrived and immensely enjoyable escapist yarn, much lighter in tone than *Rebecca* but replete with what would later come to be identified as Hitchcock 'touches' and worthy of its Best Picture nomination at the next Academy Awards.

In September 1939, war had finally broken out in Europe. Alma and Hitch, thousands of miles away from their respective families, suddenly felt very homesick. Alma had at least managed to persuade her mother and sister to make the journey to America where her husband's income ensured that they could all enjoy a comfortable life in the safety of California. Hitchcock's mother, however, was not about to be uprooted. Emma was too old or too stubborn to move and she refused point blank to join Hitch in the States; it was all he could do to persuade her to move out of the centre of London to Shamley Green, where at least she would be removed from German bombing.

Hitchcock, who was in no physical state to participate in the hostilities, suddenly found himself criticised in the London papers by Michael Balcon, among others, accused of putting his own personal safety before the national interest. Fretting over his mother and watching impotently from afar as the threat to what he still regarded as his own way of life grew daily, Hitchcock continued to seek refuge in food and drink, and he now tipped the scales at a massive 360lbs. While Selznick expressed concerns over the director's drinking, stories of Hitchcock's eccentricity also started to circulate around Hollywood. On one occasion, he was alleged to have taken Carole Lombard and Loretta Young to dinner at Chasen's and fallen sound asleep in the middle of the conversation.

There was another problem in the director's life; not quite a mid-life crisis—that would be too dramatic for the 40-year-old Hitch—but something of a mid-life blip. Since Pat's birth, his relationship with Alma had become in his own word 'chaste' and, as she could no longer contribute directly to his films in the way that she once had, a divide had opened up between the two of them on both a personal and professional level.

The first person to fill this gap was Joan Harrison, the personal assistant who had accompanied the Hitchcocks when they left England. Harrison had been considering a career in journalism when she saw an advert in a newspaper for a secretary at Gaumont-British. Having survived her initial encounter with Hitchcock's toilet humour and sarcasm, she had established herself as indispensable factotum to the great man. She had risen from secretary to continuity assistant to dialogue editor, before finally becoming his closest associate. Hitch respected Harrison's intelligence (she had been educated at Oxford and the Sorbonne) and judgement, and they had developed a bond that was rare between the director and his staff. Harrison was one of the small entourage that travelled with the family to California, where she quickly established herself as a script editor, writer and finally producer in her own right.

Joan Harrison provided the extra stimulus that the director needed. Just as she had been a regular guest of the Hitchcocks in England, so she and Hitch would return from the studio to Hitchcock's house where Alma had the evening meal waiting. As if they did not see enough of her during the week, she was also a weekend guest at the Hitchcocks' home and would be there for holidays, Christmas and New Year. It was a curious *ménage à trios*; Alma seemed to accept that she was allotted a largely, though not exclusively, domestic role in Hitchcock's life while Harrison filled the role of trusted advisor and collaborator on set. However, the two women had a genuine affection for each other, and it was not unknown for she and Alma to settle down in the evening with a clutch of red pens and a troublesome script for a little last minute doctoring.

There is no question that Hitchcock's feelings for Harrison were unrequited. Also, Alma must have been aware of the feeling that was there and accepted it for what it was—the vague and undefined whimsy of a rather sad, middle-aged man. 'There are only two women I ever could have married,' Hitchcock once said, 'Alma, whom I did and Joan, whom I didn't.'

If Hitchcock's domestic situation had reached a tranquil plateau, there still remained the problem of finding a subject that appealed to him *and* his demanding employer. Remakes of *The Lodger* or *The Man Who Knew Too Much* were suggested as projects that could be mounted quickly and cheaply but nothing came of either. Over the next few years, titles such as *The Man in Half Moon Street*, *Letter from an Unknown Woman* and *Treasure Island* would all be associated with the Hitchcock name, but none would come his way. Coping with the full-scale industry that *Gone with the Wind* had become had paralysed Selznick International Pictures as a production company and it would continue to distract David Selznick from producer duties until 1944. In the meantime, Hitchcock was on a weekly wage, so something had to be done to ease the burden on Selznick's cash flow; accordingly, Selznick let it be known that Hitch was available for duty elsewhere, if the price was right.

RKO eventually came forward with the best bid, and Hitchcock was duly handed over to a studio that was already struggling with one cinematic genius, Orson Welles, and his bloated albatross, *Citizen Kane* (1941). Hitchcock was engaged for a more modest effort—a screwball comedy about a couple who may or may not have been legally married and the comic 'chaos' ensuing from their dilemma. Provisionally titled *Before the Fact* and finally emerging as *Mr and Mrs Smith* (1941), the picture was intended as a vehicle for Carole Lombard, with Cary Grant initially pencilled in as the petulant husband; budgetery constraints would eventually see Grant ousted in favour of the more economically-priced Robert Montgomery. Despite a witty and elegant script by Norman Krasna and charming performances from the leads, the resultant film falls flat, with Hitchcock showing little sympathy either for the material or for the genre. Hitchcock—as he often did with his misfires—insisted that he had never wanted to make the film in the first place and did so only because Lombard begged him.

The fact that any major studio would think that Hitchcock could direct a comedy says a great deal for the success of the director's personal publicity campaign. He was talked about as being the 'greatest thing to hit Hollywood', and his interviews and press releases were carefully engineered to ensure that he was given all the credit for his successes. Hitchcock had even started to believe the hype himself; soon after the success of *Rebecca,* he publicly claimed that he was entitled to benefit from the financial windfall gained by Joan Fontaine's overnight stardom, completely ignoring the fact that she had been 'discovered' by Selznick at a dinner party, tested and signed to a contract, and *then* introduced to Hitchcock. Nevertheless, Hitchcock revelled in his newly-acquired reputation as a star-maker.

Hitchcock was on surer ground when he returned to RKO to make *Suspicion* (1941)—for which he successfully prised Fontaine away from Selznick on a one-film loan deal and cast her as another introspective Englishwoman, this time falling for a charismatic ne'er-do-well. The plot hinges on whether this rogue is planning his new wife's demise or whether he is merely misunderstood. In the book, the husband is a murderer and the wife allows herself to be killed, preferring to die by the hand of the man she loves than live a life without him. Hitchcock certainly had no doubt that

Mr and Mrs Smith (Robert Montgomery, Carole Lombard)

Suspicion (Joan Fontaine, Cary Grant)

Saboteur (Norman Lloyd, Priscilla Lane)

he was making a film about a wife-murderer but the studio had other ideas: Cary Grant was cast as the duplicitous Johnny Aysgarth, and he gives a finely-judged performance with just the right shade of grey, but RKO was concerned that one of its prize assets was being portrayed as a villain and ordered Hitch to tone the content down and ensure that the whole 'misunderstanding' is cleared up at the close. Alma and Joan Harrison toiled away in the evenings to make sense of this change—a collaboration which won the two women in Hitchcock's life a shared screen credit.

Hitchcock remained unhappy with the constant tweaking of the script, which he felt was undermining the carefully-contrived suspense. His misgivings transferred to the cast; Grant and Fontaine did not get on (the actor jokingly suggesting that he would happily strangle her for real). Fontaine, cast again in a passive role, was miserable about the way she was being directed; despite her post-*Rebecca* fame, she still lacked confidence in Hitchcock's presence and adopted a submissive pose. 'Hitchcock,' she complained, 'wouldn't let anyone near me. He kept me in a cocoon.' She found his attention stifling, and she tried in turn to keep him at arm's length. Hitch took this as rejection and became sullen and taciturn. Nevertheless, Joan Fontaine was to turn in a career-best performance, one that earned her an Academy Award the same year.

A salary increase notwithstanding—he was now on a creditable $3000 a week—Hitch constantly complained about money. He looked enviously at the amounts paid to the studio's top stars and felt that as the 'creator' of the film, he was massively underpaid. His argument, that he found the project, shaped the script, oversaw the design of the film and directed the action, cut no ice with Selznick, who pointed out that it was the likes of Cary Grant and Joan Fontaine who brought the customers to the cash registers: a paradox that the director would work strenuously over the next two decades to address in his favour.

In the meantime, the relationship with Selznick boiled over into open antipathy—one of the few times in his life when Hitchcock failed to control his temper. Faced with the prospect of yet another loan-out at an inflated rate, Hitchcock asked his boss for a greater share of the fee, a request which was declined. He then asked for a bonus for Joan Harrison, which was also declined by a now-intransigent Selznick, who saw Harrison as no more than Hitchcock's personal secretary and said as much. Enraged, Hitchcock stormed out of Selznick's office and refused to work. The walk-out prompted a furious exchange of tersely-worded memos and letters. But despite the uncharacteristic display of pique, Hitchcock was not about to break a lifelong habit; direct confrontation was avoided and a sullen Hitch soon returned to work.

It was something of a relief to both parties when Hitchcock reported to Universal to work on *Saboteur* (1942), a tale of Fifth Columnists at large in the American heartlands. With a script credit shared by Peter Vietel, Dorothy Parker and Joan Harrison, the film is awash with some of Hitchcock's favourite motifs: mistaken identity, an espionage ring, a glamorous blonde (Priscilla Lane) kidnapped by the leading man, and the inevitable prolonged chase. In many ways, *Saboteur* plays like an American version of *The 39 Steps*, but the shooting proved to be a difficult experience for Hitch and one that would evoke sad memories; not only did Joan Harrison choose this film to end their professional relationship for the foreseeable future (and by association their friendship, as the they were one and the same to Hitch) but he had to hear of Carole Lombard 's death in a plane crash. (The 33-three year old actress was returning from a War Bond rally in her native Indiana.)

To escape the memories at Lombard's house, Hitchcock uplifted his family into their first permanent home since leaving London—a modest but elegant house, nestling amid trees on Bellagio Road, in the Bel Air district of LA. Over the weeks and months that followed, the house was transformed into a home as Hitch bought up chintzes, polished brasses and dark wood panels, to lend the most Californian of houses a distinct air of the Surrey countryside. With a stash of imported Dover sole and bacon carefully packed in refrigerated storage in Los Angeles, Hitchcock's lifestyle was matched as close as possible to the routine with which he had been familiar in Britain, right down to the newspapers (particularly *The Times*) which he had flown over, albeit weeks out of date. (The Hitchcocks later added a weekend house in Northern California near Santa Cruz to their property portfolio, which acted as a stand-in for Shamley Green.)

However, any joy to be found in their new home was tempered by the news that Emma's health was deteriorating and it seemed likely that she would never fully recover. Travel to and from London was virtually impossible and contact by telephone was intermittent and unreliable. Hitchcock was reduced to poring over newspapers and radio reports for signs of a recovery in Britain's fortunes. Having 'lost' Joan Harrison, and still upset at the tragic death of Carole Lombard, Hitchcock began to craft another film for Universal about a homicidal killer hiding out in the family home of his sister.

Shadow of a Doubt (1943) became one of Hitchcock's favourite pictures, partly because the location shooting turned into a family event with both Alma and Pat staying close by and frequently visiting the set. The congeniality continued after the crew returned to Universal's studios for the interiors, with Hitchcock particularly enjoying the company of his leading players: Joseph Cotton and Hume Cronyn. Seasoned Hitchcock observers also attribute his fondness for the film to a raft of autobiographical touch-points dotted throughout the script, particularly involving Cotton's murderer, 'Uncle Charlie'. The character's back story could have been lifted straight from the director's childhood: in one speech, written by Hitchcock, Charlie is described as 'such a quiet boy, always reading', and what follows is a long anecdote about a boy who is under the thumb of an overbearing father and who resorts to 'mischief to let off steam'.

Hitchcock had always professed fascination with the rotten underbelly beneath society's civilised façade and *Shadow of a Doubt* offered him an ideal opportunity to explore that dark world. Charlie's words, again written by Hitch, sum up a lifelong cynicism and bitterness: 'Do you know, if you rip off the fronts of houses, you'd find swine? The world's a hell. What does it matter what happens in it?'

(*Shadow of a Doubt* had another autobiographical side which must have evoked mixed emotions. The mother figure in the movie is named Emma, and while Hitchcock denies any conscious connection to his own mother, the characters have similarities, not least of which, the film's Emma is in the final throes of a terminal illness and stubbornly refuses any help to combat her infirmity.)

In Shamley Green, Hitchcock's mother was dying, her last days spent at home and in pain, having refused to be moved to a hospital where she could have been made comfortable. *Shadow of a Doubt* was still filming when word came through that the 79-nine year old had passed away. Hitchcock's brother William had been with her at the end. Hitch himself could not return for the funeral; instead, he did what he always did when faced with an emotional upset—he continued to work. Much of the fascination that critics have with mother figures in Hitchcock's films has been traced back to this point in his life, when he was powerless to ease Emma's suffering and had to endure the agony of not being at her side in her final hours.

Selznick was enjoying his role as a wheeler-dealer—both buying and selling properties and people—far too much to settle down into production again and, to Hitch's annoyance, he sent the director out on loan once more, this time to Fox.

Shadow of a Doubt (Joseph Cotten, Teresa Wright)/Theatrical poster

Not that Hitchcock felt in any way inclined to work with Selznick, but he hated the disparity of Fox paying around $300,000 for his services while he received only half that. But *Lifeboat* (1944), the story of the survivors of a U-boat attack huddled in a lifeboat and waiting, none too patiently, to be rescued, turned out to be an interesting distraction for Hitch, and it allowed him to dabble with what was to become one of his favourite experiments: shooting a film on a self-contained set.

Soon after completing *Lifeboat,* Hitchcock arranged a brief trip to London. War was still raging across Europe, but the tide had turned irrevocably in favour of the Allies and many of the restrictions on overseas travel had been lifted. For Hitchcock, the journey was something of a pilgrimage: he needed to visit Emma's grave, to pay his respects, ask her forgiveness and assuage his conscience.

As ever with Hitchcock, personal conceits were never enough; the return home, perfectly understandable in the circumstances, had nevertheless to be dressed as a business trip. There was also the outstanding matter of contributing something to the war effort and restoring any damage to his reputation that his Californian exile might have wrought. Crossing the Atlantic in the back of a US air force bomber, Hitchcock travelled for the first time without Alma and stayed just long enough in England to make two French-language short films for the Ministry of Information, intended as propaganda in France. He also used the trip to see his old friend Sidney Bernstein, who was Head of Films at the Ministry of Information, about setting up a film production company after the war. Hitchcock was comfortably ensconced in California, but he wanted to be seen to be doing something for Britain and a production company that would alternate its output between America and the UK seemed ideal.

The trip to England and a sojourn alone at the now-deserted Shamley Green reinvigorated Hitchcock and, brimming with ideas, he arrived back in New York intending to start work on the first of a series of his most personal and revealing films to date.

Hitchcock had found a 1927 gothic melodrama by 'Francis Beeding' called *The House of Dr Edwardes*—a hodgepodge of brooding mystery and madness set within the confines of an insane asylum in France—and he persuaded Selznick that it was ideal source material for a film. The producer, a passionate advocate of psychoanalysis, snapped up the rights and despatched Hitchcock and his chosen writer, Ben Hecht, on a tour of asylums on the East Coast to soak up atmosphere. Working to Selznick's requirements, Hecht and Hitch concocted the film's basic premise and turned the original pot-boiler into *Spellbound* (1945), a tale of murder and mayhem in New England; at the heart of the narrative would be a love story between psychoanalyst Constance Petersen and the newly-appointed superintendent of the asylum, Dr Edwardes, a man who may or not be all he seems; Hitchcock saw the roles filled by Ingrid Bergman and Cary Grant, their onscreen love affair unfolding against a dazzling backdrop of dreams and nightmarish visions.

In a repeat of what had happened on *Rebecca*, Hitchcock and Selznick clashed throughout both the pre-production and production processes. Selznick smarted at Cary Grant's salary demands and imposed his own contract artist, the relatively-inexperienced Gregory Peck, onto the film in the role of Dr Edwardes. Hitchcock accepted defeat in that instance, but he rejected the choice of Dorothy Maguire for the part of Constance and held out for Bergman. The Swedish actress was also signed to Selznick International, but she was less than impressed with the script and her employer had to remind her of the small print on her contract before she agreed to appear in the film.

Selznick also criticised Hitchcock's decision to use Salvador Dali, the Spanish

Ingrid Bergman

surrealist, to design the elaborate dream sequences, and he hired a Dr May Romm to furnish advice and technical expertise on the finer points of psychoanalysis. When Romm criticised a number of scenes claiming factual inaccuracy, Hitchcock sourly reminded her that this was the cinema, not real life. Selznick's usual barrage of memos, comments and criticisms continued to drive Hitchcock to distraction, and the filmmaking process soon became a tiresome slog—so much so that the director fled the studio as soon as *Spellbound* wrapped, leaving the shot footage in the hands of his producer. Selznick supervised the excising of around twenty minutes from Hitchcock's version but as an olive branch, he arranged for him to receive the rare privilege of 'above-the-title billing', and the finished film became *Alfred Hitchcock's Spellbound.*

Despite the antagonism, *Spellbound* turned out to be one of Hitchcock's most successful collaborations with Selznick, grossing $6m and earning itself six Academy Awards. However, it also represented the breaking point for the two of them: Hitch made a very public show of setting up his own Anglo-American company, Transatlantic Pictures, which would start to make films just as soon as he was free of his commitments to Selznick.

Alfred Hitchcock and Ingrid Bergman

Spellbound had a more lasting significance for Hitchcock. Working with Ingrid Bergman, he established a close bond that would drive his creative thinking for the next four years. The director had formed such attachments before, with Madeleine Carroll and Joan Fontaine, but his affection for Bergman was more like a crush than professional respect. Hitchcock, as was his want, told a story which varied in detail over the years but always came down to Bergman waiting for him after filming and begging him to have sex with her—an invitation which, in all the versions of the tale, he declined. Patrick McGilligan, in *A Life in Darkness and Light*, hypothesises that this anecdote might be given more credence than is normally attributed to it as Bergman had affairs with a number of her directors, including Victor Fleming and Roberto Rossellini.

Whether the incident was real or imagined, Hitchcock became a close confidant of Bergman's and he knew that her marriage to Petter Lindstrom was in trouble; the couple were frequent guests at Bellagio Road and the atmosphere between them was often far from genial. Hitchcock's growing fascination with Bergman became clearer in his next movie—*Notorious*—in which the female lead was crafted with the actress specifically in mind. Working with Ben Hecht once more, Hitchcock created a beautiful but morally ambivalent character called Alicia Huberman, the daughter of a Nazi spy, who is prepared to go to any lengths to appease her current lover, even sleeping with a man she despises. In what becomes a warped love story, Cary Grant was cast as a US agent, a taciturn bachelor who admits that he has 'always been scared of women' and who stifles his own yearnings for Alicia to use her as a honey-trap to capture his adversary. Hitchcock called it the 'degradation of love', and this concept of a man having such complete control over a woman that she will do anything for him would appear more explicitly in his later work.

Selznick liked the idea and allowed Hitchcock to develop the script under his auspices, but too distracted by *Duel in the Sun* (1946) to give it his full attention, he sold the whole package, Hitchcock included, to RKO. This at least allowed Hitchcock the creative freedom to shoot the way that he wanted, and in a much more convivial atmosphere; it also meant that he was given more freedom to explore the outer-reaches of what was acceptable in terms of taste, within the confines of censorship. Apart from the moral ambiguities of the narrative, which would outrage many when the picture opened, Hitchcock created one of the screen's most famous and subtly-sexual embraces: a three minute kiss, cut to frustrate the prevailing restrictions on the depiction of onscreen passion.

Hitchcock's last film for Selznick was also one of his least. *The Paradine Case* (1947) was an overwrought courtroom drama which the producer had sat on for two decades without it getting to the screen. The story concerns an English lawyer who is infatuated with the client that he is defending on a charge of murder and Hitchcock, who was developing a project for Transatlantic that would reunite him with Bergman, had only a passing interest in the film. Hecht came in as a favour to try to save the script but wisely insisted on the proviso that he was not to receive a screen credit. With the budget for *The Paradine Case* weighing in at over $4m, Selznick once again felt the need to interfere; Hitchcock's official biographer, John Russell Taylor, reports Hitch as saying as a result, 'What am I to do? I can't take it any more—he comes down every day, he rewrites the scene, I can't shoot it, it's so bad.' The bickering extended to Hitchcock accusing Selznick of skimping on costs, while he accused Hitch of shooting too slowly.

Hitchcock's frustrations on the set of *The Paradine Case* were relieved briefly by the opening of *Notorious* in August, 1946. The avalanche of praise both for his direction and his handling of Bergman spurred Hitchcock to wrap *The Paradine Case*, but his indifference to it was all-too apparent onscreen and the resultant film was a huge flop.

Finally free to start work on *Under Capricorn* (1949), Hitchcock found that his muse had other priorities and had meanwhile accepted a role on Broadway. Rather than cool his heels waiting, Hitch occupied his time by adapting a play by Patrick Hamilton entitled *Rope*. This was Hitchcock's first colour film, the first under his new Transatlantic banner, and the first with James Stewart—although Grant had been offered the script originally, but he was tied to his RKO contract. *Rope* is the story of two homosexual lovers who strangle a man whom they consider to be their social inferior, purely to experience the thrill of murder (Hamilton had drawn inspiration from real-life 'thrill-killers' Leopold and Loeb); they then proceed to hold a dinner party in the apartment in which the body is hidden. Montgomery Clift was offered the role of one of the murderers but declined, as the covertly gay Clift did not want to be associated with an overtly homosexual part, and John Dall signed on instead. Farley Granger was cast as the other murderer. Stewart was to play their college teacher and a guest at the party, who begins to suspect the truth.

Rope was Hitchcock entertaining himself with an intellectual challenge and trusting that the audience would join him for the ride—not unlike *Lifeboat*, where the novelty of shooting outweighed any interest in the script. In this case, the picture was to be constructed entirely of 10-minute takes, and the 80 minutes of screen time would cover exactly 80 minutes in the lives of the characters. Hitchcock, who described the approach as a 'stunt', soon came to hate the whole concept, as did the cast and crew. Stewart was particularly unhappy; he felt that he was miscast and he struggled to cope with the technical demands and Hitch's hands-off style, the stress of the process telling on even this most placid of screen actors. Hitchcock displayed characteristic patience and uncharacteristic sympathy with his star, but the result of all their efforts was unengaging and dull.

With Ingrid Bergman now restored to him, *Under Capricorn* had the additional bonus of a return to England—Elstree Studios to be precise—for a gothic melodrama of misplaced love and devotion in the Antipodes of the 19th-century. But the very reason that Hitchcock had wanted to make the film would prove to be its undoing. Bergman was simply too big a star for the small, independent production. 'At the time, she was the biggest star in America and all the American producers were competing for her services,' Hitch said. 'I admit that I made the mistake of thinking that to get Bergman would be a tremendous feat; it was a victory over the rest of the industry.' Typically, he later insisted that he only made the film because Bergman had talked him into it: 'From that,' he concluded solemnly, 'I learned that it was better to look at Ingrid than to listen to her.'

The actress was under some strain at the time because of her failing marriage, and she was intolerant of Hitchcock's chosen technique—he initially set out to repeat the pattern of *Rope* and shoot the film in a series of lengthy scenes (this approach was abandoned half-way through shooting). The pressure took its toll on her relationship with Hitch; at one point, she turned her back on him and launched

***Under Capricorn* (Michael Wilding, Ingrid Bergman)**

into a tirade against everything to do with his approach to the film. Refusing to be drawn, Hitchcock turned and walked off the set; legend at Elstree has it that Bergman continued to rant for many minutes more before realising that the target of her anger had left for the day!

Under Capricorn also flopped, which put the future of Transatlantic Pictures in doubt. A surly Hitchcock decided to stay away from Hollywood for a while and he returned to London to film *Stage Fright* (1950), a collaboration between Hitch and Alma and the last time that she would take a formal credit on one of her husband's films. Hitchcock described the project as 'running for cover', which meant finding something lightweight and innocuous that could be made quickly and easily.

Stage Fright, based on *Man Running* by Selwyn Jepson, fitted that bill admirably and having committed Transatlantic funding to his two previous pictures, Hitch took the project to Warner Brothers as part of a new four-picture deal. The story offered an interesting twist on an innocent man accused of murder by having the handsome suspect, played by Richard Todd, revealed as a twitching psychotic at the close. That aside, it offered little else to interest cinemagoers; it was not well received.

The architect of the Warner's contract was Lew Wasserman, Hitchcock's agent at MCA, who also looked after the interests of James Stewart, Bette Davis and Frank Sinatra. He and Hitchcock had developed a strong bond of mutual respect and affection, and Wasserman was one of the few men in Hollywood whom Hitchcock turned to for advice and guidance.

Hitchcock's second film for Warners, *Strangers on a Train*, was intended to be written in collaboration with 'hard-boiled' detective novelist Dashiell Hammett. But he and Hammett could not find a suitable window in their respective schedules and Raymond Chandler signed on instead to help the director wrestle the script into shape. But the pairing failed to gel and Czenzi Ormonde, who worked as an assistant to Ben Hecht, stepped in, while Hecht himself was to contribute further surgery.

After the lightweight *Stage Fright* and the heavy weather of *Rope* and *Under Capricorn,* Hitchcock was at work on a story about which he could be passionate and he poured his time and energy into the project, constructing an elaborate, multi-layered script. The Hitchcock 'touch' is evident throughout the movie—a mirror motif, for example, has the protagonists echo each other in terms of their personal circumstances, behaviour and actions—as are his predilections: the emphasis that he puts on a homosexual undertone in the unspoken attraction between two men who meet by chance and agree to 'swap' murders. The sexual element is not explicit but it was too much for religious groups throughout America who condemned the film. However, audiences were not put off. In *Strangers on a Train*, Hitch succeeded in constructing a dark and disturbing tale about guilt and retribution; it hit a nerve with the paying public and was an enormous success.

Now on something of a high, Hitchcock started to work on *I Confess* (1953), the tale of a murderer who confesses his guilt to the two people who are in no position to expose him, his wife and his priest (and to add a degree of complication, the murdered man was blackmailing the priest's former lover). Warner Brothers was far from keen and Hitchcock offered to offset its risk by making an additional film for the studio, over and above the ones to which he was contracted (*The Wrong Man* was to discharge this obligation in 1956).

Montgomery Clift, who was cast as the priest, was a neurotic alcoholic struggling to come to terms with his own sexuality, and his encounter with Hitchcock would do little to prop up his fragile ego. Clift was an insecure and over-sensitive 'Method' actor working for a director who was not in sympathy with the Method (when asked by one such actor what his character's motivation was, Hitch deadpanned, 'Your pay-cheque'). Tension between actor and director was further heightened by the appearance on set of Clift's acting coach, Mira Rostova. Hitchcock fumed quietly or resorted to sarcastic remarks to vent his annoyance at the intrusion.

The critics were generally indifferent to *I Confess*, but the box-office was steady if unspectacular. Hitchcock, who would trade good takings for good reviews any day of the week, put on a public show of satisfaction with the film while admitting in private that it had been something of a disappointment, and claiming that he had been forced to make too many compromises over script and casting. At this stage, Hitch still hoped to resurrect Transatlantic Pictures in order to make his films under his own control and he still had several projects in various stages of development. He resolved that his next film would be shot the way that *he* wanted to, with a cast and script of his own choosing.

The film that Hitchcock was eventually to make was far from the personal subject that he had planned. He would attach himself to an inappropriate and frustrating project, but it was one that would ultimately change his life, not because of what it was but with whom he would make it...

Chapter 2

Jack Kelly's Girl

Grace Kelly (left) with her father and sister Lizanne

'We were always competing. Competing for everything—competing for love.'
—Grace Kelly

I suppose I wasn't the sort of child anyone would hold up as an example to others. Ever since I was seven or eight I've found myself sharper than most. If I got in a mess I always managed to slide out of it, and most times I avoided the mess. So by the time I was nineteen I thought pretty well of myself.
—*Marnie*, Winston Graham (1961)

To millions of American moviegoers, Grace Kelly's transition from socialite to starlet and on through to princess was swift and effortless. The fact that the actress epitomised the virtues that they expected of royalty—poise, elegance, sophistication—and that her family were rich beyond the dreams of ordinary mortals made that journey seem almost to be pre-ordained. But Kelly's image was a carefully-constructed façade; she was no fairytale princess, and the Kellys may have been rich but they were a long way from blue blood.

Jack Kelly, Grace's father, was a second-generation American who never lost sight of his working-class roots or his Irish heritage; his own father, John Henry Kelly, had been born in County Mayo and had crossed the Atlantic in the 1860s to settle among the large emigrant communities that were dotted along the Eastern seaboard of the US. In 1869, he married a 17-year-old Irish colleen named Mary Costello, whose family also originated in County Mayo. John and Mary were to have ten children in all: Patrick, Charles, Walter, George, Jack, Ann, Mary, Elizabeth, Grace and John junior, who died of sunstroke soon after birth.

According to the accounts of his children, John was a man of limited ambition; he eked out a living as a casual labourer and so long as there was bread on the table, he considered his obligations to his family fulfilled. As he scoured New England for work, his wife and her growing brood were dragged from one sparsely-furnished house to the next. It was not until he had found work at a textile mill on the banks of the Schuylkill River that the family had anything approximating stability, in that at last they were able to call the ramshackle district of East Falls, Philadelphia, home.

Mary, who bore the brunt of raising the children, was different from her more diffident husband; intelligent and strong-minded, she abhorred domestic drudgery and the itinerant lifestyle, and she resented a society that expected the working classes to be content with their lot. By the time the Kellys were settled, Mary's frustration had transferred to her offspring in the form of driving ambition and a refusal to accept second best. In this respect, it was Mary, rather than John, who sowed the seeds of the remarkable Kelly dynasty.

The oldest Kelly boys, Patrick and Charles, had their father's physical strength and work ethic but they were their mother's sons: having started out as manual labourers, they soon outgrew the building sites and set up a successful business together. Mary was equally delighted when her other sons opted for the arts, rather than industry. Walter enjoyed a successful career on the stage, where his signature act, 'The Virginia Judge', enjoyed a brief spell of popularity in vaudevillian revues. (He would go on to appear in Broadway productions, usually comedies, and even enjoyed a period in Hollywood, where he recreated his act for a number of movies.) George Kelly also started out in revue but found his vocation as a playwright, penning eleven plays in all, with his most famous work, *Craig's Wife*, earning him a Pulitzer Prize in 1926. Hollywood showed an interest in George Kelly as well, and a number of his plays made the transition to the big screen. He even spent a (largely unhappy) time working for MGM in Los Angeles, but he soon returned home to New England. George had little in common with his more outgoing brothers, who took his bachelor status to be an indication of artistic eccentricity.

Jack Kelly was the youngest of the surviving boys and, later in life, he liked to give the impression that he was a self-made man—a living tribute to the 'American Dream' and the rewards of hard work. This image was particularly evocative when he was running his campaign to be Mayor of Philadelphia but, while there was some truth to it, the notion played fast and loose with a number of important facts. Jack was certainly a working man; he had left school and joined his older brothers to learn a trade but as his bosses' younger brother, he was not expected to follow a traditional apprenticeship route and, in fact, was allowed the freedom to pursue his one great passion: rowing on the Schuylkill River.

Even as a teenager, Jack had a powerful build and the determination, bordering on obsession, of the committed athlete. When he became a fully paid-up member of the elite Vesper Rowing Club, courtesy of his brothers, he channelled his energies into his chosen speciality: the single sculls. Every spare moment before, after and even during working hours was spent on the Schuylkill and, if the weather was too bad to row, he would lift weights to develop his physique. His determination to succeed won him six US national championships and three Olympic gold medals, including the double sculls—the first rower to achieve such a feat. In the immediate post-war years, rowing was immensely popular in America and by the early 1920s, Jack Kelly was a household name. But there was one prize that eluded him: he wanted to beat the best that England could offer and lift the coveted Henley Diamond Sculls.

Jack came close to competing at Henley, only to lose out at the eleventh hour because of the Royal Regatta's archaic rules excluding working men from this 'sport of gentlemen'. He never forgot nor forgave the sleight; after winning the Olympic gold medal, and beating the Henley champion in the process, he boasted to the American press that he would send his racing cap to King George V with a covering note exclaiming: *'Greetings from a bricklayer'*.

In his early twenties, Jack Kelly met 15-year-old Margaret Majer, a striking blonde who shared his passion for physical exercise (she would go on to take a degree in PE and became the first woman to teach the subject at the University of Pennsylvania). Margaret, a Lutheran by birth but a later convert to Catholicism, had appeared on a number of magazine covers, but she was handsome rather than beautiful and had a down-to-earth attitude completely at odds with most girls of her age. She wore unfussy clothes, avoided ostentatious jewellery and never put on heavy make-up or nail polish. In time, the couple became constant companions, but Margaret would not consider marriage until Jack could prove that he was capable of supporting a family. Showing the same single-minded determination that he brought to his sport, Jack borrowed $7000 from his brothers and founded his own brickwork company. Then, by shrewdly exploiting his fame to attract business, he built up a thriving order book and by the time he and Margaret were married in 1924, they were well on their way to their first million.

While Jack was running his empire, Margaret, or 'Ma' to all who knew her, was raising their new family. The couple's first child, Peggy, was born in 1927, followed, much to Jack's delight, by John junior. As his only son, John—or 'Kell', as he was known—bore the weight of his father's sporting ambitions and he would become an Olympic rower in his own right; he never quite managed to match his father's achievements, but Kell did exact revenge on behalf of the family by winning the Diamond Challenge Sculls (single scull) at Henley in 1947 and then repeating that victory in 1949.

Margaret had two more daughters—Grace in 1929 and Lizanne in 1933—by which time, the family was living in a luxurious red-brick mansion on affluent Henry Avenue, overlooking the district of East Falls. With seventeen rooms on three stories, the Kelly 'palace' came complete with tennis courts, landscaped gardens and live-in servants, and the children grew up with all of the privileges that money could buy. But despite fame and fortune, Jack Kelly was never accepted into the upper echelons of Philadelphia society, where 'new money' ran a poor second to breeding and heritage and the measure of worth was not the number of cars on a drive but whether a name could be traced back to colonial aristocracy. The Kelly girls, in particular, were ever on the periphery of this class system: they never became debutantes or made the much coveted 'social register', the bible of American blue bloods. Ma Kelly, true to her Lutheran principles, dismissed such social climbing with a shrug of her broad shoulders, but Jack turned his bitterness into inverse snobbery and potential suitors for his daughters' hands would be arbitrarily dismissed as not being 'good enough'.

Behind the façade of the contented family man, however, there were recurrent stories about Jack's affairs—usually with office girls or secretaries—and whispers about weekend 'business trips' and secret gifts. Margaret, if she was aware of the gossip, turned a blind eye and focussed on her duties as housewife and mother; she ran an efficient household, not without humour but with a Germanic sense of structure and discipline. When Jack was there, the house was noisy and boisterous, but when Ma was on her own, the children were taught the virtues of respect and consideration for others. It was Ma Kelly who instilled the idea into Grace that marriage was for life and that propriety must be maintained above all.

Grace Kelly, aged 12

In her early years, Grace was overshadowed by her more outgoing siblings. Even little Lizanne, four years her junior, seemed more robust; when the others played, she would sit quietly with her dolls or read a book. Peggy was the leader: she excelled at sport and was a natural show-off and Jack doted on her. Kell was his father's son and was being trained as an athlete almost as soon as he could walk. Compared to the others, Grace was pale and fragile and Jack, denied the rough and tumble with her that he enjoyed with the rest, christened her the 'runt' of the litter.

To please her father, Grace tried her hand to a number of sports, but she never excelled in a house of prize-winners and quickly realised that she would never stand out as an athlete. Various biographers have insisted that Grace was shy and self-conscious because of the chronically-poor eyesight that required her to wear glasses from an early age. But this was a temporary phase and as she matured, she grew into an attractive and confident teenager. At school, her teachers thought her a serious-minded, diligent, though generally unremarkable pupil.

The Kelly children: Grace, John jnr, Peggy and Lizanne

By her mid-teens, Grace had turned her attention to the stage. Jack indulged her interest, but only with the level of enthusiasm that was required of his position as a Democratic Party politician; he liked to be seen to support the arts but could find them of no practical value. Uncle George, the famous playwright, became Grace's mentor instead, and she would spend many hours in his company, listening to his tales of the theatre and Hollywood. Grace was fascinated by her uncle and years later told one reporter: 'He is the most wonderful and intelligent man I have ever known. Whatever he talks about he makes you understand all its beauty and hidden meaning.' It was George, much to Jack's amusement, who encouraged Grace to join the local amateur theatrical group in East Falls—a society run by another uncle, Midge Majer. As the niece of the group's director, to say nothing of her relationship with one of the state's most celebrated writers, she was guaranteed a central role and, in 1942, she made her stage debut in *Don't Feed the Animals.* While Jack drilled Kell on the Schuylkill River, Grace was cycling to rehearsals or to her Uncle George's for tips and advice about acting.

When she was 14, Grace switched from a convent-education at the Academy of the Assumption to the private Stevens School in Philadelphia, which placed as much emphasis on deportment as it did on academe; Jack, it seems, was determined that Grace would have the bearing, if not the breeding, of an aristocrat.

At Stevens, Grace garnered a few close friends but seldom participated in group events; she was undistinguished in appearance until she matured—and then she began to catch the attention of the local boys. Years later, Ma Kelly told a reporter, 'Every last boy and man who went out with her fell a little in love. Our house was everlastingly full of mooning boys.' Jack showed little tolerance for his daughter's choice of suitors and few, if any, lasted more than a single visit to Henry Avenue. But Grace soon became adept at keeping her male escorts out of sight of her father's disapproving eyes.

In 1947, Grace Kelly graduated from Stevens with her parents assuming that she would apply to a women's college in Vermont. However, this was the same summer of brother Kell's triumph at Henley, and the parental focus was elsewhere. The few colleges which still had places available were ruled out by a mediocre academic record, so when she suggested the American Academy of Dramatic Arts in New York, the idea was tacitly accepted.

Grace Kelly, aged 17, dances with her father

Grace may not have inherited her father's love of sports, but she did possess his burning ambition and, at the age of seventeen, she proved that she was a quick learner by throwing herself around the neck of her brother Kell on his triumphant return from Oxford in front of the massed ranks of the nation's press. The next day, front-page photographs all featured the 'mysterious blonde'. Not content with mastering the art of publicity, the pretty teenager was accomplished at manipulating people to her advantage. When the Kellys were informed that the roll for the AADA was closed and the Academy was not in a position to accept more students, Grace appealed to her Uncle George, who called the secretary of the Board of Trustees and she was promptly invited to a private audition. The nervous teenager managed to forget everything that she ever had learned in drama and rattled off scenes from Shakespeare and, of course, a play of George Kelly's—*The Torch Bearers*. In case anyone missed the connection, she wrote on her application that her ambition was to become, 'so accomplished a dramatic actress that some day my uncle George will write a play for me.'

Confronted with the earnest but clearly nervous young lady, secretary Emil Diestel made the following notes:

Temperament:	*Sensitive*
Spontaneity:	*Good youthfulness*
Dramatic instinct:	*Expressive*
Intelligence:	*Good*
General Remarks:	*Good, promising, youthful*

Diestel's main concern was the weakness of Grace's voice, which he described as 'nasal' and 'improperly placed', but he felt that it could be worked on and developed. Naturally, he also made a point of noting that Grace was the 'niece of George Kelly' and the aspiring actress was duly accepted into the Academy.

Jack and Margaret Kelly may have been willing to accept the idea of their 17-year-old daughter living in New York, at least for as long as she lasted at the AADA, but they were not about to allow her to be exposed to the habitual lot of acting students: dusty garrets or the YMCA were not considered appropriate for their girl. An application was submitted instead for a room at the exclusive Barbizon hotel on East 63rd Street.

Built in 1927, the Barbizon was a red brick, 23-storey bastion of feminine virtue; secure behind a 'women only' policy (the first male occupant was not admitted until 1980), the hotel had been aimed at the new class of young, professional females in New York and it protected its exclusivity by insisting that all guests forwarded three letters of reference. An air of quiet sophistication permeated its plush facilities, which included a library and a boutique; in the afternoons, tea was served in the lounge to young ladies and their beaus—the only time that men were allowed in the building (by means of a special pass). But despite its austere image, the Barbizon had no problem attracting clientele of the likes of Joan Crawford, Lauren Bacall and Gene Tierney.

Grace had no difficulty in being accepted into the Barbizon and her mother took comfort in the hotel's strictly-enforced Code of Conduct, which included a ban on male companions beyond the ground floor. But the Barbizon was not the prison camp that it appeared. With so many single women located in one place, it had become something of a magnet for every hot- bloodied young buck in town, and the clubs and bars that proliferated in the vicinity offered ample opportunity for a single girl to have fun.

The nuns and teachers at the Academy of the Assumption and Stevens School had done a good job with Grace; on the surface, she was refined and demure—the epitome of a well-bred young lady. Hugh J Connor, the manager at the Barbizon, recalled, 'Grace kept a great deal to herself. I used to see her in the dining room most nights, sitting with her glasses on reading a book through dinner.' However, the veneer of propriety was only skin-deep: Kelly biographer James Spada insists that she was sexually active before she moved to New York, having lost her virginity to a man 'several years older'. Certainly, she was no diffident wallflower and she wholeheartedly embraced all the distractions offered by the big city. The restrictions imposed by Connor and the Barbizon provided little in the way of deterrence; if anything, the prospect of doing something naughty or forbidden added spice. Within weeks of taking up residence at the hotel, Grace was reported to have smuggled men up to her rooms and was alleged to have cavorted naked in the hotel swimming pool with a rich playboy. Throughout her life, she was to adopt the same brazen attitude with regard to her various romantic liaisons.

During the daytime, Grace applied herself conscientiously to her studies. The AADA had an enviable reputation and could count Spencer Tracey, Edward G Robinson and Jason Robards amongst its alumni. Like its British equivalents, the AADA concentrated on the techniques of poise, delivery, diction, and the physical action that was required primarily of Shakespearean theatre, like fencing—which was taught equally to male and female students. But its approach was increasingly seen as old-fashioned and out of touch. In his 'Actor's Studio' in New York's 'Hell's Kitchen', celebrated acting coach Lee Strasberg was pioneering a new form of the art, the Method, which encouraged pupils to draw upon personal experience and 'live' emotions, rather than simply mimicking them parrot-fashion. Method students—Clift, Karl Malden and Marlon Brando among them—were making their own mark and would soon transform acting on Broadway and in Hollywood.

Grace had little difficulty mastering the mechanics of her craft; she read the right books, practised in her room and worked hard in her classes and at rehearsals. To help her with her delivery, she took lessons from a number of voice coaches, including Edward Goodman, an Oxbridge-educated Briton, who made it his personal mission to rid her of her Philadelphia twang. In short order, she was displaying what her tutors considered to be an ideal theatrical accent, complete with well-rounded vowels, approximating that of the English upper-class.

But she was less successful at exhibiting emotional range. Grace knew what was required and went through the right motions, but she remained stubbornly self-aware. This problem would return to haunt her when she finally made her breakthrough on the screen; the most common criticism of her later film performances, with the possible exception of *The Country Girl* (1954), was that she failed to show depth of feeling convincingly.

Grace had little social contact with the other students in her classes, and it was clear to at least one of her teachers that she was not popular among the student body. Don Richardson was her second-year tutor and though he was aware of the pretty but quiet girl in his class, he paid little attention to her until one day finding her in tears. Other students had been teasing her and when she ran from the school, it was Richardson who consoled. Grace responded to this 'knight in shining armour' by leaping, literally, into his arms.

Richardson, a graduate of the Academy, had directed a Broadway play and a number of radio shows. But in several important ways, he could not have been a more inappropriate choice for a romantic attachment: not only was he several years older than Grace and already married—albeit separated and in the process of a divorce—but he was Jewish and broke. On the other hand, dating the class tutor had advantages for an ambitious starlet; apart from the benefits in term-time, Richardson was well-connected in the theatrical scene and was soon taking his teenage protégé to all the right showbusiness parties and introducing her to producers and casting directors. Such a relationship would certainly have been frowned upon by the AADA Board, but Grace avoided drawing attention to herself by dating other students at the Academy, including Herb Miller, a regular boyfriend who remained blissfully unaware of her relationship with Richardson. 'She was so proper, people thought of her as a nun,' Richardson related. 'But when we were alone together, she used to dance naked for me to Hawaiian music. And if you don't think that was an incredible sight, you're crazy. She was a very sexy girl..'

So long as Jack Kelly's monthly cheque arrived, there was no need for Grace to take any casual work to fill in the time when she was not studying. But she was determined to prove to her family that she could stand on her own two feet, and while not about to start waiting on tables or serve in a bar to prove the point, she did manage to find a lucrative sideline. Herb Miller had taken photographs of her which he felt were good enough for publication. Grace was dismissive of the idea, but he sent them to a friend at *Redbook* magazine, who responded with an offer to publish. Grace grabbed at the chance with typical Kelly gusto; she promptly assembled a portfolio and signed on with a model agency. Within the year, her picture was on the cover not only of *Redbook*, but also of *True Romance* and *True Story*.

Grace started out on her modelling career on $7.50 per hour. However, the novelty soon wore off and she grew bored with the forced smiles and constant frock-changes. It was with diminishing enthusiasm that she lent her name (and face) to a raft of products ranging from cigarettes to beer and soap. The svelte teenager made an unusual choice for a 'girl next door', but she had the right blend of looks and sophistication to appeal to both male and females alike. Photographer Ruzzie Green told *Time* magazine: 'She's not a top model and never will be.. No glamour, no oomph, no cheesecake. She has lovely shoulders but no chest.' Despite her lack of 'oomph', her popularity with advertisers grew and, by the time she graduated from the AADA, she was commanding $25 an hour and was sought after for photo-shoots in Paris and Bermuda. But she never regarded modelling as anything more than a means to an end, and she was dismissive about her abilities in that regard: 'I was terrible. Anyone watching me give the pitch for *Old Gold* [cigarettes] would have switched to *Camels*.'

Aside from introductions, Richardson offered Grace an opportunity that all her wealth could not have bought: he chose her for the lead in the Academy's end-of-term production of the romantic comedy, *The Philadelphia Story*. As scripted, the role of Tracy Lord, a spoiled society girl whose forthcoming nuptials are complicated by confusion over who should be the real man in her life, could have been created specifically for Grace Kelly, but the faculty was not convinced that she had the qualities to pull it off on stage. Her voice was still thought too weak and her lack of presence worked against her; there were murmurings as to how she had won the coveted role.

The end-of-term play was more than a show for proud parents; it was considered to be a showcase for aspirants, and the audience was augmented by invited guests from the world of the theatre, including agents and producers. There are no reviews of Kelly's performance in *The Philadelphia Story*, but MCA talent scout Edith Van Cleve was watching from the stalls and immediately offered her a contract with the agency.

(A former Broadway actress, Edith Van Cleve had moved into casting in the early forties and quickly established herself as a major talent spotter who could count Brando and Clift among her 'discoveries'. She had an extensive network of contacts in the New York theatre establishment, as well as considerable influence in Hollywood, where endorsement by Van Cleve was considered a significant boost to any actor's career. Over the next few years, she would work exhaustively to convince the right people that Kelly had potential.)

If the MCA contract was good news, things got better for Grace when then she picked up her first professional engagement playing Florence McCricket, an amateur actress, in George Kelly's *The Torch Bearers* at the Bucks County Playhouse in New Hope, Pennsylvania. Being a provincial theatre, the Playhouse survived largely on 'summer stock' shows, but it managed to attract its fair share of theatrical talent

Only one soap
gives your skin this
exciting Bouquet
Cashmere
Bouquet
"For a TREAT instead of a TREATMENT
— have an
Old Gold"
Old Gold

Grace Kelly—model

Publicity shot for The Father

in the process, including Helen Hayes, Lillian Gish and Farley Grainger. It also offered an ideal opportunity for Grace to appear before a paying audience, and the Kelly family took up an entire row on opening night and cheered loudly at curtain call.

Jack Kelly's support was more than just vocal; the artistic director of the Playhouse was a passing acquaintance and was so keen to demonstrate friendship that when the programme was published, it hardly mentioned Grace but managed to name-check most of the rest of the Kelly family, including Kell! Jack and Ma became increasingly supportive of their daughter's new career and, while neither had much interest in the performing arts, they accommodated her ambitions financially and made an effort to see her whenever she appeared on stage. This included a trip all the way to Colorado when she performed there in the summer of 1951.

Appearing at New Hope meant that Grace had temporarily to vacate her New York base and commute to the Playhouse from Henry Avenue on a daily basis—an arrangement which signalled that the time had come to introduce Don Richardson to the family. Invited to spend the weekend, Richardson was to discover just how far he was from Jack Kelly's idea of the ideal son-in-law. While Jack took him on a whistle-stop tour of Philadelphia, pointing out the buildings that he had built, Ma rifled through his luggage and found not only condoms but the as-yet-unsigned divorce papers. The reception that awaiting him when he arrived back at the house could best be described as 'frosty'. In a letter to friend Prudence Wise, published in the *Daily Telegraph* in 1994, Grace wrote: '*The whole situation could not have been more gruesome. They dislike Don immensely and the fact that I could fall in love with a Jew was just beyond them. Then my mother pops out with the news that he was married and he was asking for a divorce. I told her I knew all about it. On and on it went.*' Before the visit had even begun, Richardson had packed his bags and headed back to New York, leaving a tearful and embarrassed Grace in his wake. The Kellys then extracted a promise from Grace that she would not see Richardson again.

Grace kept to her word, after a fashion. When she also returned to New York, she picked up the keys to Jack's latest present: a plush apartment in Manhattan House—an exclusive, newly-opened block on East 66th Street—built by one Jack Kelly. Manhattan House was a highly-suitable address for a young lady of Grace's background, if a little lavish for a wannabe actress, and it gave her a degree of independence that she was not allowed at the Barbizon. Richardson found himself gradually eased out of her life and, while she continued to see him on and off in the coming years on a casual basis, any romance was effectively ended.

If anything, Don Richardson's immediate successor in Grace Kelly's affections was even less suitable by the exacting standards of the family. But the 40-year-old, twice-divorced Claudius Charles Philippe was well placed to obtain for Grace the sort of introductions that Richardson could only dream of. Philippe was employed as the 'banqueting manager' at the exclusive Waldorf-Astoria Hotel in Manhattan and, belying his lowly title, was one of the most sought-after and influential social arrangers in New York. Philippe's address book contained such 'personal friends' as the Duke and Duchess of Windsor, the Vanderbilts and Marlene Dietrich. To the New York social elite, a soiree without the input of 'Philippe of the Waldorf' was unthinkable. Philippe not only opened the right doors for Grace, he quietly tutored her on the finer points of cuisine and fine wines. Grace already had the money; Philippe now added the class.

One of Philippe's current contacts was the Shah of Iran, Mohammad Reza Pahlavi, who was staying at the Waldorf-Astoria on an official state visit. Philippe introduced his girlfriend and promptly bowed out when the Shah invited her to join him on a sightseeing tour of New York. In the full blaze of publicity, Grace accompanied one of the most famous men in the world—and notorious womaniser—to restaurants and nightclubs, happy to be seen posing on his arm for the benefit of the cameras. On one occasion, a beaming Grace Kelly arrived with her date at the opera, and the press reported that the entire audience rose to give the couple a standing ovation.

Back in Henry Avenue, the novelty of seeing their daughter's photograph splashed across the society pages soon wore off for Jack and Ma when one newspaper revealed that the Shah had presented the unknown starlet with some extremely expensive jewellery, including a gold vanity case with thirty-two diamonds in the clasp. Ma was dispatched to New York to instruct Grace to be more discrete and, for the sake of decency, to return the Shah's gifts. (Grace kept the jewels and used them as presents for her bridesmaids at her wedding.)

Actor Raymond Massey, who was set to direct a new version of August Strindberg's *The Father* with himself in the role of The Captain, cast Grace as his daughter Bertha. The play was to open on Broadway in November 1949, after previewing in Boston. Massey was also an old friend of George Kelly's, but he at least had the sense to keep the wider Kelly family out of his programme notes, and he made a great show of surprise when the clan descended on one of his Boston previews! Two days after Grace's 20th birthday, *The Father* opened at the Cort Theatre and ran for a disappointing sixty-nine performances. The critics on the whole offered mixed reviews, but Grace received some kind notices and was reassured when she was announced as the recipient of *Theatre World* magazine's award for 'Most Promising Personality'. Despite the brevity of the run, it had given her a solid Broadway debut.

The early closure of *The Father* left Grace out of work but more determined than ever to build on the progress that she had made. Over the next few months, she tried out for some forty productions, among them the role of the ingénue in a production of *The Country Girl*. However, no-one came forward with a firm offer. Years later, she would reflect that she was always considered to be 'too tall, too skinny, too young. I was always "too" something.' One great disappointment was *The Wisteria Trees*, adapted from Chekov's *The Cherry Orchard*, which was to be directed by Joshua Logan and star Helen Hayes. Hayes's daughter Mary had been a class-mate of Grace at AADA, and the girls had stayed in touch. Grace made sure that Hayes and Logan were aware of the connection and was confident that it would help her land the role. But the actress was not to be swayed by such considerations and she rejected Grace, claiming that her voice was too weak.

Despite her lack of progress, casting agents continued to show interest. The resourceful Edie Van Cleve realised that Grace needed experience more than she

Lights Out—'The Borgia Lamp' (Grace Kelly)

needed exposure, and she pushed her into auditioning for television. The television industry was still in relative infancy, but it was beginning to entrench itself as the entertainment choice of the masses. In 1948, there were approximately one million television sets in the US; by the end of 1950, there would be some eight million sets and over one hundred TV stations. Grace was still appearing in commercials at the time, so she was already a familiar face to television viewers, even if they did not know her by name. Reluctantly, she accepted Van Cleve's argument that she could not refine her craft if she was not working and that television would at least offer her the chance to do so.

TV shows were broadcast 'live', with actors called in at short notice and expected to pick up parts quickly; it was an approach that favoured the technical aspects of acting and it suited Grace's strengths. In a short space of time, it gave her the opportunity to play leading roles in *Bethel Merriday*, *The Swan* and *Rockingham House*. She soon established herself as a reliable and attractive performer and made appearances in some of the most prestigious series on the small screen: *Somerset Maugham TV Theatre*, *The Actor's Studio*, *Lights Out* and *Hallmark Hall of Fame*, as well as a raft of guest-spots in regular shows like *Danger* and *Suspense*. By the time that she had appeared in some sixty productions between 1950 and 1953, Grace was considered successful enough to be included in *Life* magazine's feature on 'TV's Leading Ladies'.

Grace continued to use personal relationships to promote her work on television. Manny Sachs, one of Jack Kelly's closest friends and head of Columbia Records, had taken a close interest in her career since her move to New York and had used his own contacts to get her modelling assignments. Now that the actress had broken into TV, he was in a better position to put her in front of the people who mattered; Sachs introduced her to many of Columbia's biggest stars, including Frank Sinatra. Grace also cultivated a friendship with Fred Coe, head of production for NBC in New York, who would cast her in a number of prime-time shows, such as the prestigious *Philco Television Theatre*.

Despite her small-screen success, Van Cleve was having no luck in obtaining that elusive Broadway breakthrough for Grace. Instead, she sent her to audition for Gregory Ratoff, who was about to start work on a movie called *Taxi* (1953). Ratoff was looking for an actress to play an innocent young Irish girl, cast adrift in the big city while looking for her husband. With her Nordic looks and patrician bearing, Grace was hardly the typical colleen; she arrived late for the audition and the part went to raven-haired Constance Smith. But Ratoff was impressed enough to send the test footage back to California, with his recommendation that she would be worth considering for other things in the future.

Van Cleve was more successful with *Fourteen Hours*, a melodrama set in New York with Richard Basehart as a man determined to end it all, who spends said time on a window ledge awaiting an opportune moment. Grace made the trip to Los

Fourteen Hours (Grace Kelly)

Angeles for the test but made it clear to producers 20th Century Fox that she was not interested in a long-term contract. That intransigence cost her the larger role of Basehart's girlfriend in the film (ultimately played by Debra Pagett, who professed no such qualms) but she was awarded a small part as a woman in the building opposite who catches sight of the would-be suicide. 'If you sneeze,' Grace told her sisters, 'you will miss me.' Veteran director Henry Hathaway, whose work included *The Lives of a Bengal Lancer* (1935), was impressed enough with her contribution to ignore her objections and send a contract offer to Van Cleve anyway, but Grace turned it down without even reading it. But *Fourteen Hours* provided her with a screen debut and a mention from one or two eagle-eyed critics. It even resulted in a fan club—which which amused her no end.

Fourteen Hours was also to put Grace's picture on the desks of a number of

Theatrical poster for High Noon

Hollywood producers, and Van Cleve saw to it that her face was brought to the attention of Jay Kanter, a rising star in MCA's Los Angeles operation; at 25, Kanter was already looking after the West Coast interests of a number of Van Cleve's clients, such as Brando and Clift. Kanter respected Van Cleve's judgement and agreed to forward Grace's details to Stanley Kramer, the producer of Brando's film *The Men* (1950), who was casting a western called *High Noon* (1952). The film was still in pre-production and Kanter had been pushing Brando for the lead role of Will Kane, a US Marshall forced to confront a band of gunmen who are out to kill him. Kramer, writer/producer Carl Foreman and director Fred Zinnemann were persuaded to sit through the *Taxi* footage and were impressed by what they saw. Grace was summoned to Hollywood to test for the role of Kane's wife Amy, a timid Quaker woman whose wedding day looks set to end with her as a widow. Grace arrived in tinsel-town in her trademark white gloves and was immediately offered the part. A shooting date was set for the summer, conditional upon the signing of a suitable leading man.

Traditionally, the western genre offered little opportunity for actresses to shine; a man is generally left to do what a man has to do while the little lady looks on. While *High Noon* was in no way to be a conventional western, it still offered little beyond that basic premise. When Marshall Kane fails to persuade any in the local community to come to his help, Amy is only required to appear fretful. Even the introduction of a voluptuous saloon girl from Kane's past elicits little more from Amy than sullen pouting. The dramatic potential in the role was there, if anyone had cared to develop it—Amy has to battle not only her convictions on non-violence but her feelings of inadequacy as well. As it was, Messrs Kramer and Foreman were more interested in the political allegory, and any human drama in the script was reserved for the plight of husband Will.

Throughout the spring and early summer of 1951, Kramer continued with his

Kelly poses for an early studio publicity shot

preparations for *High Noon*. Producing the film independently through his own company (part-financed by Columbia in exchange for distribution rights) gave him a certain amount of freedom to shape the project the way that he wanted. However, it also meant that he had to work harder to attract a suitably bankable male star, and the subversive theme—a thinly-veiled attack on the 'witch-hunting' politics of Senator Joseph McCarthy and his House Un-American Activities Committee—put off more conservative stars. Among those who gave *High Noon* a wide berth were John Wayne, Charlton Heston and Gregory Peck. The decision to dress the allegory in the garb of the Old West rather than give it a more contemporary setting also alienated Zinnemann's preferred choices of Brando and Clift, neither of whom wanted to appear in a routine 'cowboy movie'. Running out of options, the producers returned to the one name which had come up earlier in discussions but had been dismissed out of hand.

In 1941, Gary Cooper was the highest-paid actor in Hollywood and the star of classics like *A Farewell to Arms* (1932), *Beau Geste* (1939) and *Sergeant York* (1941). A decade later, Cooper's contract with Paramount had come to an end and a run of unsuitable roles had given him an air of 'yesterday's man'. Added to the actor's problems, his marriage to Veronica 'Rocky' Balfe was in difficulties, much to the delight of the salacious Hollywood press. Since their marriage in 1933, Rocky had endured without comment a series of indiscretions by her errant husband but in 1949, Cooper had gone too far when he embarked on a destructive affair with Patricia Neal; the fling was short-lived but Rocky and Cooper separated in March, 1951. The upheaval in his personal and professional life had taken its toll on the actor; he suffered badly from stomach ulcers, was in constant pain with back problems and, in the late summer, underwent surgery for a hernia.

Cooper had been ruled out of the casting process relatively early, partly because of his own view that he was too old and too tired to play the role. But with the more obvious choices ruling themselves out, the producers turned back to him and persuaded him to accept a low salary against a percentage share of the profits.

The casting of Gary Cooper could have had a significant impact on Grace Kelly; the actor was acutely conscious of the age difference between Will Kane and his new wife—in Cooper' s words, it looked 'like I was marrying a child'. With time running against them, Kramer and Foreman decided that it was a risk worth taking and in August, they confirmed the start-date for the film with Edie Van Cleve.

The one-film contract for *High Noon* appealed to Grace, who was still insisting

Publicity shot for High Noon (Gary Cooper)

that she wanted to be a stage actress and not a film star. However, the timing of the production cut a swathe through her stated ambition and forced her to make a clear choice between stage and screen. Van Cleve, cognisant of the vagaries of the film industry, anticipated that *High Noon* would not start filming until the autumn and signed Grace to two late-summer engagements. The first of these would mark her return to the Buck's County Playhouse, this time playing a secretary to an ageing writer in *Accent on Youth*. The short run did not go well and the actress left New England with the guffaws of the critics ringing loudly in her ears. The second and more important engagement was at the Elitch Theatre in Denver, Colorado, where Grace was signed for the season: ten productions in eleven weeks, ranging from T S Eliot's *The Cocktail Party* to Kaufman and Hart's *The Man Who Came to Dinner*.

Publicity shot for High Noon (Grace Kelly)

High Noon (Katy Jurado, Grace Kelly)

The grand old Denver theatre had been hosting summer stock companies since the 1890s and counted Sarah Bernhardt, Cecile B De Mille and Douglas Fairbanks among previous casts. For $125 a week, Grace was being offered a valuable and exhilarating experience, as well as the sort of basic grounding in theatre-work that would have taken her years to acquire on Broadway.

By the time word came through from Kramer, Grace had started to enjoy herself at the Elitch and was about to take on one of the most challenging roles in the whole of the run: the damaged, haunted Laura in Tennessee Williams's *The Glass Menagerie*. The colourless Amy Kane and four weeks in California's San Fernando Valley offered little of the professional challenge or amiable atmosphere of Denver, but it did hold out the promise of film stardom. However, her main concern was not for the role she was about to play or her commitment to the company, but that the management of the Elitch would not let her leave the company at so crucial a juncture. Van Cleve put her mind at rest and assured her it that happened all the time: the theatre was told, rather than asked, that she was going to Hollywood. Pausing just long enough to let her mother in on the news and agreeing to accept her sister Lizanne as a temporary room-mate/chaperone, Grace Kelly packed her bags and headed west.

Grace and Lizanne checked into the comfortable Chateau Marmont, a French-style hotel in West Hollywood which had gained a reputation as something of a lover's hideaway. Grace would later take full advantage of the Chateau's discrete cottages when she returned to film *Dial M for Murder* during the late summer of 1953 but, for the moment, her focus was very much on preparing for the job at hand—or it was until she met her co-star.

Gary Cooper's physical discomforts showed in his face and he was looking for nothing more from *High Noon* than to prove to Hollywood that he was still employable—he certainly was not looking for any new romantic complications. But

Grace was adept at bringing out the father-figure in men, and soon the 'too old/too tired' actor was offering his young co-star lifts to and from the location, and spending the time between setups chatting to Grace or running her through her lines with her. The crew knew the signs; actors of Cooper's stature simply did not spend time with unknowns unless something was going on. To add to the speculation, there was talk that Grace was seeing Zinnemann on the side. Actress Katy Jurado thought so. Cast as the 'other woman', Jurado (who was Brando's girlfriend at the time) had been given the meatier role, but she felt that she was being unfairly sidelined for Kelly and complained vociferously—to no avail. Writer Bob Slatzer was on set as a guest of Cooper's and also noted that Grace seemed to be getting more than her fair share of close-ups: 'I thought Zinnemann had a thing going for Grace and I found out later that I was right. Miles of her on film ended up on the cutting-room floor.'

When the blonde starlet began to follow Cooper around the set like a faithful puppy-dog, gossip columnist Hedda Hooper sniffed a story and canvassed him for a quote. In the first of what would become the pattern for press statements from older co-stars, Cooper paid bland tribute to the actress while playing down any talk of romance: 'Grace,' he insisted, 'was very serious about her work.. She was trying to learn, you could see that. You can tell if a person really wants to be an actress. She was one of those people you could get that feeling about, and she was pretty..'

Whatever the cast and crew thought, Grace was disappointed by the lack of support from Zinnemann who, perhaps sensing that Cooper had staked his claim, left the actress largely to her own devices. She told *Photoplay*: 'Mr Zinnemann is the quiet type. He has a penetrating knowledge of how to delineate on the screen the light and shade of human emotions—he makes the player readily respond to that knowledge.' In later years, she would qualify that statement by stating that the director ignored her, to the detriment of her performance.

Grace's fears about her performance proved well-founded. At *High Noon*'s preview in Riverside, California, reaction was almost entirely negative and columnist James Brown reported that 'half the picture was close-ups of Grace Kelly', which not go down well with an audience anticipating a Gary Cooper movie. Harry Cohn, whose Columbia studios had helped to finance the production, declined his option to distribute the film and branded it 'a dog'. In desperation, Kramer brought in editor Elmo Williams to work with Zinnemann and recut the film; among the more telling changes was a series of close-ups of a ticking clock, which created a palpable atmosphere of tension. The tinkering further resulted in the addition of the Tex Ritter theme song, *The Ballad of High Noon*, which helped to increase the film's marketability. Williams's efforts earned him a well-deserved Academy Award.

The re-editing may have saved the film commercially, but Grace regarded *High Noon* as a personal disaster which highlighted her inexperience and made her look stiff and awkward. Her inadequacies in this regard are most exposed in her scenes with Katy Jurado, who had a point to prove, and the fiery brunette completely blows the pallid Amy off the screen. Grace was appalled at the result: 'With Gary Cooper, everything is so clear,' she told *Time*. 'You look into his face and see everything he is thinking. You looked into my own face and saw nothing. I knew what I was thinking but it didn't show. For the first time I thought, "Perhaps I am not going to be a great star; perhaps I'm not any good after all."' Shaken by the whole experience, she returned to New York to lick her wounds. 'I'm not turning my back on Hollywood, but I feel I can do stage and screen while headquartering in New York,' she assured the readers of *Picture Show*, adding weakly that she would 'still be anxious to play a good role if producers want me.'

The truth was that film producers could see nothing in Grace Kelly that they

Kelly poses for a studio publicity shot, circa 1952

could not find in a hundred other starlets, any of whom were more eager for the work. She had admirers in Hollywood, Zinnemann and Cooper among them, as well as the steadfast support of Jay Kanter and MCA boss Lew Wasserman, but instead of working the system to her advantage, Grace chose to sit in Manhattan House and wait for producers to come to her. (*High Noon* finally opened in July, 1952, while Grace was in Africa. After a shaky start, it became a respectable if unspectacular hit: its reputation would continue to grow, but for his investment of $750,000, Stanley Kramer banked a satisfactory $3.5m on its initial North American release.)

'Doesn't a woman's reputation count for anything here?'
—Linda Nordley (Grace Kelly), *Mogambo* (1953)

With no better offers on the horizon, Grace returned to television for a part

in *The Rich Boy*, from a story by F Scott Fitzgerald. She also played a small role in the Broadway comedy, *To Be Continued*, which opened at the Booth Theatre on April 23, 1952. Her character in the play is listed as 'a young woman', but *To Be Continued* was discontinued after only thirteen performances with hardly anyone noticing. (The production is worthy of a footnote now because it was to be the last time that Grace Kelly would appear on Broadway.)

By the early 1950s, the all-powerful studio system which had dominated the American film industry since its beginnings was in decline. With the Hollywood Antitrust Case of 1948 (the 'Paramount decree', as it became known), the Federal government forced the major studios to off-load their interests in exhibition and distribution and without their theatrical outlets, they could no longer control what films were seen, or when. The demise of 'factory' production led directly to the rise

Publicity shot for Mogambo (Clark Gable, Ava Gardner)

of independent producers—Kramer now prominent among them—and the nature and style of films changed. In 1949, less than 20% of Hollywood's films came from independents; within a decade, it would be nearer 60%. At the same time, actors were flexing their own muscles and some of the biggest stars in Tinseltown were refusing to sign long-term contracts. Agents had begun to negotiate lucrative deals for one-off productions, frequently with percentage shares of the profits. The old style moguls, Cohn at Columbia, Zanuck at Fox and Jack Warner at Warner Brothers, were still in their upholstered offices, but their day was going and their replacements were being forced to adapt to a very different environment.

At MGM, founding father Louis B Mayor had handed over the reins to Dore Schary, but despite this change at the top, there was little change in the studio's business model. Under the straight-talking New Yorker, the company had tried a platform of realistic pictures which had met a lukewarm response and it quickly retreated behind the same old diet of overblown action movies and musicals. Like his predecessor, Schary clung to the studio's stable of stars, regarded by many to be as much a trademark of MGM as its famous 'Leo the Lion' logo.

MGM was in need of a film for star Clark Gable, the one-time 'King of Hollywood', who was coming to the end of his contract and almost to the end of his shelf-life as a leading man. Actor Stewart Granger, also on MGM's payroll, had suggested a remake of Gable's 1932 *Red Dust* as a vehicle for himself and Marlene Dietrich. Schary liked the idea but decided that it would be a better goodbye present for the 'King', and Gable was duly cast in his old role, but with a new name. Veteran western director John Ford was given the chore of directing, while *Red Dust* writer John Lee Mahin was instructed to rework his own script for the post-World War 2 generation. The result was *Mogambo*.

Set against the rugged backdrop of Africa's 'dark continent', *Mogambo* was to pit Gable's all-action hero against a panting floozy with a past and a repressed but sensuous married woman. *They fought like sleek jungle cats!* MGM's publicity ads screamed. *A flaming love feud! The jungle strips two civilised women of all but their most primeval instincts!* Schary looked no further than the studio's own roster for the hard-drinking, hard-talking Eloise 'Honey Bear' Kelly and cast the hard-drinking, hard-talking Ava Gardner in the role. Grace, who until then had been no-one's idea of a feline predator, was the surprise choice for the third side of the triangle—the mousy Linda Nordley.

John Ford, who had notched up two Oscars (his third would come during the shooting of *Mogambo*), had seen Grace in *High Noon* and been understandably unimpressed. 'All she did was shoot a guy in the back,' he said. 'Cooper should have given her a boot in the pants.' But he liked the *Taxi* footage, in which she better suited the character that he had in mind; as a result, she was offered a return ticket to Hollywood to test for the role of Linda.

While professing that her long-term goal of stage stardom remained the same, Grace was finally prepared to compromise her principles and accept the fact that theatrical producers would need an incentive to find their way to her door. The contract that came with *Mogambo* was therefore the first step towards the creation of 'Grace Kelly—movie star'. In later years, she would claim that it was the enticement of Africa that brought her into the Hollywood star system: 'If *Mogambo* had been in Arizona, I wouldn't have done it,' she said—an odd remark for a woman who always had the wherewithal to afford an African adventure anytime that she liked, without the need to work during daylight hours. By signing over exclusive claim on her services to MGM, Grace Kelly would effectively consign her film career to a studio that was at least a decade behind the current trendsetters in terms of its thinking. But that is what she did. She arrived in Hollywood on September 3, 1951, to test for the role of Linda Nordley in *Mogambo*, on the clear understanding that if cast, she would sign a long-term contract. John Ford, who described the character she was to play as a 'frigid dame that's really a pip between the sheets', was convinced by what he saw and instructed the studio to sign her up.

Jay Kanter led for MCA in discussion with MGM and enlisted support from Wasserman. Poor word of mouth on Grace's contribution to *High Noon* and lack of significant progress in her career put them in a weak bargaining position; Lucille Ryman Carroll, formidable head of MGM's Talent Department for over a decade, conceded that she saw no discernable potential in Kelly. Nevertheless, she gave permission for her pursue her career on stage and to stay in Manhattan when not required for film work. In return, Grace agreed to a seven-year contract, renewable

Mogambo (Grace Kelly, Ava Gardner)

half-yearly, at $750 a week; to put that into perspective, the average newcomer at MGM was on $1500 per week and an established star would be on $4–$5000.

For his part, Schary was intent on pulling out all the stops to make *Mogambo* a success. MGM press releases would promise 'scenes of unrivalled savagery and awe-inspiring splendour', and director John Ford, his cast and crew were to spend a gruelling sixty-seven days trudging through locations in Kenya, the Congo and Uganda. *Mogambo* was to be the biggest film ever shot in Africa, with the production unit of almost two hundred personnel, supported by three hundred local bearers. Their base camp on the banks of the Kagera River was comprised of three hundred tents, which included catering, wardrobe and recreational facilities. There was also a purpose-built airfield to fly supplies in and film stock out, as well as a private army of thirty hand-picked guards working for the famous white hunter, 'Bunny' Allen. In the centre of this, Ford and his actors toiled away to make movie art out of a massive logistical undertaking.

Like most who were involved in *Mogambo*, Ford later claimed he took the film on as an adventure; he told Peter Bogdanovich, 'I never saw the original picture [*Red Dust*], I liked the script and the story, I liked the set-up and I'd never been to that part of Africa—so I just did it.' But the attraction quickly wore thin for the director: he hated the heat, the flies and the lack of amenities. Never an easy man at the best of times, Ford took his frustration out on the cast: he shouted at Gable for wasting time and slumming his way through the film; he raged at Gardner for her drinking and her incessant chattering, and at Kelly for her dithering. Gardner called Ford, 'One of the crustiest sons of bitches ever to direct a film.. the meanest man on earth, thoroughly evil.' At least Gardner could match his acid tongue and vulgarity, and a grudging respect developed. Grace, who visibly wilted whenever he stared at her, could do no more than endure the onslaughts.

To abbreviate things in the hope of returning to the US faster, Ford took to rewriting the script in the evenings, cutting down the location work and removing as much of the 'awe-inspiring splendour' as he could get away with. This tactic brought him into conflict with his producer, Sam Zimbalist, who watched in increasing desperation as the picture's main selling point was whittled away. The bickering between the two men left Ford even less inclined to indulge his cast and, in an effort to speed things on, he dispensed with rehearsals and instead barked instructions at the actors. Donald Sinden, as Grace's husband, recalled the director's style in his autobiography: 'The script merely indicated: The boat arrives and the scientist and his wife get off. Over the walkie-talkie we heard, "Roll 'em. Action" and the boat started to chug forward. Suddenly Ford's voice screamed over a loud hailer: "Grace—Donald—get below. OK Donald—come on deck. Look around at the scenery. Call Grace. Put your arm around her. Point out a giraffe over to your right. Get your camera—quickly. Photograph it—the giraffe. Smile at him, Grace. Grace—look at the hippopotamus on your left, get Donald to photograph it. A crocodile slides into the water. You're scared. Grace—you're scared. OK. OK. You're coming into the pier. Look around. What's in store for you? Natives are running to meet you. OK. OK. Cut. Print it."'

Kelly on location for Mogambo

There was no time for retakes; no discussion on motivation; the actors were there to do whatever Ford ordered them to do. Ford had no interest in character development; he may have thought Linda Nordley a 'pip' in bed but if Grace struggled to convey that on the screen, that was her problem not his. As a result, where the script required Linda to be smouldering, Grace simpered like a schoolgirl—a far remove from the 'sleek jungle cat' of the poster.

There was some respite from the daily grind. In the evenings, Grace, Gable and Gardner would sit up drinking and discussing movies, with the 'King' in full flow about how his career would pick up when he could throw off the shackles of MGM. Gable, openly contemptuous of Hollywood, promised that he would look after Grace and that she would star in his first film as an independent, and she seems genuinely to have believed the ageing matinee idol would be able to revive his career in the autumn of his life. The three would put the world to rights into the wee small hours until Grace, a novice drinker in comparison to the others, could take the pace no longer; on more than one occasion, she had to be carried back to her tent. Donald Sinden told of stumbling into Gable's tent one evening by mistake and, seeing the outline of a naked woman in the shadows, mumbled an apology and beat a hasty retreat. Sinden was too much of gentleman to name names in print, but the crew of *Mogambo* were sure that they knew who was sharing the 'King's' camp-bed.

Clark Gable was single but not exactly unattached; he had divorced wife Sylvia Ashley in April 1952 and although he was 'seeing' French model/actress Suzanne Dadolle, he had made it clear that this liaison was on a casual basis. Gable's formidable reputation as a Lothario was largely based on his Rhett Butler screen image and tall tales from a string of publicity-hungry starlets, but the years had not been kind to him and he was in poor physical and mental shape. Ava Gardner, commenting on his declining memory, said, 'He's the sort of guy—if you say, "Hiya Clark how are ya?"—He's stuck for an answer.' For all his failings, the 'King' remained a fantasy figure for a generation of women throughout the world, and the suggestion that the 52-two year old actor might be carrying on with a woman half his age was a dream come true for the scandal-hungry media.

Rumours of an affair between Gable and Kelly were fed back to Hollywood and Louella Parsons, the shrew-like gossip columnist of the powerful Hearst group of newspapers, used her friendship with Gable to ask him outright. 'This is the greatest compliment I've ever had,' he insisted through her nationally-syndicated column, 'but I'm old enough to be her father.' The speculation continued regardless, spurred on by the studio's publicity department, which thought that a few hints here and there might add some spice to the on-screen passions: the official press releases made as much as they could of Grace knitting a pair of socks for Gable's Christmas present, or teaching him rudiments of the local dialect. The couple, film fans were told, liked nothing better than an early morning hunting trip; Gable armed with his rifle and Grace trotting behind in her 5th Avenue khaki shorts, with nothing more threatening than a camera. It may have been the slowest of slow-burning affairs, but the slew of publicity helped to revive interest in Gable while at the same time giving Grace the sort of media coverage that any aspiring actress needs.

Nominally, *Mogambo* was an MGM-British production (most of the crew were English), and as soon as he had finished in Africa, Ford decamped to Borehamwood in Hertfordshire to shoot interiors. Arriving in London, Grace found that her mother had crossed the Atlantic to keep an eye on her. Ma began by putting reporters right on a few basic points. 'I was only too aware of the emotions that our Gracie could arouse in men,' she said, but she went on to insist that the Kelly/Gable romance was 'nothing more than a schoolgirl crush'. There was no truth, she told them, in the rumour that Gable was about to propose marriage.

Gable himself was in complete agreement; long nights in Africa with nothing else to do were one thing, but London was altogether too close to Paris for comfort—especially with a certain French model watching his every move—and he decided that it was time to put some distance between himself and Grace. When she and her mother booked into the Savoy, he checked into the Connaught, and when they

Publicity shot for Mogambo (Grace Kelly, Clark Gable)

***Mogambo* (Donald Sinden, Grace Kelly, Clark Gable)**

did meet up socially, it was always in the company of Ma Kelly, tabloid interest notwithstanding.

Even winning the Best Director Oscar for *The Quiet Man* (1952) did nothing to improve John Ford's temperament; if anything, it made him more anxious to finish *Mogambo* and get back to California. His failing health did not help; Ford had contracted amoebic dysentery in Africa and he suffered debilitating stomach cramps. He had also developed cataracts in his eyes, leaving his vision blurred and light-sensitive. *Mogambo* was now a test of endurance; he wanted it done and he cared about little else—especially the sensitivities of his pampered cast, of whom Grace had become a singular example. By the time the production restarted in England, he and the actress were barely on speaking terms; when he did deign to talk to her, he addressed her only as 'Kelly'.

Grace was relieved when she finally finished her scenes and she saw no reason to stay on in London. Despite the presence of a maternal chaperone, MGM's publicity team had one last card to play, and it persuaded Gable to escort her to Heathrow airport for a fond farewell. The actor appeared visibly annoyed at being dragged out of his hotel to put on a show, while Grace looked suitably distraught, but the press went into something of a frenzy. The fact that it was a carefully-orchestrated publicity stunt seemed to elude most of the reporters, and the tearful goodbyes and renewed talk of 'love affairs' made front pages across the world.

Director John Ford followed suit soon afterwards, leaving it to producer Sam Zimbalist to put together a coherent movie.

Back in New York, Grace unpacked her mementoes of Africa and fretted over the state of her career and her latest movie. In a private letter published in 1994, she complained: 'Gable and Sam Zimbalist are cutting the picture to pieces, which breaks my heart. I'm not speaking to Clark these days and neither is Ava but don't tell anyone that.'

Grace Kelly and Clark Gable

Edie Van Cleve continued to look for work for Grace on the stage, but her image was no more acceptable to theatre producers in 1952 than it had been two years earlier. *High Noon* had since opened, but her role was so overshadowed by those of her co-stars that she barely registered in most reviews. Van Cleve and Kanter both advised patience, and pointed out that MGM was struggling to generate enough work for their established talent—Elizabeth Taylor, Deborah Kerr, Lana Turner and Debbie Reynolds among others—let alone find suitable parts for a virtual unknown. Dore Schary was in no hurry either; he had seen the unedited footage of *Mogambo* and been unimpressed by Grace's screen persona. It was clear that she did not fit with the current vogue for brassy, vulgar sex symbols, *à la* Marilyn Monroe.

MGM had a break-point written into Grace's contract which allowed it to terminate early if it so chose and on the evidence of *Mogambo*, Schary was inclined to exercise his option. If she had been on a higher salary, MGM might well have cut its losses, then and there. But as things stood, Schary was prepared to wait until the release of *Mogambo*, scheduled for the autumn of 1952, and let the public be the judge as to whether he had an asset or a liability on his hands.

With no interest emanating from Hollywood, Grace was faced with the option of going back into television—a move that she considered with some distaste—or sitting it out in New York. And she might have been left to stew in Manhattan House had MCA's Lew Wasserman not intervened on her behalf..

Alfred Hitchcock was about to start shooting his latest movie in Los Angeles and he was struggling to find a leading lady. He needed either an English actress or one who could convince as English; she also needed to be pretty and available more or less immediately. Whether she could act or not, so far as Hitch was concerned, was immaterial; he had already cast the rest of the roles and was getting uncomfortably close to his start-date. And that was when Wasserman called him to say that he thought he had the very actress that Hitch was looking for...

Chapter 3

Dial M for Murder

Kelly and Hitchcock on the set of Dial M for Murder

'Do you really believe in the perfect murder?'
—Margot (Grace Kelly), *Dial M For Murder* (1954)

'We did an interesting colour experiment with Grace Kelly's clothing. I dressed her in very gay and bright colours at the beginning of the picture, and as the plot thickened, her clothes became gradually more sombre.'
—Alfred Hitchcock

In the early summer of 1953, Alfred Hitchcock and Grace Kelly were introduced for the first time. Jay Kanter and Warner's casting office in LA had arranged a short, informal meeting in Hollywood in lieu of a screen test which, given Kelly's recent track record at auditions, must have come as something of a relief to the actress. That is not to say that the prospect was entirely stress-free. Kelly would have been aware that Hitchcock had a stated intolerance of actors as a breed and a total indifference to the idea that acting was an art-form—the fact that she had not been furnished with a script spoke volumes about how he viewed her relative importance to the process; nor would her disposition have been helped by the knowledge that MGM's Dore Schary was looking to terminate her contract if she failed to demonstrate her earning potential, or by the news from her agents that she had not even featured in the shortlist of potential candidates when Hitchcock started to cast his film.

Returning from her stage-managed fond farewell to Gable in London, Kelly reluctantly accepted the temporary hiatus in her film career while *Mogambo* was being assembled and instructed Edie Van Cleve to find her any work that she could in the meantime, preferably on stage in New York. With nothing suitable on Broadway, Kelly agreed to a run in Philadelphia as a virginal actress fending off the attentions of two playboys in Ernest Laszlo's *The Moon is Blue* at the Playhouse in the Park, a theatre partly sponsored by her father.

Television also offered a reprieve from 'resting' when Kelly was cast in a Philco Playhouse production entitled *Way of an Eagle,* co-starring Jean-Pierre Aumont, a handsome French actor who was equally popular on American television. By the time the play was broadcast on June 7, 1953, she and Aumont had become lovers. Such romantic interludes may have provided some distraction, but what Kelly really wanted a good role in a play or film of quality.

For his part, Hitchcock shared John Ford's view that Kelly had been weak in *High Noon* but the Englishman was rather more diplomatic than the cantankerous Ford, and described her performance only as 'mousy'. Nevertheless, Kelly came recommended by the one man whose opinion Hitchcock respected above all others: Lew Wasserman. That Kelly's résumé suggested she was the least qualified of the candidates that he had considered was of limited importance to a director who was supremely confident of his ability to tease a performance out of any actor. If anything, it played to the prejudices of a man who often stated that the less experience an actor had the better—the less they would have to 'unlearn'.

There was another reason why Kelly might have attracted the attention of Hitchcock prior to his meeting with her; behind the persona of an urbane gentleman, Hitchcock loved gossip, and the more scandalous the better. Despite her limited exposure to the film industry, there was a great deal of murmuring circulating about the starlet; in Hollywood at the time, Grace Kelly's name meant one thing: sex. Writer Gore Vidal summed it up succinctly: 'Grace almost always laid the leading man. She was famous for that in this town.'

Hitchcock had shrugged off the disappointment of *I Confess* and thrown himself back into his work, wrestling with two projects dear to his heart: a Frank Iles story about a timid man driven to murder his wife (for which he had been keen to see Alec Guinness in the role) and an adaptation of David Duncan's *The Bramble Bush*, about an opportunist thief who assumes another man's identity only to find that he is wanted for murder in his new guise (an idea that would turn up again as the premise of Michelangelo Antonioni's *The Passenger* in 1975). Both scripts had stubbornly resisted adaptation to the screen and he and Warners had grown increasingly frustrated by the delays in getting his fourth and final film for the studio underway. Hitchcock was particularly keen to move on; his first post-Warner movie, *Rear Window* (1954), had already been announced, and Wassermann had negotiated a deal which granted him greater artistic control, as well as a considerable increase in his earnings.

In a BBC interview in the 1960s, Hitchcock said that the coming of sound was one of the worst things that could have happened to films, encouraging lazy producers to plunder the theatre for subjects, completely ignoring the opportunity to make visual art. In the present circumstance, he had opted for expediency over principle and had scoured the trade papers for suitable subjects from Broadway or London's West End. The logic had been to capitalise on something already in the public arena, which would require minimal input from him. 'I was running for cover,' he later admitted to Peter Bogdanovich. 'When your batteries run dry, when you are out creatively, and you have to go on, that's what I call running for cover.

Take a comparatively successful play that requires no great creative effort on your part and make it.'

It was Jack Cardiff, Hitchcock's cinematographer on *Under Capricorn*, who had solved the dilemma by drawing the director's attention to a play by Frederick Knott, called *Dial M for Murder*. Originally shown on BBC television, the reaction had been so positive that Knott had adapted it for the stage and, when it opened at the Westminster Theatre in London in June, 1952, it was an immediate hit.

Dial M for Murder relied on suspense rather than mystery, ignoring the well-worn whodunit template of authors like Agatha Christie, and instead drawing the audience into a cat-and-mouse game between the killer and the police. Cardiff thought that the complex plot machinations, love-triangle element, duplicity and brutal murder, all lent themselves to a perfect Hitchcock picture, and he had urged the director to see the play when it opened on Broadway in October the same year. Hitchcock was so impressed that he returned to see the production a second time and, recognising that an end to his Warner Brothers career might finally be in sight, had instructed his agents to snap up the screen rights.

(Obtaining the rights had proved to be less straightforward than Hitchcock imagined. Investigation revealed that they had already been acquired by Hungarian-born British film mogul Alexander Korda for a nominal $3500. On hearing that Warners was interested, and having little by way of capital to mount the film himself, Korda was more than happy to sell the rights on for more than $100,000—a healthy return on his modest investment!)

Hitchcock had a preference for writers with a theatrical pedigree and he was delighted when Knott agreed to come out to Hollywood and work with him on adapting his play for the screen. Born in China of English parents, Knott had graduated from Cambridge with a degree in law before enlisting in the Royal Artillery at the outbreak of World War 2 and rising to the rank of major. *Dial M for*

Kelly and Frederick Knott

Murder had taken him eighteen months to write and over two years to sell, it was turned down by seven separate theatre managements before finally being accepted by the BBC; he would pen only two other plays, both of them thrillers: *Write Me a Murder* and the much better known *Wait until Dark*, which would be filmed in 1967 with Audrey Hepburn. Following his play from West End to Broadway, Knott had decided to make New York his home and he was only too willing to fly to the West Coast to collaborate with Hitchcock on the script. The added sweetener—that the director had agreed to stay as faithful to the source as possible—was probably not necessary; Knott had already accepted a number of amendments for his Broadway version, including changing the villain's adolescent crime from misappropriation of funds to drug-dealing. Hitchcock opted to adapt the London version of the play rather than the more 'Americanised' version but otherwise stayed true to his word, and the only significant changes were to the characters' names. With Knott on board, Hitch envisaged the adaptation being complete in a matter of weeks, in keeping with his view that *Dial M for Murder* would be 'an average movie, photographs of people talking. It's ordinary craftsmanship.'

> *Tony Wendice is a man in an unusual position: he has discovered that his wife, Margot, is having an affair but instead of confronting her, he has given up his glamorous life as a professional tennis player and taken a more mundane job selling sports equipment. He appears to all intents and purposes to be working hard to be the ideal husband. Believing that Tony has turned over a new leaf, Margot decides to end her fling with Mark, a mystery-story writer, and burns his letters—all except one, which subsequently goes missing. Determined to make another go of her marriage, she breaks off contact with her lover.*
>
> *Behind his new-found commitment to wedlock, Wendice is hatching a devious plan to rid himself of his faithless wife while at the same time ensuring that he keeps his hands on her private fortune. He bumps into an old school-friend, Swann, who has a dubious reputation, and blackmails him into killing Margot and making it look like a robbery that has gone wrong. At the same time, he concocts a scheme to manoeuvre Mark into providing him with a watertight alibi. Things go wrong when, after a violent struggle, Margot overpowers and kills Swann instead—but the quick-thinking Wendice turns the situation to his advantage and manipulates the evidence to suggest that she lured her attacker into their flat in order to kill him. Margot cannot explain away inconsistencies in her version of events and she is arrested and convicted of murder. Even Mark thinks her guilty and fails to convince Wendice to lie to save her from the gallows, leaving him heir to her wealth..*
>
> *It seems that Wendice has successfully outwitted the justice system itself, by having it aid and abet him in committing the 'perfect murder'...*

Frederick Knott arrived in Hollywood in June to start work on the script for *Dial M for Murder* and he and Hitchcock hit it off immediately—so much so that when shooting started, Hitch would be happy to have the writer on set and even afforded him the privilege of a chair with a picture of a reef 'knot' embroidered onto the back of it, in jocular reference to his name! With Knott making good progress on the script, Hitch had committed himself to a start-date at the end of July. Easing the pressure on Knott was the director's decision to shoot the film on a single set, constructed on a sound stage at Warner's Burbank studios and arranged exactly as it had been in the theatre. In so doing, Hitch was ensuring the production of a significant saving in cost and, more importantly from his perspective, a much-truncated shooting schedule. The scenes were also to be shot in the sequential order of the story itself.

Aware that its relationship with Hitchcock was drawing to a close, Warners was keen to extract as much benefit from *Dial M for Murder* as it could. Hitchcock's three previous films for the studio were hardly the most lucrative of his career and, with the notable exception of *Strangers on a Train*, could best be described as mediocre performers at the box-office. Not only had the financial rewards been disappointing, but Warners could not even draw comfort from a claim to artistic merit; while *Stage Fright* and *I Confess* had their share of admirers, they remained minor entries in the director's canon.

The premise of *Dial M for Murder* does have echoes of *Strangers on a Train;* both films feature professional tennis players with inconvenient spouses. In the case of *Strangers on a Train*, Guy Haines (Farley Grainger) is awaiting a divorce so that he can marry a senator's daughter. Both scenarios then introduce a third party unconnected to the victims who is blackmailed into committing murder; in *Strangers*, psychotic mother's boy Bruno Anthony (Robert Walker) meets Guy by chance on a train and offers to 'swap' murders. Hitch always insisted that any similarity between the films was coincidental, but their common elements might well have been an added attraction for the director. Jack Warner would certainly have welcomed a commercial repeat of *Strangers on a Train*; his studio was in financial trouble, staff had been asked to accept a pay cut and production schedules had already been purged of all expendable projects. Hitchcock may have been 'running for cover' and looking for a stop-gap feature, but Warner Brothers was hoping that its last Hitchcock would also be one of its bigger hits.

Realising that the story itself presented limited opportunities for extravagant marketing, Warner vetoed Hitchcock's preference to shoot in black and white in favour of Warnercolor, believing it would enhance the film's box-office appeal. He then went one step further and surprised many in Hollywood by announcing that *Dial M for Murder* would also be shot utilising the studio's much-vaunted 3-D process. Hitchcock's opposition to the whole 3-D 'phenomenon' was public knowledge: he regarded it as 'anti-cinema', arguing that audiences were constantly being reminded that they were watching an artificial contrivance and were unable to suspend their disbelief. He may have had a point but he was not one to let principle stand in the way of personal vanity; his cameo appearances in his films had the same effect, reminding viewers that they were sharing an in-joke with Hitch—indeed 'Hitchcock-spotting' had become as much a feature of his work as the thriller-element!

Warner was one of the most prominent proponents of the 3-D process, and his company had invested heavily in the new technology, believing that this would be the cinema's main weapon in its war against television. His view was reinforced by the enormous success of the studio's *House of Wax* (1953), starring Vincent Price, a little-altered remake of a creaky 1933 horror-thriller called *Mystery of the Wax Museum*, which was actually to mark the box-office zenith of the current 3-D 'craze'. At the beginning of 1953, the *Hollywood Reporter* had predicted that there would be more than a dozen 3-D films in the following twelve months and, by announcing a raft of titles including *Rear Guard* (later *The Command*), *Hondo* and *Phantom of the Rue Morgue,* Warner Brothers was intent on marching at the forefront of the technological revolution.

The process proved to be popular with cinema audiences looking for something new, but with some notable exceptions, such as John Wayne in *Hondo*, the 'extra' dimension was being left to second-string actors in exploitation and horror movies, where characters and script were considered surplus to requirements. The public

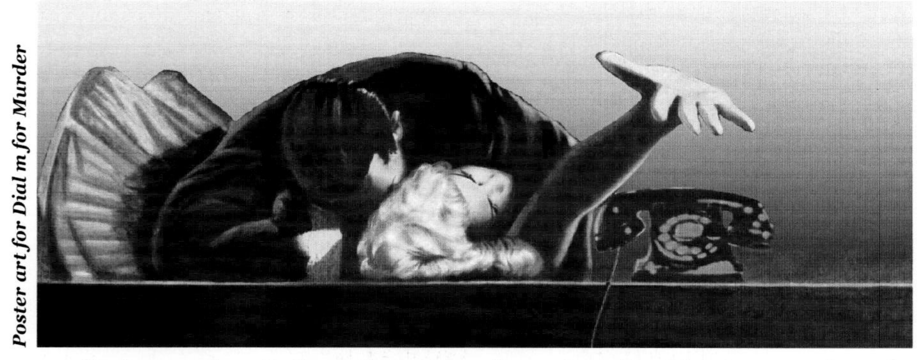

Poster art for Dial m for Murder

was likely to endure *It Came from Outer Space* (1953) or *The Creature from the Black Lagoon* (1954) only for so long before the novelty wore off and the need to wear uncomfortable cardboard 'sunglasses' to watch films in 3-D would begin actively to discourage audiences. The warning signs were there before *Dial M for Murder* started shooting, and Hitchcock was already of the opinion that the short-lived fad was over. Warners nevertheless decided to fly in the face of this growing discontent and, believing that a director of Hitchcock's stature would legitimise the process and reinvigorate the box-office, it allocated a budget of $1.4m to *Dial M for Murder*—over twice that of *House of Wax*. Even then, the cash-strapped studio was not exactly being over-generous: *Notorious,* made ten years before, had cost more than $2m, and that without the benefit of colour or the complexity of 3-D.

Unlike previous 3-D movies, in which audiences had been bombarded with all manner of items hurled at them from the screen, Hitchcock decided to shoot *Dial M for Murder* more or less flat, restricting the dimensional effect to shots of characters coming and going through doorways. The exception comes in the murder scene, which was staged to take full advantage of the technology and has Margot thrown violently back onto a table and reaching out into the auditorium in desperation.

Pandering to the needs of 3-D necessitated the digging of a camera pit, which restricted the actors' movements and gives a very static feel to an already slow narrative, but even this relatively modest use of the medium required a great deal of patience and preparation. The film employed M L Gunzberg's 'Natural Vision' 3-D camera rig, as per *House of Wax*, which required the use of two synchronised cameras shooting simultaneously. This huge rig was noisy, unreliable and too heavy to be used for tracking shots, even when not constrained by the pit. If the movie had been a more personal project for Hitchcock, he may well have fought tooth and nail to resist 3-D, but he simply did not care enough about *Dial M* to argue and by utilising the process to enhance an existing script rather than alter the script to advertise the process, he managed to fashion a work that continued to live long after 3-D itself disappeared and, arguably, created the much-maligned genre's one truly memorable film.

Hitchcock's passive acceptance of the 3-D process was mirrored to a large extent in his attitude towards the casting. Frederick Knott, contentedly typing away in Chateau Marmont, suggested that they hire from either the London or Broadway casts of the play. Hitchcock was inclined to go along with the idea, but once again the studio intervened and insisted that the lead roles be filled by familiar—if economical—faces. This presented Hitch with a challenge when he came to consider the part of Tony Wendice.

Film actors are more protective of their images than are their counterparts in the theatre, and finding a leading man who would be willing to play a ruthless lady-killer was never going to be easy. Maurice Evans, the charismatic English actor who had enjoyed a long and successful career on the American stage, had essayed a roguishly-charming Wendice on Broadway, but despite the critical plaudits, his name meant little to cinemagoers—or Warner executives. At Hitchcock's suggestion, Cary Grant had watched the play in New York and had formed the opinion that it might represent an opportunity for him to extend his range. Grant, at various times in his career, had tried to subvert his popular image, most notably in 1941's *Suspicion*, when Hitchcock horrified RKO by casting its top star as a conniving thief and murderer. Jack Warner was not convinced that Grant was right for the role, however, and the actor's hefty price tag, plus contracted profits-percentage, was a contributing factor in the decision not to offer it to him.

Hitchcock needed a star who was a big enough name to attract the crowds but not so big that he would break the budget. Warner also wanted an actor who was instantly recognisable to American audiences; he was concerned that the film was looking increasingly like a British picture—which could be box-office poison with the domestic audience. Welsh-born Reginald Alfred Truscott-Jones, better known as actor Ray Milland, seemed to fit the bill perfectly.

The former guardsman in the Royal Household Cavalry had begun his film career in Britain in 1929, appearing in a number of minor roles before striking out for California in 1930. Milland's military bearing, puckish good looks and easy charm kept him in constant employment throughout the thirties, as undistinguished support to the likes of George Raft and Fred MacMurray in a number of routine features. Paramount eventually took a shine to him and, recognising his utility value, signed him to a long-term contract; the studio became a home from home for Milland for the next decade. He gradually worked his way up the pecking order and contributed solid performances to *Beau Geste* (1939) opposite Gary Cooper, and to Cecil B De Mille's *Reap the Wild Wind* (1942) with John Wayne. Milland's public image of a quiet, unassuming man seemed to carry over into his private life: he had married Muriel (Mal) Webber in 1933 and the couple had shunned the spotlight to enjoy a comfortable and sedate life with their son Daniel and adopted daughter Victoria. But despite the outward veneer of respectability, it was generally felt that Mal had learned the secret of a long and happy marriage in Hollywood—knowing when to turn a blind eye. Within the film community itself, Milland had earned a reputation as a discrete but persistent philanderer, a situation which gained the long-suffering Mal much sympathy.

Without ever displaying an abundance of talent, Milland traded on solid dependability; his loyalty to Paramount was rewarded when he was persuaded to play a desperate alcoholic in Billy Wilder's *Lost Weekend* (1945). His uncharacteristically gritty portrayal of a man coming apart at the seams won him a deserved Best Actor Oscar, but the stress of creating and maintaining such an unstable character took its toll. Struggling to separate the extremes of life and art, Milland buckled under the pressure and spiraled into a bout of depression that almost wrecked his marriage. Standing by her man despite his very public breakdown, Mal found herself elevated to something like sainthood by other Hollywood wives—a breed not noted for its solidarity.

Unwilling or unable to maintain the career impetus that was required to be a major star, Milland drifted back to undemanding roles in second-rate fare. By 1953, he was in his late forties and his time as a leading man was almost up; he had been released from his contract by Paramount and, while he kept himself busy, was clearly beginning to settle into character parts. From Warner's perspective, Ray

Kelly and Ray Milland

Milland was ideal: he was a household name, he had the credibility of an Oscar-winning performance behind him, and he was more than capable of portraying the duplicitous Tony Wendice. He would not bring the public flocking to the box-office in the way that Grant might have done, but given the film's modest budget, he was a safe bet. The Welshman was duly engaged to star in *Dial M for Murder*.

Having been persuaded to hire a Hollywood actor for the lead, Hitchcock stayed faithful to the London and Broadway productions by selecting John Williams to play the genial Chief Inspector Hubbard, a role which had won him a Tony award. Williams had worked with Hitchcock on *The Paradine Case* in 1947 and had established himself as one of the director's favourite supporting players. The part of the would-be murderer, Charles Swann, proved more challenging; like Williams before him, character actor Anthony Dawson had played the role on stage in London and on Broadway but Hitch thought his screen persona too obviously seedy for him to be convincing as a successful confidence trickster. Louis Hayward, another Hollywood star of the forties, best-known for *The Saint in New York* (1938) and numerous costume roles from *The Man in the Iron Mask* (1939) on, was approached instead. Hayward might have made a debonair and charming criminal, the perfect match for Milland, but his salary demands would have taxed the film's budget to breaking point. Opting for the line of least resistance, Hitchcock relented and hired Dawson.

For the role of Margot's erstwhile lover, Mark Halliday, Hitchcock settled for the studio's suggestion of Missouri-born Robert Cummings, a lightweight leading man who previously had starred for the director in his wartime espionage thriller *Saboteur* (1942), though he had since become better known for comedy and spent much of his latter-day career on television. To accommodate Cummings, the part of Halliday was also Americanised—the one concession made to US audiences by a script which was to remain stubbornly British from its dialogue to its title (a punning reference to the Maida Vale telephone exchange in London).

Hitchcock's first choice for the luckless Margot had been Deborah Kerr, star of *The Life and Death of Colonel Blimp* (1943) and *Black Narcissus* (1947), who at 33 had the age and bearing to play the rich society wife of a former tennis champion. Kerr was considered to be one of the best actresses of her generation and a series of movies for MGM (which had her under contract) had established her as a popular star. But films like *King Solomon's Mines* (1950), *Quo Vadis* (1951) and *The Prisoner of Zenda*, (1952), the first and the last opposite Steward Granger, had barely stretched her as an actress and had given her a slightly matronly image, which Kerr abhorred. A more interesting role had come from Fred Zinnemann, who had just cast her as the bitter, sex-starved officer's wife in Columbia's *From Here to Eternity* (1953). When Hitchcock was casting his film, Zinnemann's Pearl Harbour epic had not yet opened, but word of mouth had it that Kerr's performance was a scorcher, and her swimsuited lovemaking with Burt Lancaster—the iconic 'sex in the surf' scene—was predicted to be box-office gold. To Hitch, the fact that she was Scottish by birth was a technicality; on screen, she was as English as a Lancashire rose and possessed all of the characteristics that he looked for in a leading lady: she was always on time, she hit her marks, and she exuded the same aloof, understated sex appeal of Bergman. Hitchcock had no need to see her in a passionate clinch on a Hawaiian beach to know that she had hidden depths. 'I am not a believer in the sexy type,' he insisted. 'I think it should be discovered in a woman. If you take the English woman, North German or Nordic types, you know they all look like school teachers, but I gather that they are murder in bed. The English woman is the most promiscuous type.'

...and Robert Cummings

But Warners was not the only studio touting for Kerr's signature; after ten years in leading roles, the actress was suddenly considered 'hot' again. Kerr was offered the part of the passive Margot Wendice—on the face of it, something of a let-down after the 'sexual awakening' of *From Here to Eternity*. Nevertheless, she acquiesced and Warner's publicity department, unable to contain its excitement, immediately sent out announcements to the trade papers. While Hitchcock and Jack Warner were smugly congratulating themselves on a casting coup, Kerr received a better offer in the form of her Broadway debut, no less, and a leading role in Robert Anderson's powerful *Tea and Sympathy*, as a teacher's wife who seduces one of her husband's pupils. Deborah Kerr, much to Hitchcock's chagrin, promptly bowed out of her verbal commitment to Warner Brothers and signed to a play that was to run for over 700 performances and keep the actress from the big screen for the better part of two years.

Having failed to secure the female star that he had wanted for the film, Hitchcock re-thought his strategy. Margot in both play and script is excruciatingly dull and, despite the duality in her nature—dutiful wife and passionate mistress, she never quite comes to life as a character in her own right. With Deborah Kerr out of the running, the role was relegated in Hitchcock's mind to the level of a plot device and he now felt that it no longer merited the participation of an 'A-list' actress. With Jack Warner's box-office expectations being carried by Ray Milland and 3-D, Hitchcock excused himself from the courting necessary to cast a major player and plumped instead for a relative unknown. Rather than interview Hollywood's finest, he started to sift through all of the screen-test footage that the studio could make available to him.

Grace Kelly's two most ardent supporters at MCA, Edie Van Cleve and Jay Kanter, have both laid claim at various times to having suggested Kelly to Wasserman for the Hitchcock film, and each may have put her name forward independently of the other. The fact that they both remained convinced of her star potential, despite a general lack of interest in New York and Hollywood, must have impressed Lew Wasserman, and it was the MCA chief who urged Hitch to see the *Taxi* test reel and who intimated that Kelly might be an ideal replacement for Deborah Kerr.

For the portly director, who was never a great socialiser, Lew Wasserman and his wife were Hitchcock's most habitual social contacts. He seldom entertained fellow directors and so would have been unaware of Kelly from either Fred Zinnemann or John Ford—the latter having had nothing good to say about her anyway. So Hitchcock the film director would have been largely unaware of Grace Kelly; Hitchcock the incorrigible gossip would certainly have heard her name. While most filmmakers liked to study scripts or talk to cast or crew about the next setups, Hitch would share a cup of tea and the latest tittle-tattle with his assistants. The stories circulating about Kelly would certainly have solicited his interest; not only had she been romantically linked with both of her leading men, Cooper and Gable, but the reports from the set of *High Noon* suggested that Fred Zinnemann was either already sleeping with her or desperately desired to do so.

There was nothing in *High Noon* to interest Hitchcock. For all of Zinnemann's supposed yearnings, he had done little to bring out any star quality in Grace Kelly. But the failed *Taxi* audition, of which Kelly herself was scornful, was enough for Hitchcock to ask to see some of the footage from *Mogambo*, which was still awaiting release. Hitchcock, always reluctant to share credit, liked to suggest in later years that he alone had been the one to discern something special about Kelly. In an interview in *Time* in 1955, he insisted, 'From the *Taxi* test, you could see Grace's potential for restraint.' He went on, 'I always tell actors don't use the face for nothing. Don't start scribbling over the sheet of paper until we have something to write. We may need it later. Grace has this control. It's a rare thing for a girl at such an age.' But Hitchcock could have spotted Kelly's fragile beauty, unfilled yearnings and repressed sexuality in the clips from *Mogambo*, and he may have played up the *Taxi* footage to avoid acknowledging Ford's contribution. Kelly's playing of Linda Nordley was not a great performance (despite its Academy Award nomination), and she is elbowed off the screen by the sheer physicality of Ava Gardner, but there was enough in it for Hitch to have considered that there might indeed be 'fire in her belly'.

Word came back through Wasserman that Hitchcock wanted to see Kelly, and it was Jay Kanter who convinced her to return to Hollywood for an 'informal meeting'; but he may have done too good a job of overstating its importance to her career: By the time she arrived, the actress was a nervous wreck and she was incredibly relieved to find that there would be no formal screen test. As was his usual practice, Hitchcock met Kelly over tea and they discussed practically everything except the film; instead, they chatted about food, travel and movies in general. Kelly assumed that Hitch was just trying to put her at ease and would at some point wish to discuss the role, but the closest they came to talking about Margot Wendice was when he told her that he planned to have Margot dressed in bright colours in the early scenes and as her circumstances changed, her clothes would become more subdued and drab. He made a point of explaining that Margot's wardrobe would all be off-the-peg, the only exception being a glamorous gown—scarlet, of course, to emphasise promiscuity. Kelly later recalled that she had been so nervous that her brain had 'turned to lead', and she was convinced that she had come across as a 'silly' girl. She was so sure that she had lost the role that instead of waiting around in Hollywood to hear the bad news, she returned immediately to New York to look for alternative work.

Kelly in a costume test for Dial m for Murder

Hitchcock's only comment with regard to their meeting was that Kelly's voice was too 'light' and would need some work. He later conceded that he was taken by her good manners, as well as her deference to him (she would always thereafter call him 'Mr Hitchcock' and he, in sharp contrast to John Ford, would address her as 'Miss Kelly'). Hitchcock was also impressed with her natural elegance and air of innocence, and he would build upon these qualities to emphasise Margot's vulnerability in the film and make the assault on her the more disturbing.

Kelly was back at the family home in Philadelphia when the call came through from Jay Kanter, confirming that Warner Brothers wanted her for the part of Margot Wendice and had already approached MGM for a loan-out; she was expected to fly back to Hollywood straight away to begin costume fittings. Jack Kelly had been unhappy about his daughter filming in the wilds of Africa, far from parental supervision, and the prospect of her once more jetting off to Hollywood was only marginally less unsettling. In that curious way in which the Kelly family operated, he gave his blessing only if sister Lizanne were again to accompany Kelly to Los Angeles as chaperone.

The deal hammered out between MGM and Warner Brothers saw Grace Kelly reporting to Burbank for the tidy sum of $24,000, with a modest increase in her own weekly salary to $1000—though that was still well below the market rate for a leading lady.

Whatever the qualities that Hitchcock had seen in her, Kelly was considered an unusual choice for the role of Margot. Austrian actress Gusti Huber had played the part on Broadway and had created a mature and intelligent Margot, making the Wendices seem a well-matched couple. Knott's play, or screenplay, made no suggestion that the only female character in the story is a child-bride, or a trophy wife, and with Kelly's relative youth and outstanding looks, it is hard to shake the idea that she was simply miscast. But Hitchcock was unconcerned; in an interview for the American Film Institute in 1970, he declared, 'I have never been very keen on women who hang their sex around their neck like baubles. It is more interesting to discover sex in a woman than to have it thrown at you, like a Marilyn Monroe or those types.' But in 1953, he was talking of Grace Kelly in terms that could easily have confused her with Marilyn Monroe, such as promising the *Los Angeles Daily News* that he had a 'blonde, sexy newcomer with an appeal that will give the boys something to think about'. On and off the set of *Dial M for Murder*, Kelly was about to give the 'boys' a great deal to think about.

With his Margot Wendice in place, Hitchcock finished the remainder of the casting with commendable precision. Patrick Allen, who played Detective Pearson in the film, recalled: 'I arrived on the set and was immediately sent to wardrobe to be outfitted in what I suppose they thought a London bobby might be wearing these days. About a dozen of us then lined up on the set in costume and Hitchcock went along the line saying, "you, you, not you and you". That was it; I think I was the second "you"!'

Having conceded ground on the big issues of 3-D and the leading players, Hitchcock dug his heels in on the minor details. Memos in the Warner Brothers archives reveal that he was concerned with the most trivial of matters: the 'black cap', for example, as worn by Old Bailey judges when passing sentence in capital cases, had to be authentic, and photographs of the genuine article were sent from Warner's London office along with detailed descriptions of court procedures and judicial etiquette (in the event, the courtroom made no appearance in the film). Hitchcock also insisted that background sounds should have a distinctly British feel and refused to even consider the stock of tapes in the studio's sound library; new recordings had to be made in London and shipped out to California.

As he had often done in the past, Hitchcock intended to act as his own producer on *Dial M for Murder*. This not only freed him from interference on a day-to-day basis but satisfied his need to be in control of every aspect of the filmmaking process. This was Hitch very much in his element; he may have selected a project that required relatively little creative input on his part, but he still insisted on planning everything down to the smallest detail. Using tried and trusted crew-members also relaxed him and a relaxed Hitchcock meant a happy, friendly atmosphere on set. As always, he made efforts to surround himself with people he knew and felt that he could rely upon, and he included a number of his regular collaborators on *Dial M for Murder*—among them cinematographer Robert Burks and set designer George James Hopkins, both from *I Confess* and *Strangers on a Train*.

Shooting was scheduled to run through to the last week of September, 1953, with a short interruption already scheduled for August 13—Alfred Hitchcock's birthday. This had become something of a ritual for the director's staff whenever he was shooting on that day: they would summon cast and crew, produce a giant cake while Hitch feigned surprise, and then he would pose for the stills cameraman, holding some appropriately murderous-looking carving implement. After a short period of rehearsal—a rare luxury for Kelly after her experiences in Africa—Hitch, his cast and crew gathered together on the Burbank sound stage on July 30 to begin principal photography on *Dial M for Murder*.

Working with Hitchcock, particularly during the early stages of the film, was something of a revelation for Grace Kelly. She found him patient, open, and always willing to discuss the finer points of craft or characterisation. Compared with Zinnemann, who had stayed away from her, or Ford, who had barked instructions, Hitch was a delight. The fact that they used courtesy titles with each other, and that he spoke quietly and politely to her, also appealed to her sense of finesse, and she felt comfortable with his careful approach to the filming, and his sense of order and insistence that production ran strictly to office hours.

It was not unknown for Hitchcock to be attentive to his stars, but it was a relative novelty in a director who seldom cared to discuss the finer points of anything with mere actors. As a rule, he was not interested in collaboration between director and actor; he took the view that he had his job to do and they had theirs. While his approach varied a little from film to film, he could be brusque with even the most valued of performers. When Ingrid Bergman raised a query about psychology on the set of *Spellbound*, Hitchcock dismissed her concerns with, 'It's only a movie, Ingrid,

don't take it so seriously.' But the crew of *Dial M for Murder* felt nevertheless that Grace Kelly was being singled out for special treatment, and she responded to Hitchcock's attitude towards her in just the way that he wanted. She listened attentively—dotingly, even—to his instructions and advice, and she followed his directions to the letter; she adopted the pose of a dutiful child, eager to please a favourite uncle.

From the outset, the nature of the relationship between Kelly and Hitch was less that of employer and employee and more that of mentor and pupil. It was an arrangement which Hitchcock would find as professionally rewarding as it was personally satisfying. He boasted that his daily coaching successfully lowered the pitch of his protégé's voice and improved her delivery; at the same time, he set out for the studio each day knowing that he had one of the most beautiful and desirable creatures in Hollywood hanging on his every word. On more than one occasion, Hitchcock identified himself with 'Svengali', the manipulative hypnotist of George du Maurier's *Trilby,* who exercises such a degree of control over the novel's titular heroine—an impressionable young singer—that she can barely function out of his presence. Hitchcock's influence over Kelly was hardly akin, but the notion took hold in the director's mind; the more he came to know her, the more he was fascinated by the elegance and reserve that she exuded and the contrast that was evident from the tales that were circulating of her nocturnal activities. The contradiction between angelic demeanour and whorish disposition, and the almost total reverence, in which she held him, excited and aroused Hitch. But after a lifetime trapped in what he described as an 'ugly, fat body', he had long accepted that his fate was to look at beauty through the lens of a camera but never to possess it.

As the only woman in the cast, Kelly naturally attracted the attention of her fellow actors on the film. Patrick Allen fell under her spell: 'I was totally in love with her, as was everybody on the set,' he said. 'She was so beautiful, glamorous and had a real star quality about her. Although she wasn't a big star—not then anyway—she always seemed to carry herself like she was.' From the first day of shooting, Kelly's dressing-room was filled with flowers as admirers vied for her attention, and they were not limited to the denizens of Burbank: powerless to enforce her role as chaperone, Lizanne recalled that Kelly's Chateau Marmont apartment seemed to be under virtual siege from would-be suitors. Hitchcock, whose lunchtime sessions with a few close friends would inevitably turn to studio gossip, was invariably

Dial M for Murder (Ray Milland, Robert Cummings, Grace Kelly)

bemused by the latest tittle-tattle about his star, particularly the news that she was 'associating' with some of the crew. Kelly biographer Robert Lacey reports him as commenting on the situation some years later: 'That Gryce,' Hitch is alleged to have remarked. 'She fucked everyone! She even fucked little Freddie, the writer!'

Kelly's romance with Frederick Knott had attracted the attention of the press; the *New York Post* devoted a paragraph to the production and reported that, 'Grace Kelly who stars in it and Frederick Knott who wrote it are hand-holding after *Dial M for Murder* hours.' The fact that Kelly and the 37-year-old Knott were both booked into Chateau Marmont made the 'hand-holding' less troublesome. Knott fitted Kelly's preferred male model perfectly: not only was he intelligent and worldly, but the royalties from *Dial M* had made him a wealthy man. Moreover, he was single—though he was romantically linked with actress Ann Hilary, whom he would later marry. Knott was also a skilled athlete and talented tennis player; it was only the outbreak of World War 2 which had prevented him from competing at Wimbledon.

When he was made aware of the mutual attraction between actress and writer, Hitchcock could not resist playing matchmaker and Kelly and 'little Freddie' were invited to dinner at Bellagio Road, where they were to become regular guests in the first weeks of shooting, enjoying the ritual of home cooking and after-dinner anecdote-telling. Hitchcock liked and respected Knott and thought he and Kelly made a charming couple; more importantly, Knott was not about to usurp his own position as Svengali to Kelly's Trilby. But this happy arrangement was not to last: Kelly soon switched her amorous attentions from Knott to co-star Ray Milland.

So far as the press was concerned, there was a certain inevitability about Kelly falling for Milland and repeating the pattern that she had already established on both *High Noon* and *Mogambo*. Milland was an older and more sophisticated figure than Knott, ever ready to give her his undiluted attention and approval—in other words, a classic father-figure for a little girl who had always strived to be noticed by Jack Kelly. Milland's status in Hollywood was fading rapidly but, despite that, he remained a well-liked and respected personality and Grace Kelly's relationship with him seems to have been based on a genuine affection, even love.

Hitchcock directing John Williams

The crew may have sniggered at Ray Milland's toupee and old-fashioned charm, but Kelly fell for him and the couple embarked on what was to prove a passionate but damaging affair. By all accounts, Milland was an old hand at the game but Kelly would show herself to be a quick learner. Initially at least, they both observed the traditional rules for illicit affairs and kept a suitably low profile. But they were soon the talk of the Burbank sound stages. Losing sight of the delicate nature of their situation, Kelly and Milland gave up the attempt at discretion and allowed their romance to spill out from the Marmont's discreet cottages and into some of Los Angeles's more fashionable night spots. It was not long before the lovebirds were also the talk of Hollywood.

When the famously-waspish gossip columnist Hedda Hopper began to drop some startlingly-unsubtle hints in print, Mal Milland confronted her husband, who denied the affair outright. Having tolerated his behaviour for longer than she could remember, she had reached the end of her tether: she then arranged for her errant spouse to be followed after filming finished for the weekend and he claimed to be going on a business trip. The hired detective watched Milland and Kelly and as they left the studio and drove to the airport to spend the weekend in a romantic hideaway. When Ray Milland returned to home, he found his bags packed and his wife in no mood to discuss things any further. Far from cooling Kelly's ardour, Milland's eviction inspired her to talk to friends about him in terms of a possible husband.

Although MGM had profited from the publicity that surrounded the Kelly-Gable 'affair' on *Mogambo*—and gone to great lengths to ensure that it stayed in the public eye—the studio realised that there was a considerable difference between a romantic interlude in the wilds of Africa with a popular *single* star and what was now a scandal on their own doorstep. Kelly was warned that if she continued to see Milland, her reputation might be tarnished beyond the studio's power to save it. Warner Brothers was also concerned and raised the subject with Hitch, who simply shrugged; he was, he insisted, powerless to influence his actors after they had left his set.

The days when film studios could have 'bad' news suppressed with a mixture of bullying and blackmail were gone, and now neither MGM nor Warners had the means to influence the press; instead, they relied on goodwill and mutual dependency. This 'gentleman's agreement' worked in everybody's interest when the studios were dealing with the mainstream press, but they were about to come up against publisher Robert Harrison's unscrupulous new scandal-sheet, *Confidential*—a magazine that operated in a twilight world entirely its own.

Confidential, which specialised in the type of scandals that today are the domain of *News of the World* or *National Enquirer,* had been founded six months earlier on the promise that it would 'tell the facts and name the names'. Its editorial policy employed a somewhat elastic definition of the word 'fact', and it relied upon hack journalists and a network of informants who were willing to sell out anyone for a quick buck. *Confidential* quickly established a niche for itself as 'a sewer-sheet of supercharged sex,' in the opinion of *Time*. It was to become one of the top-selling titles in the US (though few people would actually admit to reading it!) and despite a series of high-profile law-suits, it would continue to peddle its particular brand of low-brow sensationalism for over two decades.

Harrison played by his own rules and when he got wind that an Oscar-winning actor had moved out of the family home and checked into a local motel, he sent one of his 'journalists' to interview the neighbours; it was not long before they dug up dirt. 'After one look at Gracie,' *Confidential* told its readers, '[Milland] went into a tailspin that reverberated from Perino's to Ciro's. The whole town soon heehawed over the news that suave Milland, who had a wife and family at home, was gaga over Grace. Ray pursued her ardently and Hollywood cackled. Then Mama Milland found out. She lowered the boom on Ramblin' Ray, and there followed one of the loudest, most tearful nights their Beverly Hills neighbours can remember.'

Rushing to close the gate after the horse had well and truly bolted, the Millands issued a statement which confirmed their decision 'that it might be best for both of us to separate temporarily. The problems which have ended in this decision are purely personal. There is no third party involved.'

Dial M for Murder (Grace Kelly, Ray Milland)

Grace Kelly might have been advised to take a leaf out of Groucho Marx's book: following an article in *Confidential* implying that his TV show game show was fixed, he wrote to the magazine announcing, 'Gentlemen, if you continue to publish scandalous articles about me, I'll feel compelled to cancel my subscription.' Instead, she tried to bluff her way out of the situation by flatly denying any involvement with Milland and insisting that they did not 'even have lunch alone in the commissary'. For the Millands to deny that anyone else was involved was understandable, and seasoned observers of the Hollywood scene respected their right to be economical with the truth, but with Kelly, denial was viewed as an absurd hypocrisy and it only alienated her further from many in the film community. She was already unpopular in the town, due to what was regarded as an 'open-minded attitude' towards married men, but now she became the number one hate figure for any Hollywood wife with a husband under the age of 60.

With *Confidential* having broken the story, the mainstream West Coast press felt free to join in the fray and, given the popularity of Mal Milland, it was Kelly who was singled out for reproach. The *Los Angeles Mirror-News* declared: 'Miss Kelly's supposed to be so terribly proper, but then look at all those whispers about her and Ray Milland.' When the story went national, Kelly tried belatedly to adopt a lower profile but there was nowhere to hide from the press. The *New York Journal American*, one of the highest circulation papers in the Big Apple, ran a feature on her sudden departure from the society pages, which it headlined, 'Grace Kelly hasn't got anyone's husband. She's just got a cold'. Kelly confided to a friend that she felt like a 'streetwalker'—it was an evocative image and one that many Hollywood wives would not have disagreed with. The stigma of the Milland affair was to tarnish her reputation for many years to come.

Lizanne, a mere 20-year-old herself, was just not up to her role as chaperone.

Grace Kelly and sister Lizanne

At the start of her assignment, she was dutifully reporting to Jack and Ma that Grace was staying in every night to study her lines, and that the pair of them were attending chapel every Sunday like good Catholic girls. By the time the tales of Kelly's philandering were all over the papers, she was informing her parents that she and Grace were out on the town every night and, with just a hint of desperation, that predatory men were 'everywhere'. She later conceded that keeping her sister from male admirers was something of an uphill struggle. 'They were round her in scores,' she wrote. 'They used to compete as to who could send her the most flowers until they ran out of vases and the place looked like a funeral home.' Reaction in Henry Avenue was predictable: Jack was enraged, and after despatching the strong maternal hand of Ma to Los Angeles to take charge of the situation, he also engaged a professional PR agent, Paul H Conlon (known as 'Scoop'), who worked for the *Los Angeles Times*. Conlon's role was to orchestrate a damage-limitation exercise. Margaret Kelly's instructions were more straightforward: she was to ensure that Grace returned to New York the minute that shooting ended.

Picture Show, August, 1954

The Kelly family need not have worried: a thoroughly chastened Ray Milland would eventually chalk the whole affair up to a mid-life crisis and slope back to his wife and family. Grace Kelly herself, who had been genuinely convinced that Milland had the backbone to divorce Mal and marry her, swallowed her pride and listened to Conlon's advice. Having endured insult if not injury at the hands of the press, she now turned to that same media to smooth her path from would-be harlot to heartbroken patsy. In a public relations coup, Kelly granted an exclusive interview to the influential Louella Parsons, whose syndicated column appeared in literally hundreds of papers and whose intolerance of those who refused to pander to her whims was legendary; more than just another acid-mouthed gossip columnist, Parsons counted Mal Milland as one of her closest friends. Kelly turned on the contrition and her charm melted the notoriously-cold Parsons heart. 'I happen to know when Grace began *Dial M for Murder*, she thought Ray was separated from his wife,' she wrote, adding with a twist of the knife, 'Later he did leave home, but it was not the first time that he had walked out on his beautiful wife, Mal.' The use of the adjective 'beautiful' was calculated to assuage her friend, but this one article nevertheless contrived to rewrite history and cast Kelly as the victim of a inveterate womaniser.

Kelly preferred this version of events and stuck to it throughout her life. In the 1970s, she told her friend Gwen Robbins: 'I really thought the marriage was over. I did not know he had many affairs, and that I was just one of them.' If that was the truth, then she must have been the only person in Hollywood who thought Milland a dutiful husband. To his credit, the actor maintained a gentlemanly silence about the episode; having moved back with Mal, the couple remained together

***Look*, June 1954**

for the rest of their lives, and neither of them felt the need to comment publicly on Grace Kelly. In the 1960s, columnist Shelia Graham, a friend of Mal's, revealed to the *New York Mirror*, 'It came over him in a rush; that whole thing, whatever it was, had been make-believe, and that he had been in love all the time with his very understanding wife, Mal.' The closest Ray Milland ever came to a confession was in his witty autobiography of 1976, *Wide-Eyed in Babylon*, in which he never mentions Kelly by name but does furnish this intriguing comment: 'I have been paid fabulous sums to frolic with and make bogus love to the most beautiful women in the world, which on one or two occasions turned out to be not so bogus. My life in those days was one long saga of agony and ecstasy'.

Much as he liked to gossip about such 'agony and ecstasy', Hitchcock would never have thought to interfere or even raise the matter with 'Miss Kelly'. For one thing, it was not an appropriate conversation for a gentleman to have with a lady; for another, he had come to value her trust too much to jeopardise it with studio hearsay. Kelly, for her part, understood how to cultivate friendships and she made certain throughout the shooting of *Dial M* that she was always free for dinner with Alma and Hitch when required, even after Frederick Knott departed from her life. Ray Milland, with whom Hitchcock found little rapport, did not enjoy the same access to the director's inner circle. While Kelly's love life was a topic of discussion for every runner on the lot, everything remained as it was meant to be in Alfred Hitchcock's world: his beautiful new star was always on time, she knew her lines, and she was deferential to his needs. In fact, she had transformed what had seemed destined to be a tiresome and mundane shoot into a working week to which to which he could now look forward. Whatever else was going on in her life was of no concern to him.

As filming progressed and Hitch grew more confident and relaxed with Kelly, he started to inject his particular brand of blue humour into their conversations; much to his glee, she reciprocated. On one occasion, he introduced himself to a visitor on set and, aware that she was standing within earshot, remarked, 'Call me Hitch, without a cock.' He then turned to Kelly with a grin and enquired, 'Are you shocked, Miss Kelly?' Kelly shrugged and replied, 'I went to a girl's convent school. I heard all those things when I was thirteen!' It was the sort of retort that amused Hitchcock, and he later commented that he thought Kelly was practically 'unshockable'—though that did not prevent him from trying! Director and actress discovered that they shared a similar sense of humour and they would play word-games together, like dropping the initial letter from celebrity Christian names, a jape that Hitchcock devised after

On set: Alfred Hitchcock, Grace Kelly, Robert Cummings

meeting actress Lizabeth Scott; he and Kelly would come up with variations on the theme, such as Rank Sinatra, and then giggle like schoolchildren.

It was at such times, both on set at Warners and over dinner at Bellagio Road, that Hitch came to realise there was more to Kelly than a mere starlet with a taste for her leading men. He was given glimpses of what lay beneath the glacial surface and it excited him enormously. Years later, he explained her appeal to journalist Oriana Fallaci: 'She's sensitive, disciplined, and very sexy. People think she is cold. Rubbish! She is a volcano covered with snow.'

Although they were from different generations, Kelly and Hitch shared a strict Catholic upbringing—he with the Jesuits at St Ignatius and she with the nuns at the Academy of the Assumption—and while neither could be described as practising Catholics, they would both evoke the tenets of the Church from time to time. Kelly always maintained that her faith was important to her, but she was more than capable of turning her back on its teachings when it suited. Hitch, on the other hand, seemed to take his religion more seriously. The grocer's son and the bricklayer's daughter also found common ground in their familial backgrounds: both were born into strong patriarchal families, dominated by father-figures more concerned with putting food on the table than spending time with their offspring. As children, she and Hitch were both quiet and introspective and, to some extent, the 'runts' of their respective litters, to quote Jack Kelly—Hitchcock, because he was youngest and weakest; Kelly, because she was the most timid.

On set, this new-found familiarity and understanding between teacher and pupil still had its boundaries though, especially when it came to the shooting of Margot Wendice's 'murder' scene. Fellow film director and Hitchcock buff François Truffaut once said: 'Hitchcock filmed scenes of murder as if they were love scenes and love scenes as if they were murders.' The attempted murder of Margot in *Dial M* was to blur the distinction between the two.

Strangulation was a favourite murder-method of Hitch's; it was implied in *The Lodger*, *Shadow of a Doubt* and *Notorious*, then used to great effect in *Rope* and *Strangers on a Train*, and he would return to it with disturbing results in *Frenzy* (1972), nearly two decades later. Death by strangulation was more intimate and personal than shooting or poisoning; perpetrator and victim need to be physically close, almost in a sexual embrace. Strangulation and autoerotic-asphyxiation are forms of sexual perversion—something which Hitchcock had hinted at in *Rope*, and would later explicitly depict in *Frenzy*.

The attempted murder of Margot in *Dial M for Murder* represented the only real violent action in the film; it was also imbued with a strong sexual undercurrent. Hitchcock rehearsed Kelly and Anthony Dawson for a week, choreographing their movements and coaching them in the actions that he wanted to see. The question that vexed wardrobe designer Moss Mabry throughout the process was what Margot should wear to her prospective demise. Hitchcock had wanted to give the scene an additional *frisson*, and he had made it clear early in the planning that she should wear as little as possible, but when confronted with Kelly's natural refinement, he lost his nerve—though not his cunning. During the rehearsals, he produced a heavy velvet robe claiming, rather unconvincingly, that it would create vivid contrasts of light and shadow. Kelly reacted as he hoped she would but did not dare to suggest. 'I was very unhappy about it,' she said, 'and I told him I didn't think it was right for the part.. I don't think that this woman is going to put on this great fancy robe if she is getting up in the middle of the night to answer a ringing phone and there's nobody in the apartment!' Asked by a querulous Hitchcock what she had in mind instead, Kelly volunteered, 'I wouldn't put on anything at all, that I'd just get up and go to the phone in my nightgown.' When filming proper began the following week, Kelly found herself clad in a figure-hugging silk nightdress, believing it to have been her own idea.

Despite the extensive rehearsals, filming of the sequence went slowly and it took Hitch a week of shooting before he pronounced himself satisfied—by which time Kelly was covered in bruises after Dawson had been urged by his director to make things look more authentic. For most of those five days, Hitch had sat only feet away as Grace Kelly, beautiful but dishevelled, was repeatedly abused by a stranger.

Hitchcock was aware that the fate of his movie depended upon the success of this scene—it had to look terrifying and real, and it had to look sexual; the director was effectively filming an attempted rape. To emphasise the sexual sub-text, there is a fleeting but noticeable shot of Margot's bare legs pushing against those of her attacker, just as Swann overpowers his victim and pushes her backwards across the desk, into a position of sexual submission. (The Warner Brothers publicity department was also alert to the erotic content: the scene appeared on the film's poster, where it was deliberately contrived to look like a sexual assault.) The use of 3-D during this scene, with Margot's hand reaching 'out' of the screen in desperation, makes the attack all the more shocking, particularly given the limited use the process during the earlier scenes. Hitchcock said later that he thought the scene had been 'nicely done but there wasn't enough gleam to the scissors, and a murder without gleaming scissors is like asparagus without the hollandaise sauce—tasteless'.

Had Hitchcock employed the same level of care in the rest of the film, *Dial M for Murder* might have been seen as a classic of the genre; as it was, it emerged as passably entertaining but not much more. The decision to stick so rigidly to Knott's text creates a very static drama, that all too clearly reflects Hitchcock's decision to point his cameras and 'film people talking'. The elements of the story that engendered suspense in the theatre come across as curiously unengaging on the screen.

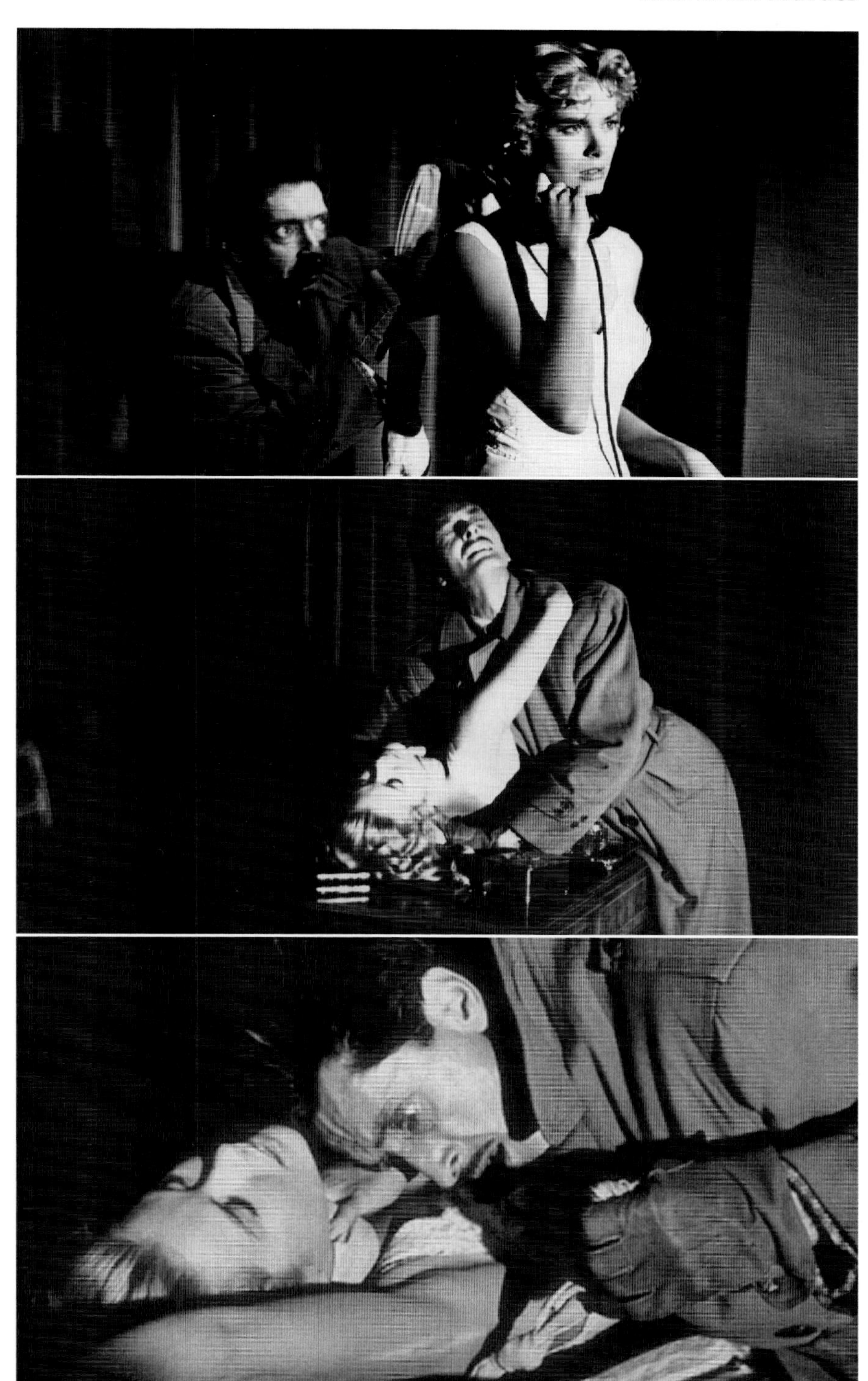

Only in the attempted murder of Margot Wendice, and the lead up to it, does Hitchcock's direction come to life. Particularly effective are shots of Tony Wendice, nervously glancing at his watch during a party that he has contrived to provide himself with an alibi, intercut with scenes of the hired assassin prowling the darkened apartment. When Swann concludes that Wendice has called things off and determines to leave the apartment, the tension is palpable. Then the phone rings—and the attack that follows is one of the most startling and distressing that Hitch had filmed to date. Margot's frantic struggles as Swann subdues her are genuinely uncomfortable to watch, while the would-be murderer's demise is sickening. Having plunged her sewing scissors deep into Swann's back, the *coup de grace* is not delivered by Margot but by Swann himself, as he falls and lands excruciatingly on his back, skewering himself to death. Having exhausted his creative energies on this scene, Hitchcock all too quickly returns to the conceit of filming a play and the tension rapidly dissipates.

The single living-room set of the Wendice's London home was meant to evince a feeling of claustrophobia—instead, it looks cheap and stagy. Cutaways to the street outside and some comings and goings only serve to point up the artificiality of the environment that Hitchcock had created for his principals. Margot's imprisonment and trial presented an opportunity for Hitch to 'open out' the proceedings, but he decided that it was too late into the film for a new level of drama. Instead, the trial is conveyed in montage over close-ups of Margot; in Knott's play, the scene is missing entirely and her death sentence merely reported.

Even in his most famous films, Hitchcock was happy to fudge the finer points of plotting; his oft-quoted 'MacGuffin' is typical of a director who invariably felt that details took second place to atmosphere and tension. In the case of *Dial M,* he allowed Knott too much freedom and plot becomes all-important. Mark, a mystery writer, owes most of his lines to the need for someone on screen to grasp the intricacies and then explain them to the audience. The result is swathes of exposition. The unravelling of the convoluted plot takes on a mechanistic air, and the climax of the film is an elaborate trick that appears to exist only to show how clever is John Williams's Chief Inspector. It is almost a relief when Wendice accepts his undoing with good humour and thus spares the audience any further explanations.

Of the performances, Ray Milland quite steals the show in a part that required him to be unambiguously villainous while at the same time not alienating the viewer. He exudes charm and menace in equal degrees, and he works hard to present the conniving Wendice in such a way that his roguish appeal is undiminished by his homicidal bent; much of the enjoyment to be gleaned from *Dial M for Murder* comes from watching his duplicitous twists and turns. If the drama has any lasting force, it comes from the illicit desire to see the cuckolded Wendice get away with (attempted) murder, rather than a cathartic need for the morally-compromised Margot's last-minute salvation—a typically Hitchcockian double-bluff.

Bob Cummings's Mark comes across as a colourless bore—there is little if any magnetism between he and Margot—however, Williams and Dawson, as policeman and potential killer, are both excellent and display a clear understanding of the material. Williams is particularly good as the archetypical British sleuth, fastidiously combing his moustache and interspersing lengthy tracts of dialogue with nuggets of dry humour.

Grace Kelly comes out of the proceedings better than anyone who saw *High Noon* might reasonably have expected, though Knott was not generous to Margot in his script and the character remains resolutely one-dimensional. She does, however, demonstrate clear signs of growing maturity as an actress; Hitch was correct in claiming that her delivery was improved and her voice is noticeably stronger. She is also more than competent in the early sequences, when Margot is alternating flirtatiously between husband and lover—though in her scenes as a penitent, she largely fails to evoke audience sympathy. 'I don't seem able to feel anything,' she mumbles, by way of superfluous explanation, but her lack of emotional range has already given that impression.

Hitchcock, for all his talk of fire and ice, did not quite manage to release the smouldering interior in *Dial M for Murder*, but Kelly was more confident than in previous screen outings and she was happy to credit him with the improvement. She told *Film Parade*: 'Working with Hitchcock was a tremendous experience and a very enriching one. As an actor, I learned a tremendous amount about motion picture making.' The subtle change in Grace Kelly's screen demeanour was something that Hitchcock was keen to promote. 'Remember Grace Kelly in *High Noon*?' he asked the *Hollywood Reporter*. 'She was rather mousy. But in *Dial M for Murder* she blossomed out for me splendidly, because the touch of elegance was always there.'

Unfortunately, Hitchcock's haste to remove himself from Warner Brothers was uppermost in his mind and the minute that the shooting was over, and cast and crew had been despatched to pastures new, he lost whatever passing interest he had in the project. This indifference shows in the sloppiness of the post-production and of all Hitchcock's pictures, only *Marnie* a decade later would look as slapdash. Margot's collection of press cuttings, for example, are clearly blank on one side and could not have come from newspapers, and in an early scene, she mistakenly refers to Mark as 'Bob'. (A more explicable goof is the obvious employment of a giant wooden finger to dial 'M' on an over-sized prop telephone. The 3-D cameras could not be configured to shoot the requisite close-up!)

In later life, Hitchcock had little time for *Dial M for Murder* and dismissed it as a 'minor work'; it was a view that was shared by at least some of the critics at the time of the film's release, *Variety* among them, which suggested: 'There are a number of basic weaknesses in the setup that keep the picture from being a good suspense show for any but the most gullible.' But other reviews were more positive, such as that in the *New York Times*: 'Mr Hitchcock has presented this mental material on the screen with remarkable visual definition of developing intrigue and mood. Grace Kelly does a nice job of acting the wife's bewilderment, terror and grief.' The *Hollywood Reporter* went further: '*Dial M for Murder* is as suspenseful a murder yarn as has been screened for some time.. flawlessly acted.. superbly directed. Milland is excellent as the charming, cunning parasite and Miss Kelly turns in a brilliant performance as his wife.'

The notion that Kelly had delivered a 'brilliant performance' was picked up by a number of sources and added to a growing reputation—by the time the film opened, she had received her nomination as Best Supporting Actress for *Mogambo* (she was to lose out to Donna Read in *From Here to Eternity*). But consolation would come in the form of a Best Actress Award for Margot Wendice from the New York Film Critics and National Board of Review. Even the British, who were generally less inclined than their American counterparts to favour pretty young actresses, found her accent and performance worthy of note and honoured her with a British Film Academy nomination for Best Foreign Actress.

Hitchcock, who was never to win an Oscar for direction, picked up a nomination from the Director's Guild of America for 'Outstanding Directional Achievement in a Motion Picture', but with characteristic cynicism, he put that down to appreciation for someone having finally made a watchable 3-D film rather than for any inherent quality in *Dial M for Murder*.

'The New Queen of Hollywood'–Picturegoer, July 1954

Warner Brothers felt that the sex angle of the plot was the best way to sell the movie—not only did the posters imply that Margot is being sexually assaulted, but the tag-lines talked up the erotic aspect—'Kiss by Kiss.. Supreme Suspense Unfurls!' The trailers also exploited this theme and promised 'a married woman with a two-party line to her affections'. The strategy worked well enough and the film, which opened in May, 1954, grossed a healthy \$3m on its initial North American release, compared with \$3.5m for the earlier *Strangers on a Train.*

By the time *Dial M for Murder* opened, Grace Kelly was a much bigger star than she had been when she turned up on Hitchcock's set the previous July, due partly to her notoriety in the gossip columns. Her Oscar nomination and the unexpected success of *Mogambo* added credibility, but it was *Dial M* that started the conversion of Kelly from actress into movie star; it was a process that would continue under Hitchcock's supervision. Before filming wrapped in Burbank, he was hard at work on his next film, a hugely personal project: *Rear Window*. It has often been said that he was a man who kept his emotions for the screen and it was there that he conducted his 'love affairs'. If *Dial M for Murder* was Alfred Hitchcock wooing Grace Kelly, then *Rear Window* was to represent the consummation of that courtship.

Chapter 4

Rear Window

Rear Window (James Stewart)

'How far does a girl have to go before you notice her?'
—Lisa Carol Freemont (Grace Kelly) *Rear Window* (1955)

Sure, I suppose it was a little bit like prying, could even have been mistaken for the fevered concentration of a Peeping Tom. That wasn't my fault, that wasn't my idea. The idea was, my movements were strictly limited just around this time. I could get from the window to the bed, and from the bed to the window, and that was all. The bay window was about the best feature my rear bedroom had in the warm weather. It was unscreened, so I had to sit with the light out or I would have had every insect in the vicinity in on me. I couldn't sleep, because I was used to getting plenty of exercise. I'd never acquired the habit of reading books to ward off boredom, so I hadn't that to turn to. Well, what should I do, sit there with my eyes tightly shuttered?
—Cornell Woolrich, 'Rear Window' (1944)

On November 27, 1953, Alfred Hitchcock started shooting his 40th film, *Rear Window*, and he could not have been in better spirits. Not only did he have a witty and intelligent script by John Michael Hayes, he had a talented and trusted crew, the largest and most elaborate set yet constructed on a Paramount sound stage, and a contract from the studio that guaranteed him complete creative freedom. He also had Grace Kelly.

Throughout his career, Hitchcock maintained that the actual shooting of a picture was the least interesting part of filmmaking. After the planning and preparation were complete, directing a film was nothing more than supervising a group of professionals who had already been instructed on what to do. Visitors

to Hitchcock's sets would often express surprise at his apparent disinterest in what was happening in front of his cameras. To keep his intellectual juices flowing while he was on the studio floor, Hitch liked to balance the minimal creative effort needed to helm the current film with the crafting of the next; in the case of *Dial M for Murder*, he had coped with the monotony of the shoot and the technical frustrations of 3-D by absorbing himself in the detail of *Rear Window* and, early in the process, he had decided that he wanted Kelly for the female lead. 'All through the making of *Dial M for Murder*,' she recalled, 'he sat and talked to me about it.'

Hitchcock himself was more guarded as to when he reached his decision with regard to Kelly; at the time, he was still an employee of Warners, discussing a role in a Paramount film with a contract player from MGM! Press announcements for *Rear Window* had already been made, so it was no secret, but Jack Warner would not have been amused to learn that Hitch was any less than totally committed to his film. No doubt *Rear Window* was a topic of conversation at the dinner parties at Bellagio Road, for John Michael Hayes was a regular visitor, but if there was agreement between Kelly and Hitch about their next film together, then it was purely on the strength of verbal commitment.

Hitchcock's contract with Paramount gave him the freedom to cast his pictures, and he made it clear that the one and only choice he had for leading lady was Grace Kelly. The studio had no complaint—its later adverts for the film promised cinemagoers (or at least the men in the audience) that they 'would not be able to take [their] eyes off the glowing beauty of Grace Kelly'. But Kelly's insistence that she committed to the project from the moment that Hitch first broached the subject was overstating the situation. There was nothing predestined about her involvement in *Rear Window* and, whatever she and he discussed over dessert, it was by no means certain that she would even be able to appear in the film. The threat to Hitchcock's plans did not come from the studio bosses but from Kelly's own ambitions.

Grace Kelly had returned to New York as soon as filming finished on *Dial M*, pleased to be away from the hot-house atmosphere of LA and back in the relative sanity of Manhattan. Her first professional engagement after her return was for Dore Schary, who instructed her to attend the premiere of *Mogambo* at the Radio City Music Hall. Ava Gardner also made an appearance on the arm of husband Frank Sinatra, but Kelly was spared any repetition of the embarrassing scenes at Heathrow airport with the film's star; Clark Gable, freed from his MGM shackles, did not feel obliged to make even a token show of support. Nevertheless, *Mogambo* managed to create a stir. The studio threw the full weight of its publicity machine behind Ford's film and convinced everyone that it had what *Variety* called a, 'sexy two-fisted adventure'. With a campaign promoting the top-liners, Gable and Gardner, to the exclusion of all others in the cast, the effort produced a sizable box-office hit.

Kelly disliked having to engage in publicity chores for what effectively was someone else's film, but at least she had been rewarded with an Oscar nomination—

albeit due more to lobbying by MGM than anything the Academy members might have seen for themselves on the screen. From his point of view, Dore Schary saw the income from Warners for *Dial M for Murder* as a useful fillip for MGM and calculated that there might be some value to Kelly's contract, after all. But there was currently no suitable role available and no-one at the studio looking for one, so while her agents were instructed to find her film work, Kelly herself thought she might have another crack at the Broadway stage.

Once again, Kelly ran up against East Coast theatre prejudice against Hollywood and, despite having made three significant movies in more or less quick succession, there were no takers on Broadway for the actress whose likeness now peered out from posters urging patrons to come see, '*The BATTLE of the SEXES! The BATTLE of the GORILLAS!*' Unperturbed by the tepid reaction among theatre producers, she set her sights on the part of Roxanne, the female lead in a prestigious revival of *Cyrano de Bergerac* at the City Centre Theatre. Edmond Rostand's famous play had previously been a huge Broadway triumph for Puerto Rican-born actor José Ferrer, who had picked up a 'Tony' Best Actor award in the lead role in 1947 and followed it up with an Oscar in Stanley Kramer's big screen version; Frances Reid and Mala Powers were his 'Roxannes' in those two instances. Ferrer, now turned director, was looking to repeat his earlier success at the City Centre Theatre. The call had gone out to talent agents throughout New York that the role of Roxanne was up for grabs, and Kelly indicated interest. She also tracked down the play's original director, Mel Ferrer (no relation to José), and charmed him into giving her private tuition before being seen by José. It was to no avail; the actress had a terrible cold on the morning of the auditions and failed to make it past the first round. But Mel Ferrer turned out to be a receptive shoulder to cry on and pleaded her case for another chance. Kelly was equally poor on the second occasion. 'There, I told you. She hasn't got the experience; she's not a pro. It wouldn't have mattered if she didn't have a cold. She's not right,' exclaimed a vindicated José Ferrer. The part went to Arlene Dahl, and Kelly was forced to inform an indifferent MGM that she was still available for work.

Grace Kelly's willingness to deploy her undoubted charms to further her career has often been construed by more scurrilous sections of the press—*Confidential* magazine among them—as a sign that the actress was casually promiscuous. Don Richardson, Kelly's on/off boyfriend, was in no doubt that his erstwhile lover used sex to achieve her ambitions. Speaking to writer Darwin Porter, his views on Grace may well have been coloured by the way he was treated by her family, but he nevertheless insisted, 'She screwed everybody she came into contact with and who was able to do anything good for her. She screwed agents, producers, directors, and certainly all of her leading men, even the gay ones.' Kelly was certainly capable of exploiting friends and relations—that was a family trait and her father would have seen it as part of the natural order of things. The difference between she and many of her contemporaries was that Kelly was always in charge: she may have used her sex appeal, her charm and, if Richardson's blunt assessment is to be believed, her body, but she expected a great deal in return and she usually got it.

While Alfred Hitchcock toiled in Hollywood, thinking that he was shaping *Rear Window* for the actress, Kelly was not yet ready to demonstrate the same level of commitment. She still believed that with *Mogambo* and the forthcoming *Dial M for Murder,* she had now done enough to ensure herself a return to the Broadway stage. Had she won the Roxanne audition in the autumn of 1953, she would not have been available for *Rear Window* unless Hitch was prepared to postpone the film to the following year—an unlikely event, given that work had already started on building the hugely-expensive set in the second week in October. Not only was Kelly prepared to forego *Rear Window* for Broadway, she might even have passed on her second outing for Hitchcock if a better film opportunity had presented itself—and Jay Kanter believed that he had just such a project in mind.

Hitchcock, distracted by the complex technical issues on his Paramount sound stage and the needs of his scriptwriter, had not yet made any formal approach to MGM, although he had made it known to Wasserman and MCA that he wanted to cast Kelly. In the absence of a firm offer, Kanter approached producer Sam Spiegel, who was about to start shooting *On the Waterfront* in New York with director Elia Kazan. Kanter was familiar with the new film; his client Marlon Brando had returned the script unread, stating with characteristic disdain that he 'didn't need the money badly enough' to work with Kazan—a nod to the director's recent willingness to testify before Joe McCarthy's House Un-American Activities Committee.

Spiegel reluctantly signed Frank Sinatra—suddenly a box-office draw again after his performance in *From Here to Eternity*—for the lead, but Kazan was reluctant to accept the singer as a tough New York-Irish street-fighter; he had wanted Paul Newman. But Kanter was not about to give up. Figuring that *On the Waterfront* was potential Best Picture material, he set to work on Brando while Spiegel worked on Kazan; both men were eventually persuaded to put their differences aside in the name of art and Sinatra was unceremoniously ditched; he would later (unsuccessfully) try to sue Spiegel for breach of contract. Kazan was a founder member of the Actor's Studio and a strong advocate of Method acting and having cast the Studio's favourite son, he surrounded Brando with other leading Method lights: Karl Malden, Rod Steiger and Lee J Cobb. This was heady company for a still relatively-inexperienced actress, and putting Kelly's name forward was something of gamble. But if Kanter had one thing in his favour, it was an understanding of the mind of the film's charismatic producer.

Austrian-born Samuel P Spiegel was an old-style Hollywood mover and shaker and he had been active in the film capital since the mid-1930s, originally under the pseudonym of S P Eagle. Among his previous credits were *The African Queen* (1951) and the Orson Welles thriller, *The Stranger* (1946), and he would go on to make *Bridge on the River Kwai* (1957) and *Lawrence of Arabia* (1962). Working within the Hollywood system as an independent, Spiegel knew the value of publicity to his projects and the need to have a pretty face and/or a star name to sell a movie to exhibitors; he desperately wanted a name to play the female lead in *On the Waterfront*. The producer's preferred choice for the film was Jennifer Jones, wife of mogul David Selznick, but Jones was dragging her heels on committing to the project, so when Kanter suggested an MCA package deal of Brando and the 'fastest rising female star in Hollywood', Spiegel jumped at the chance.

Kelly may have experienced *déjà vu* in relation to *Taxi* when she learned that the part on offer was that of an Irish tenement girl named Edie Doyle who falls in love with the 'bad boy' lead. A shared Irish heritage aside, the character's working-class roots, in this case Hoboken, were a million miles away from Philadelphia's Henry Avenue and she could hardly have been considered an obvious choice. Kanter nevertheless assured her that while the part was small, On *the Waterfront* was the sort of film that she needed to be seen in if she wanted to be taken seriously as an actress.

As it happened, *On the Waterfront* was not the only game in town, and in sharp contrast with her stuttering theatrical career, Grace was suddenly *starlet du jour* when an old admirer finally broke surface. Clark Gable was back, revitalised after his global wanderings and keen to kick-start the next phase of his career on the back of *Mogambo*'s success. Gable had set up his own production company and convinced 20th Century Fox to finance *Soldier of Fortune* (1955), his first movie as an independent. Evidently forgetting the taste that the staged scenes at Heathrow had left in his mouth, to say nothing of at least two abortive marriage proposals since then, Gable wanted to reignite some of the old magic and offered Kelly the female lead. The role was not an insignificant one in itself—a feisty widow willing to go to any lengths to free her husband from the Red Chinese—but it was still second-fiddle to the male lead. Two months of shooting in Hong Kong may also have been appealing, but the prospect of Gable's undivided attention did not present much of a lure for the actress. Gable was optimistic that he could sign Grace, but *Soldier of Fortune* was the exactly the kind of undemanding action movie that Kelly could have picked up from MGM any time that she chose to do so.

When Hitchcock was advised by MCA that he was facing stiff competition for his leading lady, he contacted Lew Wasserman, who in turn asked Kanter to formally offer Kelly the role in *Rear Window*. Wasserman was strongly in favour of Kelly making the Hitchcock picture, while Kanter (and Van Cleve) both wanted to see her appear opposite Brando. None of them took *Soldier of Fortune* seriously. While Kelly vacillated, Kanter pressed her for a decision. A year later, the actress told readers of *Photoplay* about her dilemma. 'I wanted to do both,' she said. 'I was in my agent's office and he said, "Decide!" I couldn't. I told him, "I want to do both of them." He said, "You can't. You've got to decide on one. You've got ten minutes." If *Cyrano de Bergerac* had been in the mix, there might have been a different outcome, but her choices were now Hitchcock and Hollywood, or Kazan and New York: popular success in the movie capital or artistic credibility on her home turf. Kelly chose Hitchcock.

Spiegel and Brando opted for newcomer Eva Marie Saint (subsequently to star for Hitch herself) who, if anything, looked even less Irish than Kelly did but who had also studied with the Actor's Studio and went on to win Best Supporting Actress for *On the Waterfront*. Gable was less fortunate; he stalled for a while, hoping that Kelly might find time in her schedule, before Fox finally ran out of patience and foisted Susan Hayward on him and between them, they churned out an instantly-forgettable movie.

Kelly's agents had one last act to perform before she could report to Paramount Studios for her costume fittings; they had to persuade MGM to agree. But the fact that Hitchcock and MCA had already agreed a deal and effectively were only informing MGM out of courtesy was a breech of protocol and of some concern to Schary; Kelly was still an employee of his studio, and it was MGM that had the say on where she worked and with whom. Kelly had carefully positioned herself as the sole arbiter of questions related to her career and this would lead to serious conflict with the studio but, for the moment, Schary was not about to cut off his nose to spite his face and he agreed to loan her out for *Rear Window*—though she was reminded that she was an MGM employee and that *it* would negotiate on her behalf in the future.

Keen though he may have been to land Kelly, Hitchcock was not overly generous on the matter of her salary, which was arranged through his own company rather than directly with Paramount. Fox contract player Thelma Ritter, a reliable character player but hardly a star, was also loaned-out to appear in a supporting role in *Rear Window* and she was paid $4166 per week, while Kelly, the female lead, earned less than $2900 per week—paid directly to her 'masters' at MGM.

In the summer of 1953, around the same time that Frederick Knott was settling into the Chateau Marmont to write *Dial M for Murder*, Hitchcock had met with John Michael Hayes to begin discussions about the script of *Rear Window*. Hitchcock's new deal with Paramount was then common knowledge, as were its advantageous terms: in return for leaving Warner Brothers, he was to receive a step up in salary and a four-film production deal that would also grant him ownership of three out of the four, after a period of eight years. *Rear Window* was to be the first under the new arrangement, with *The Trouble with Harry* (1955) and *The Man Who Knew Too Much* (1956) following on—and all of them reverting to Hitchcock eventually. The fourth film to emerge from the deal, *To Catch a Thief* (1955), would remain the property of Paramount.

Rear Window was adapted from a short story by Cornell Woolrich (writing as William Irish) which first appeared in the February 1942 issue of *Dime Detective Magazine* under the title, 'It Had To Be Murder'. It surfaced as 'Rear Window' in 1944 when Woolrich republished it in an anthology entitled *After-Dinner Story*. The film rights were picked up for a nominal sum by producer/songwriter Buddy DeSylva but the project, for one reason or another, never made it off of the drawing board and when DeSylva died in 1950, the rights were sold to theatre director Joshua Logan. Better known for his stage musicals, Logan wrote a treatment which he sent to his agent, the ubiquitous Lew Wasserman, with the intention of using it to make his debut as a film director. Wasserman saw it as an ideal starring-vehicle for another of his clients, James Stewart, and he had suggested that Hitchcock might be willing to come on board as producer. Logan's plan had been to shoot the film in 1952, but accommodating Stewart's schedule would have pushed the start-date back to the following year. It then came to light that Stewart was unhappy about entrusting himself to Logan and Wasserman was left to engineer an uneasy compromise, without loss of face for the film's sponsor, who had taken it to MCA in the first place. He eventually managed to ease Logan out of the director's chair and replace him with Hitchcock and, in May 1953, the trade papers carried the news that the next Hitchcock film after *Dial M* would be *Rear Window*—to be produced jointly by Stewart, Hitchcock and Logan. Realising that he was likely to be elbowed out when the film went into production, Logan and accepted a modest payoff and withdrew.

While Hitchcock was directing Kelly on the Warners sound stage, John Michael Hayes worked on his treatment for *Rear Window* and the first draft was submitted

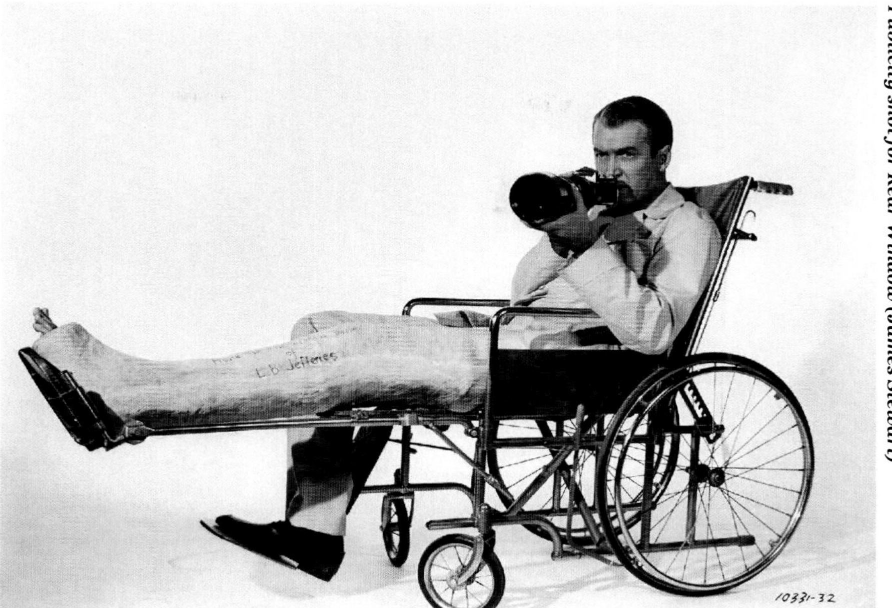

Publicity shot for Rear Window (James Stewart)

to Paramount, via MCA, in September 1953. The 33-year-old Hayes, another client of MCA, had learned his craft writing suspense dramas for radio, which had eventually led him to Hollywood to pen a series of programmers such as *Torch Song* (1953), starring Joan Crawford, and *Thunder Bay* (1953), with James Stewart. He had come to Hitchcock—following a recommendation from Wasserman—with a reputation for good plotting and intelligent dialogue.

Hayes proved to be a reliable collaborator for a director who is often associated with the *auteur* theory, the notion originated by the critics of *Cahiers du Cinema* that a director is the sole creator, or 'author', of a film. The theory flattered Hitchcock's ego and, while he was only too pleased to present himself in this exalted role in later life, he was always smart enough to allow himself some wriggle-room in the event of failure by insisting, 'Often the director is no better than his script.' In fairness to Hitch, he invariably was closely involved with all aspects of the filmmaking process at a time when many of his contemporaries in Hollywood limited themselves to hiring and firing writers and/or simply showing up on set to direct.

There has been some debate as to how much of *Rear Window* was Hitchcock and how much Hayes; the script was certainly a collaborative exercise, but Hayes told Donald Spoto: 'We sat down and broke it down shot for shot, and he showed me how to do some things much better.. The stamp of Hitchcock's genius is on every frame of the finished film.' Unlike *Dial M for Murder*, which effectively was made to order, *Rear Window* was to be a personal project for Hitchcock and the script that emerged would mirror his own obsessions.

Hayes's first treatment contained a number of enhancements to both the earlier Logan version and the original short story. Woolrich's tale was typical pulp fodder: an incapacitated protagonist, Hal Jeffries, struggles to convince his companions, a 'day houseman' called Sam and a doubting policeman named Boyne, that he has witnessed a murder. Logan's treatment had fleshed out this basic plot and introduced a love interest in the form of an actress who is too busy with her

On set: Grace Kelly, Alfred Hitchcock

career to settle down. The basic concept of a 'Peeping Tom', monitoring the comings and goings of his neighbours for his own amusement, was inherent in the original as well as in Logan's work, but Hitchcock saw the potential to take this to a more extreme level. Hitch's protagonist soon evolved from someone casually observing others out of boredom to a full-blown *voyeur* armed with a camera and telephoto lens. In doing so, his aim was to put protagonist (now renamed L B 'Jeff' Jefferies) *and* audience right into the neighbours' living rooms. Hitchcock also enhanced the various domestic dramas unfolding for Jeff's entertainment; in the Woolrich story, they were only briefly delineated, but Hayes created a series of vignettes which were designed to amuse, titillate and intrigue—almost encouraging viewers to become voyeurs themselves.

Looking to elaborate on Jeff's romantic entanglements, Hitch took inspiration from his recent past. During the shooting of *Notorious,* Ingrid Bergman had become besotted with noted photojournalist Robert Capra, but her ardour cooled somewhat when he refused even to contemplate marriage to the smitten actress. Hitchcock was fascinated with the idea that a man could be so absorbed in his own world that he could resist the charms of a beautiful and available woman; it was an anecdote that he often recounted at dinner parties. Hitch asked Hayes to work this idea into his script, and it became a central theme of *Rear Window*: Jeff was transformed into a daring action photographer, whose enthusiasm to capture the perfect shot at the racetrack has led to a broken leg, while his love interest, Lisa Freemont, became a model-cum-fashion buyer—an unfeasibly glamorous creature, who spends the first half of the film on a fruitless quest to coax him into marriage.

Having been given this template by Hitchcock, Hayes first looked to his own wife, also a model, to provide him with inspiration for Lisa, but Hitch gave very clear instructions on how the writer was actually to shape Lisa's background and personality: Hayes was invited on to the set of *Dial M*, introduced to Grace Kelly, and then instructed to acquaint himself with the actress so as to ensure that the character he was creating came as close as possible to Kelly herself. Hitchcock did

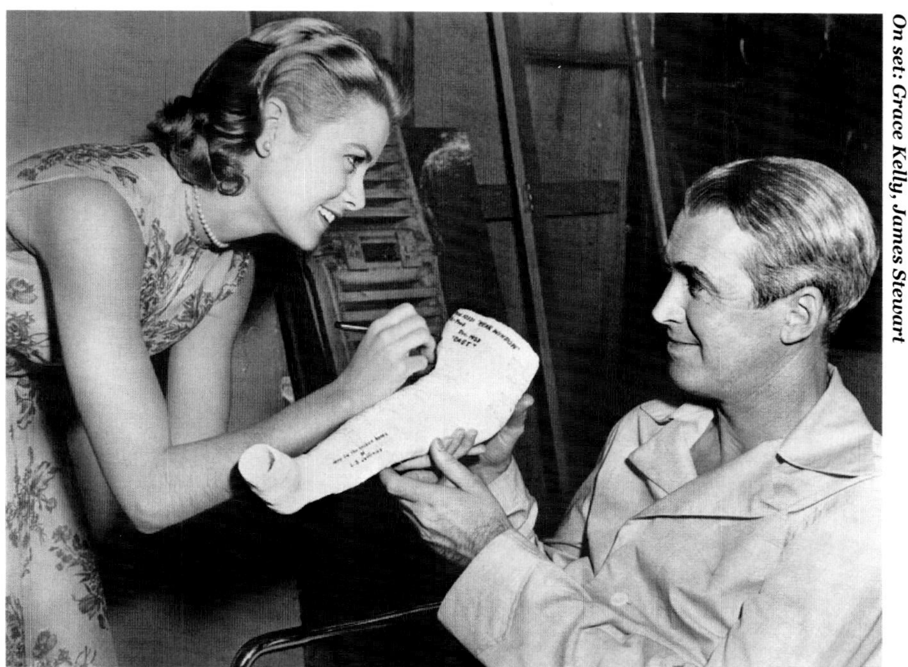

On set: Grace Kelly, James Stewart

not intend Lisa to be written for Kelly; he intended Lisa to be written *as* Kelly. Confiding in Hayes before a word had been typed, he said: 'Grace has a lot of charm and talent but she goes through the motions as if she is in acting school. She does everything properly and pleasantly, but nothing comes out of her. You have to bring something out of her, bring her to life.' After their introduction Hitchcock arranged for Hayes to spend a week in her company so that he could get to know the 'real Grace Kelly'; the result was predictable. 'I was entranced by her,' he told James Spada, 'I couldn't get over the difference between her personal animation and, if I may say so, her sexuality.'

Hayes's script highlighted the contradictions in Grace Kelly's psychological make-up: the diffident and elegant façade, and the unbridled animal lurking just below the surface. Hitch correctly surmised that the very qualities which entranced Hayes would intrigue and titillate the audience in equal measure.

L B Jefferies is bored. Having spent his professional life on the edge, taking photographs in dangerous situations, he is now wheelchair-bound with his leg in plaster. To relieve the tedium, 'Jeff' has taken to observing his neighbours across the courtyard and has come to rely upon them as his only source of entertainment: two girls sunbathing on a terrace, an artist working on a sculpture, a composer creating a new tune, and a pair of newlyweds in the first throes of passion. Jeff gives them all pet names—an energetic dancer, for example, becomes 'Miss Torso'—and in his mind, he maps their individual stories. He also watches a morose character named Thorwald as he struggles to cope with a bedridden and clearly demanding wife.

Jeff has two companions: a professional physiotherapist and his girlfriend, Lisa, whom he describes as just too perfect to marry, implying that she would not fit into the rough and tumble of his working life.

Jeff's suspicions about Thorwald are aroused when he watches him leave his apartment in the early hours of the morning carrying a heavy load. Soon afterwards, he notices that the housebound Mrs Thorwald has 'disappeared'. The police think that Jeff is deluded and dismiss his pleadings—as does Lisa, until a dog that has been digging in the yard turns up dead and Jeff convinces her that Thorwald was responsible. Jeff writes Thorwald a note asking, 'WHAT HAVE YOU DONE WITH HER?', and Lisa posts it under his door; he then arranges to meet Thorwald in a bar, so that Lisa can sneak into his apartment and gather evidence against him. But the break-in goes wrong and Lisa is arrested..

Thorwald now realises who sent him the note. Unable to leave his apartment, Jeff has no choice but to wait helplessly in the dark as Thorwald comes for him...

Hitchcock also plundered two real-life murder cases to flesh out Thorwald's crime; one was culled from the headlines of 1924, while he was still working in London. Patrick Mahon, a remorseless womaniser, convinced his pregnant mistress, Emily Kaye, to hide out in his Sussex love nest while he made arrangements to leave his wife. Mahon throttled poor Emily to death and then dismembered her body and hid the parts in a large trunk; he then began to dispose of the remains. He burned the head in the fireplace and boiled the limbs in pots; other parts were flung out of the windows of the Eastbourne to London train. Mahon was captured after his wife found a left-luggage ticket in his pocket and opened the locker at London's Waterloo Station to find yet another piece of her unfortunate rival.

The other borrowing for the film was from the case of the infamous Dr Hawley Harvey Crippen, who poisoned and disposed of his wife Cora, a former music-hall singer—telling the police that she had moved permanently to the United States. Crippen was exposed as a killer when the pawning of Cora's jewellery aroused the suspicions of her friends and neighbours. But Crippen evaded arrest and, altering his appearance, he boarded the transatlantic liner SS Montrose with his mistress, disguised as a boy. However, the ship's captain recognised the couple and the police, in the form of Chief Inspector Walter Dew, were waiting for them when they arrived in Canada. By then, the remains of Cora Crippen had been discovered in the cellar of his home. Hitchcock was fascinated by the notion that an item of jewellery, which in the case of *Rear Window* became a wedding ring, could be the key to the unlocking of a dark secret for anyone astute enough to realise it.

The influence of these two murders on the Hayes/Hitchcock script is plain, though there are notable omissions in the cinematic variant. The (off-screen) murder of Mrs Thorwald and subsequent disposal of her body is a completely bloodless activity; in fact, no body parts are so much as glimpsed, despite the grisly inspiration for the deed. The closest the film version comes to its real-life inspiration is a shot of Thorwald cleaning a kitchen knife—all else is left to the viewer's imagination. This restrained approach kept Hitchcock on the right side of the censors and allowed him to adopt a lighter approach to the situation. The other absentee is Thorwald's own mistress: the character is mentioned several times and is key to establishing his alibi, thus convincing the police that Jeff's tale has no credibility—but all without actually appearing on screen. After Thorwald is exposed and the picture rolls to a climax, the mistress disappears entirely from the narrative and her role in the murder and subsequent cover-up is never explained.

Casting the leading roles could not have been easier for Hitchcock. James Stewart was a part of the package almost from the moment that it landed on Lew

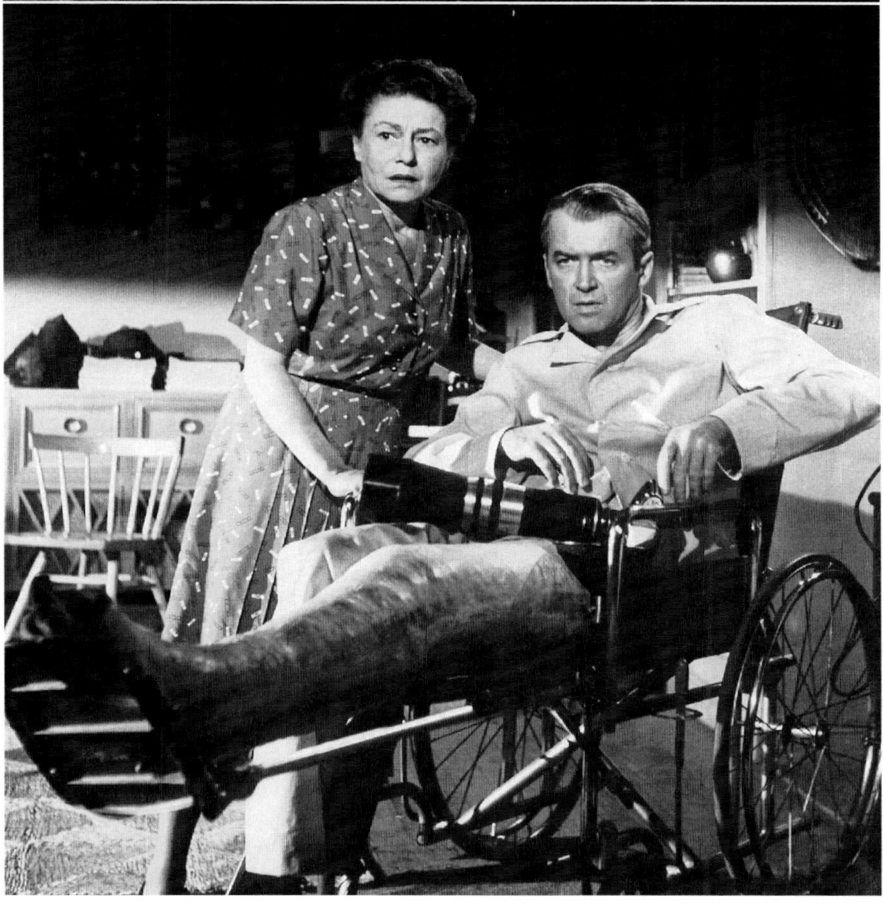

Rear Window (Raymond Burr, Thelma Ritter, James Stewart)

Wasserman's desk. Hitch had enjoyed working with Stewart on *Rope*, and the mutual respect that developed between them during the shoot was sufficient for the two men to want to work together again on a less demanding project. But though they enjoyed a successful professional relationship, Stewart and Hitch never became friends and rarely socialised away from the studio.

James Stewart was one of the biggest stars in Hollywood at the time, having begun his movie career in the 1930s and gained huge popularity in hits like *Destry Rides Again* (1939), *Mr Smith Goes to Washington* (1939) and *The Philadelphia Story* (1940). After serving with distinction in the US Air Force during the Second World War, Stewart returned to Hollywood and used his well-entrenched, folksy and easy-going screen image to rebuild his star status in a run of equally-successful films ranging from Frank Capra's *It's a Wonderful Life* (1946) to the gentle whimsey of *Harvey* (1950). By the early fifties, Stewart, a shrewd custodian of his career, had joined the growing band of big stars who were turning their backs on the studio system and signing with the increasingly-influential talent agencies: in Stewart's case, MCA. Stewart's relationship with Wasserman was pushing him in a more challenging direction, but it was his work with Hitchcock that was to show a darker side to his persona.

It has been suggested that Stewart was Hitchcock's alter ego; that his charm, intelligence and old-world manner were a self-image of the director on screen. (Cary Grant, conversely, with his good looks and sexual charisma, is thought to be how Hitchcock *wanted* to be seen.) Hitch used Stewart in four films altogether, including two of his most personal projects, *Rear Window* and *Vertigo* (1958)—in both of which he was cast against type, as a flawed character in situations containing strong autobiographical undertones for the director. These films also had close associations with Grace Kelly and, in particular, her relationship with Hitch.

Having finally secured Kelly for *Rear Window*, Hitchcock set out to redefine her screen image. To a large extent, all of her earlier screen roles, including *Dial M*, reflected aspects of her own personality: she was seen as demure, passive and somewhat aloof—though none had been written with her specifically in mind. With John Michael Hayes writing a role of Lisa to order, and modelling the character closely on the actress herself, audiences were to be given the opportunity—for the first time—to see Grace Kelly as Hitchcock saw her. The Kelly of the film is an energetic and ambitious young lady with a lively libido. (Her overt sexual advances to 'Jeff' were considered risqué for their day, when such was rarely alluded to onscreen.) She is also an extrovert, who thinks nothing of parading in a new dress for her boyfriend's (and the audience's) approval, and later features just as casually in lingerie. No longer was this the 'mousy' actress of *High Noon*—Hitchcock was exhibiting the 'Gryce' who 'fucked everyone' on *Dial M for Murder*. Kelly had looked beautiful for Zinnemann and Ford without ever being sensual; Hitchcock was the first of her directors to tap into what he described as her innate 'sexual elegance'. He later told Newsweek: 'I didn't discover Grace but I saved her from a fate worse than death. I prevented her from being eternally cast as a cold woman.'

To make sure that his star looked her very best, Hitchcock wrote in a number of costume changes, each more eye-catching than the last, and he engaged top designer Edith Head to create the spectacular outfits. Head later confirmed that Hitchcock was as closely involved with the costumes as he was with the script: 'There was a reason for every colour, every style,' she said, 'and he was absolutely certain on everything he settled on.. he was putting a dream together in the studio.'

Lisa was not only dressed to impress, she was made up to look stunning: 'An actress like Grace, who is also a lady, gives a director certain advantages,' Hitchcock claimed. 'He can afford to be more colourful with a love scene played by a lady than one played by a hussy. With a hussy such a scene can be vulgar, but if you put a lady in the same circumstances, she's exciting and glamorous.' To showcase his theory, Hitch created one of the most enticing entrances ever afforded a leading lady, filming her from Jeff's point of view to ensure that the audience shared in his vision: a shadow looms over the sleeping Jeff and she bends down in loving close-up to kiss him; then in an effort to steal him away from the distractions across the yard, she sashays across the room and introduces herself by switching on three lights in time to 'Lisa—Carol—Freemont.' Robert Burks, Hitchcock's regular cinematographer, crafted the intoxicating scene, which sets the tone for the character throughout the film. Grace Kelly never looked so bewitching.

The contrast between *Rear Window*'s Lisa Freemont and *Dial M for Murder*'s Margot Wendice could not have been more marked. In the latter, Hitchcock did very little to suggest a passionate or sensual woman, above or below the surface. The only instance of emotional contact (aside from the assault) is when Margot and Mark Halliday kiss, and the scene is shot in a very matter-of-fact way; their brief embrace seems passionate only when compared with the perfunctory peck which she reserves for her husband. In *Rear Window*, Hitch once more demonstrated what could be done with a kiss—with Lisa's face filling the screen as she lowers her head to her lover's in what seems like slow motion, her rouged lips parted and moist. For the benefit of Paramount's press office, Kelly reported, 'I'd heard that Alfred Hitchcock was a thorough director. All I can say is that he is definitely as thorough with his love scenes as he is with his mystery sequences. In one three-minute scene, for example, Mr Hitchcock had me kiss Jimmy Steward 37 times. And I mean *kiss*!'

Aside from the leads, the most significant role in *Rear Window* in terms of presence, if not actual screen time, was the morose and threatening Lars Thorwald. In casting Canadian Raymond Burr in the role, Hitchcock once again dipped into autobiographical baggage, this time in the form of a thinly-veiled swipe at his former employer, David O Selznick. Burr bore a passing resemblance to Selznick, and to underline the point for those in on the joke, Hitch had him style his hair the way that Selznick did and wear the same type of glasses; according to legend, he also delighted in coaching the actor in Selznick's mannerisms.

Hitchcock launched himself into preproduction on the film with a vigour that was barely glimpsed during the making of *Dial M for Murder*; soon the walls of his office at Paramount were covered in elaborate storyboards and shot-lists. Not only were his energy-levels up but he had his diet under control—always a sign that he was in good spirits. By the time shooting started on November 27, he boasted that he had shed some 20lbs from his ample girth. Hitch liked to tease the press that it was the stress of filming complex murder scenes that produced the weight loss; in fact, he had given Alma strict instructions to limit his calorie intake and it was the new slim-line, more relaxed Alfred Hitchcock who beamed for the cameras alongside Grace Kelly in the early publicity shots.

But it was not only Kelly who had rekindled the director's passion for filmmaking. The magnificent set for the film, designed by Hal Pereira and Joseph MacMillan Johnson, offered Hitchcock the kind of technical opportunity that he relished. The *Rear Window* set, housed in Stage 18 on the Paramount lot at 5555 Melrose Avenue, was comprised of 31 apartments— eight of which included fully-furnished rooms—as well as fire escapes, roof gardens, an alley and a street. Construction had started on October 12 and by the time it was ready to be lit, the set required a massive 36,000 amps of illumination from 800 lamps, 500 of which were over 5 kwt apiece. This elaborate lighting rig was split into three banks, which could recreate day, dawn or

The Rear Window set

dusk at the flick of a switch. The set was the talk of the studio and a 'must see' stop on every VIP tour; Hitchcock, like a child with the smartest toy in the playground, revelled in telling visitors that it cost over 25% of the film's budget and that eight of the apartments were fully plumbed and wired and fit for human habitation!

To shoot on the massive set, Hitchcock and his crew worked from 'Jeff's apartment' and he directed the actors in the building opposite through microphones hidden in their clothing; this allowed the camera to maintain a consistent point of view through practically the whole of the film—what Jeff saw, the audience were to see. The unforeseen complexities of shooting at such a remove were to add an extra fifteen days to the schedule, but Hitchcock relished the challenge. 'My batteries,' he insisted, 'were fully charged.'

The single set also allowed Hitchcock the advantage of not having to 'strike' sets when he moved to the next scene and, like *Dial M*, the film was shot largely in chronological sequence; this also gave the actors the luxury of a more structured and logical approach to rehearsals and the development of their characters. Stewart, in particular, enjoyed the more relaxed and convivial atmosphere on set—a considerable turnaround from the tension that had pervaded *Rope*. Having deferred his salary to take a stake in the production, Stewart had more to lose than his co-stars, but when instead he began to relate to his wife how well things were going, it was she who started to worry.

James Stewart had been married to former model Gloria McLean (née Hatrick) for four years; McLean had two sons from a previous marriage and they had twin daughters of their own, Judy and Kelly, born in 1951. The Hollywood press was habitual in its use of the term 'perfect marriage' about every famous couple who had not yet filed for divorce but, in the case of the Stewarts, it seemed genuinely apt. The only cloud on the horizon had come wafting in from Philadelphia with the arrival of Grace Kelly onto the Paramount stage. As it happened, little Kelly Stewart's godmother was none other than Mal Milland, the newly-reconciled wife of Ray, and thanks to the newspapers, everyone knew of the impact that Grace Kelly had made on that particular marriage.

The situation was shaping-up a treat for the 'gutter' press, with yet another middle-aged Hollywood A-lister ready to spend his working days looking into the eyes of the town's most notorious home-wrecker. Unfortunately for the tabloids, James Stewart was no Ray Milland. Pushed to offer a comment on his nubile co-star, Stewart conceded he was not immune to her charms. 'Everything about Grace is appealing,' he said. 'I'm married but I'm not dead!' Years later, Gloria Stewart revealed: 'Jimmy was working with some of the most glamorous women in the world. My constant fear I suppose was that he would find them more attractive than me and have an affair with one of them. And I can honestly say that in all the years of our marriage Jimmy never once gave me cause for anxiety or jealousy. The more glamorous the leading lady he was starring opposite, the more attentive he'd be to me.' On a regular basis, Stewart would present Kelly with a bouquet of flowers that he claimed to have picked from his own garden, but he also made sure that he went home to his wife at the end of the every day's shooting.

The press was so convinced that it would have another on-set love triangle to report on that it almost missed the story that was unfolding away from the Paramount lot, with crooner Bing Crosby emerging as an unlikely suitor for Kelly's affections. The 50-year-old star—along with screen partner Bob Hope—of Paramount's popular 'Road' comedies still dominated the record charts, and he and Kelly had met when she first arrived in Hollywood and Bing's wife, Dixie, had been terminally ill (she would die shortly before filming started on *Rear Window*). Although Crosby, like the philandering Hope, never seemed short of female companionship, Kelly was singled out to provide solace, and her own brand of distraction: stories circulated that the couple enjoyed midnight skinny-dipping in the pool of Crosby friend and neighbour, Alan Ladd. In her book *Grace Kelly's Men*, Jane Ellen Wayne tells how Ladd would entertain Kelly and Crosby to drinks then make his excuses and go off to bed; according to the author, he 'would occasionally go downstairs after midnight to make sure the door was latched and would be embarrassed to find Bing and Grace caressing and kissing on the couch.'

Grace might have been having fun, but she had learned some lessons from the Milland affair and was paying more attention to the advice offered by guardian angel 'Scoop' Conlon. She avoided the temptations posed by the Chateau Marmont and opted instead to rent a two-bed apartment on Sweetzer Avenue in West Hollywood, just off Sunset Boulevard. For once, *Confidential* missed an obvious headline: in daylight hours, Sweetzer Avenue was quiet and respectable if somewhat run down, but at night, it was a favoured haunt of streetwalkers and similar lowlife; given its previous exposés of Kelly's nocturnal activities, it is surprising that the opportunity to draw a parallel between the town's best known man-eater and the more notorious denizens of Sweetzer Avenue somehow passed the magazine by.

When she was out on the town or dining at a restaurant, Kelly presented a more refined image for public consumption and invariably ensured that she was in the company of a lady, usually her sister Lizanne or Prudence Wise, a friend from her Barbizon days who now acted as her secretary. The 'paparazzi' still followed her everywhere though, hoping for something spicer, and the presence of a chaperone did little to discourage reporters in search of a story. One popular Los Angeles daily printed a picture of Kelly and Bing Crosby looking very cosy in a restaurant and left its readers to draw their own conclusions; the fact that Lizanne had been cropped out of the photo was conveniently overlooked. Such underhand behaviour did not sit well with Kelly and she remained openly contemptuous of the press. 'At times I actually hate Hollywood,' she complained to the *Saturday Evening Post*. 'I have many acquaintances here but few friends.'

In the meantime, Kelly's own publicists were working hard to ensure that she received as much of the 'right kind' of publicity as possible—newspapers and magazines began to feature more bland and clearly-contrived stories. Even Louella Parsons no longer took side-swipes at her romantic liaisons, instead assuring her readers that 'Grace is a strict Catholic girl brought up by a strict Catholic mother'; Parsons also revealed that Kelly had once met her childhood idol, Douglas Fairbanks Jr, and, having received a peck on the cheek from the star, 'knew she would never wash off that spot on her face again'. The Parsons anecdote was typical of the cheesy articles that were now fed to journalists as part of a concerted PR plan. (Underlining this new-found maturity in her dealings with the press, Kelly would announce, some months later, that she was dating émigré Italian dress designer Oleg Cassini—the first time that she would publicly acknowledge a romantic attachment and a move designed to invest her with a solid air of respectability.)

The fact that Kelly was now keeping her affairs out of the public eye and away from the film set pleased Hitchcock. 'I think that too much sex while you are working goes against the work,' he said later, 'and that repressed sex is more constructive for a creative person. It must get out, and so it goes into the work; I think it helped create a sense of sex in my work.' There was nothing repressed about Kelly's behaviour during *Dial M for Murder*, and soon after she had begun her relationship with Milland, Hitch became uncharacteristically intolerant of the actor and he would snap at him for fluffing a line or missing a mark. On *Rear Window*, Hitch had Kelly all to himself, at least during working hours, which for him was the most important time of the day.

Their shared sense of humour served to deepen the affection that Kelly and Hitchcock felt for each other; he revelled in his role of mentor, and she believed that he was genuinely interested in her career and in helping her to develop as an actress. She found that he valued her opinion—something that she had not experienced with her father or the other older men in her life; on the set of *Dial M for Murder*, Kelly had informed Hitch of the importance of a handbag to a woman, and that nugget of 'inside' knowledge had found its way into the script for *Rear Window*.

As respect grew between the two, Hitchcock became more confident in what he asked of the actress. Four months earlier, he had been too embarrassed to put Kelly into a nightdress; there was no such modesty about lingerie in *Rear Window*. Hitch was comfortable enough to suggest that Kelly should augment her modest bosom in the scene where she is required to wear a sheer nightgown. Kelly recalled, 'Hitchcock called for Edith Head and said, "Look, the bosom is not right. We're going to have to put something in there." Well, I said, you can't put falsies in this, it's going to show—and I am not going to wear them. So we quickly took it up here, made some adjustments there, and I just did what I could and stood as straight as possible—without falsies. When I walked out onto the set, Hitchcock looked at me and at Edith and said, "See what a difference they make."' Kelly would advance this as the only time she could remember disobeying the director.

Hitchcock may have been pleased with the way that his star looked on the big screen but Joseph Breen, chair of industry censorship board, the MPAA, was less than impressed with the *Rear Window* script and voiced his own concerns about Kelly's state of undress—with or without bust enhancement. Citing various prohibitions in the Production Code, Breen's office also objected to the 'toilet' humour in Hayes's script and the prolonged and lustful kissing. But what most troubled the guardians of the nation's morals were the domestic vignettes that Hayes had served up for Jeff's entertainment, which included taboos like suggestive dancing, extra-marital sexual activity and none-too-subtle bedroom athletics from the newlyweds. The censor's most damning comments were reserved for the 'Miss Torso' character; in particular, the suggestion in Hayes's script that she would be cavorting half-naked. 'The picturization of a young girl, described as wearing only black panties, is unacceptable,' observed the official report. 'It is apparent that she is nude above the waist, and it is only by the most judicious selection of camera angles that her nudity is concealed from the audience. We feel that this gives the entire action a flavour of a peep show which is unacceptable.' Breen had missed the point that Hitch had conceived the entire film as a million-dollar peep show and, as such, the viewer had to be given something to 'peep' at!

Hitchcock was an old hand at this cat-and-mouse game with the censor and he began his usual charm offensive by inviting them to the studio to watch cast and crew in action. When Luigi Luraschi, Paramount's representative at the censor, arrived expecting a den of iniquity, he found Hitchcock at his most disarming, generously taking time out of his busy schedule to show him how the elaborate set functioned and introduce the cast, including the enchanting Miss Kelly. The director then launched in to a carefully-prepared diatribe against gratuitous displays on the screen, and how he always sought to 'suggest' rather than depict nudity and violence. In consequence, the MPAA moderated its tone and accepted Hitch's assurance that he could obviate its concerns on the floor or in the editing suite. Having pacified Breen, Hitch shot the film more or less according to the script.

With the censorship issues resolved, Hitchcock was relaxed and happy: he liked

Hayes and his screenplay, he liked the freedom that his Paramount contract was affording him, and he enjoyed working with the calm professionalism of Stewart and, of course, his female lead. Such was the thoroughness of Hitchcock's planning and the skill of his crew that Paramount records show the film's first week of shooting to have averaged a creditable 25 setups a day. Progress was so good that Hitchcock was able to take time out of his schedule to indulge in a little mischief: he announced that he was going to film some shots of Kelly's feet and had her turn up on set in costume and high heels for the close-ups. After shooting for thirty minutes, he pronounced himself satisfied and instructed the crew to move on to the next setup; when his cameraman quizzed him on why they had shot something that was not in the storyboards, Hitch deadpanned, 'Have you ever heard of a shoe fetish?'

The supposed fixation on Kelly's footwear may have been Hitchcock's idea of a joke, but it was harder to shrug off the opinion of many reviewers that *Rear Window* was crafted as a paean to sexual deviation, specifically voyeurism—something the Breen Office had missed in its pursuit of the more obvious sexual elements on the other side of the yard. Jeff's 'innocent' observation of his neighbours becomes an obsession that takes over his life to the exclusion of everything and everyone else, including the beautiful girlfriend who literally is 'throwing' herself at him. Trying everything that she can think of to elicit his interest, Lisa sits on his lap and pouts provocatively, but she still manages to raise nothing more than indifference in a man who could be said to be distracted at best. Jeff's physical impairment—a leg in plaster—may explain his lack of enthusiasm for physical contact, but the implication is that something deeper is troubling Jeff than his girlfrinds's sexual assertiveness. Immediately after rebuffing her advances, he meekly asks Lisa what she thinks of him and she responds, 'Something too frightful to utter.' It is only when she becomes a part of his voyeuristic fantasy by crossing the courtyard in front of his camera to break into Thorwald's rooms that he starts to pay her the attention that she has been craving.

Hayes's script makes no moral judgements about spying on neighbours, although Jeff's physiotherapist does point out to him that his innocent pursuit could earn him 'three years in Dannemora', New York State's maximum security prison. While one might reasonably expect a 'Peeping Tom' to be subject to punishment or humiliation, *Rear Window's* protagonist not only gets to catch a killer but prevent a potential suicide. Rather than condemn voyeurism, Hitchcock goes out of his way to make the viewer complicit in what is actually an illegal act and, by sustaining Jeff's point of view for much of the movie, the director lures the audience into becoming active participants in his deviant pastime; what he sees, we see. It was a clever trick by Hitchcock to condone voyeurism if the end can be demonstrated to justify the means; he told director François Truffaut that Jeff was a 'real Peeping Tom,' adding, 'He's a snooper, but aren't we all? I'll bet you that nine of ten people, if they see a woman across the courtyard undressing for bed, or even a man puttering around in his room, will stay and look; no-one turns away and says, "It's none of my business".'

Hitchcock's response to Truffaut's question has been interpreted as an attempt to justify his own voyeuristic tendencies, and at least one writer has suggested that during the filming of *Rear Window*, Hitch took his fixation one step further—with Kelly as participant. Kenneth Anger, the controversial Underground filmmaker and author of *Hollywood Babylon* (and its inventively-titled sequel *Hollywood Babylon II*) alleged that Hitchcock was a *scopophiliac*— literally, he 'loved to look'—the term describing a man who achieves sexual gratification from objectifying women and observing, rather than participating in, sexual activity. Anger claims in *Hollywood*

Babylon II that Kelly indulged in an act that could have sprung straight from the *Rear Window* script, in that she performed a striptease for Hitch, but from afar: 'Slowly, thoughtfully, as if returning from a night on the town, Grace Kelly disrobed. Her hat came first, then the gloves..' Anger goes on to describe the striptease in lurid detail, right down to Kelly's 'French lace panties hitting the floor'. And he states that this peep show was arranged solely for Hitchcock, who was watching from a mile away through a high-powered lens. (The story finds resonance in *Rear Window,* in the scene where Lisa announces that she will get Jeff's attention even if she has to 'move in to an apartment across the way and do the Dance of the Seven Veils every hour'.)

Both of Anger's books regurgitate famous Hollywood scandals, and many of the stories are have been circulating for years; others, like the Hitchcock–Kelly incident are presented for the first time. The common factor in all the tales is that the participants are deceased and therefore not in any position to defend themselves; Anger's sources are domestic staff, chauffeurs, and anyone with a grudge against their erstwhile employers, or cab drivers or waitresses out to make a quick buck; predictably, no names are ever given. The softcore prose and headline-grabbing style is off-putting, but Anger is adamant that the incident actually took place. His version has Kelly deciding on a whim to indulge Hitchcock's fantasies after listening for ages to his innuendoes and double-entendres.

Trade ad for Rear Window

Anger's anecdote has an air of the apocryphal and is unlikely to be independently verified; none of the many biographies of Hitchcock or Grace Kelly afford it any credence. But apart from the obvious parallels with *Rear Window* (as well as the voyeurism in Hitchcock's other films, notably *Psycho* [1960]), the episode does offer a tantalising foretaste of later events in the director's life. So far as Kelly is concerned, there is no evidence to suggest that she would have stooped to anything as squalid, even if she was no shrinking violet when it came to her dealings with the opposite sex.

Whatever did or did not occur away from the set of *Rear Window*, Kelly was a model of professionalism when reporting to Paramount each day and despite some technical hitches, shooting of the film continued smoothly to the end, although Hitchcock's casual disregard for the strictures of the Production Code came back to haunt him when *Rear Window* was submitted for approval. Breen once again voiced his objections to 'Miss Torso's' dancing, the suggestive depiction of the honeymoon couple, and the provocative nightgown worn by Kelly—which he now found to be 'too bold and unconventional'. Hitchcock had always known that he would have to give ground on 'Miss Torso' and he had taken some 'protective' shots of her in case but, much to his annoyance, Lisa's late night sauntering in Jeff's apartment was also ordered to be reduced.

***Rear Window* ('The Newlyweds')**

Despite Hitchcock's tussles with the censor's office, *Rear Window* emerged as a prime example of a director in control of his medium. The film opens with the kind of understated shot that is trademark Hitchcock: the camera pans around an apartment, over a series of photographs of Jeff's past adventures, and comes to rest on a magazine-cover emblazoned with a picture of Lisa Freemont. In a single shot, Hitch introduces the film's main characters and tells the audience all that it needs to know about their respective histories. The playing of the radio over this sequence acts as a coda to the structure of the film: Jeff is going to dip in and out of a number of stories in the way of someone surfing the airwaves with a dial; the fragmented soundtrack, with its snatches of music and song, is designed to subtly forecast the narrative texture of the piece.

Hitchcock's confidence with the material is on show throughout. He was clearly exhilarated by the opportunities afforded him by both set and cast, and his reliance on the audience being able to suspend its disbelief is nowhere more evident than in the character of Lisa, an improbable creation even for a Park Avenue debutante. Hitch makes no attempt to ground Lisa in reality; she lives in a world where a lobster dinner delivered by a fashionable restaurant is acceptable as an evening snack, and beautiful models can confront wife-murderers armed with nothing more potent than a radiant smile. Exactly why such an exotic creature would spend her days panting after a patently-disinterested middle-aged man is a mystery that Hayes's script never quite solves. At one point, Jeff describes her as, 'too talented, too beautiful, too sophisticated, too perfect'—in *Rear Window*, Grace Kelly is all of that.

The role fits Kelly like a glove, as was intended, and she gives an effortlessly-elegant and poised performance. In contrast to all of her earlier films, she has a pro-active character to play, not only in terms of her own energy levels—she is seldom still—but in her contribution to the drama: Jeff's broken leg renders him a virtual spectator until the climax of the film; Lisa, on the other hand, climbs ladders, breaks into apartments and goes head-to-head with the supposed murderer while her invalid lover looks impotently on.

Despite the attention paid to his co-star and the passivity of his role, top-billed Stewart gives a fine performance as Jeff—taciturn and tetchy, and mostly devoid of the wholesome goodness of his forties' films. In many respects, Jeff's character flaws anticipate the darker and more disturbed Scotty in *Vertigo*, Stewart's next collaboration with Hitchcock. Both stars are nevertheless helped considerably by Hayes's script, which keeps the action moving at a brisk pace while still allowing its characters ample opportunity to engage in witty repartee:

> *Jeff and Lisa—*
> ***Jeff:*** Why would a man leave his apartment three times on a rainy night with a suitcase and come back three times?
> ***Lisa:*** He likes the way his wife welcomes him home.
>
> *Jeff and Lt Doyle—*
> ***Jeff:*** He killed a dog last night because the dog was scratching around in the garden. You know why?—Because he had something buried in that garden that the dog scented.
> ***Lt Doyle:*** Like an old hambone?
> ***Jeff:*** I don't know what pet names Thorwald had for his wife!

For all its merits, *Rear Window* is not without flaws. Its short story source, for example, is all too obvious in a thin narrative which is stretched almost to breaking point by the film's bloated 112-minutes running time. Another fault is the lack of interest shown by Hitch in the peripheral characters: Jeff's neighbours remain stubbornly stereotypical or lightly-sketched and, despite the promised 'peep' behind the curtains, all nods towards social commentary are glib and superficial. Of the shows put on for Jeff's entertainment, he is most interested in the nubile 'Miss Torso' and the mousy, emotionally-fragile 'Miss Lonelyheart'. In the case of the former, his curiosity is piqued less by her fondness for semi-naked workouts and more by the all-male dinner parties that she arranges for her free evenings. Watching as she plays hostess to three admirers simultaneously, he quips, 'A queen bee with her pick of the drones..' Sex is equally explicit in the tale of Miss Lonelyheart, who is assaulted and left sobbing alone in her apartment by a 'gentleman' caller. The honeymoon couple, whose sexual antics so concerned the censor, are employed merely as comic relief via some unsubtle sexual innuendo.

The world premiere of *Rear Window* took place at New York's Rivoli Theatre on August 1, 1954, and critics on both sides of the Atlantic were generally positive. *Time* thought it 'just possibly the second most entertaining (behind *The 39 Steps*) film made by Alfred Hitchcock.' *Time*'s critic was one of those who understood what Hitchcock had tried to do and mentioned the film's 'tingling essence of sexual elegance'. The *Sunday Times* hailed Hitchcock's 'first real success with the enclosed scene: enjoyable, brilliant, using detail to produce ferocious narrative effects.' While the BFI's *Monthly Film Bulletin* sensed a director more interested in gimmickry and found the film to be 'little more than an ingenious, heartless, intermittently entertaining exercise in technique.' It was a view echoed by the *New Yorker*, which also was unimpressed by what it regarded as the director's, 'fruitless ambition to make a movie that stands absolutely still'.

As Hitchcock had intended, Grace Kelly came out of it well; *Films in Review* summed up the consensus with, 'The acting honours belong to Grace Kelly, who more than justifies the publicity build-up she's been getting. Beautiful, well-bred, exuding subdued sex, she blithely projects charm that is never pretentious and sophistication that is never phoney.' Equally cognisant of the transformation in her screen image, the *Hollywood Reporter* proclaimed, 'This gal's sailing in the romantic department—which is good box-office, but Grace is going to be one of the great stars of the picture business not because of the romantic items—Kelly's lovers—but because she is a top actress.' Hitchcock was similarly effusive, and he paid Kelly the best compliment that he could when he told the *Sunday Express* that he had found, 'the best actress to come up in Hollywood since Ingrid Bergman.'

The publicity campaign for *Rear Window* was based on the simple adage that 'sex' sells, and Paramount ignored the murder/suspense angle and instead promised, 'MISS TORSO—hot nights or cold, her shades are never drawn..' It was a blunt approach, but it hit the mark and *Rear Window* found an appreciative audience and went on to achieve a healthy gross in excess of $5.7m in its North American release, making it the fifth biggest hit of 1954.

It was clear to many, even before the film opened, that Kelly was on the cusp of stardom. Certainly, *Life* magazine thought so and briefly imposed on Hitchcock's schedule to arrange a cover-story featuring the actress. The issue in question came out in April, 1954 (nicely timed to coincide with the release of *Dial M for Murder*), and proclaimed that the year would prove to be 'The Year of Grace'. *Dial M* gained widespread recognition for Kelly, a situation which was reinforced by *Rear Window* to the extent that, by year-end, the annual Showman's Trade Review poll of cinema managers in the US and Canada had placed her at the top of the list of female box-office stars. (James Stewart topped the male equivalent.) The accolades followed: Kelly won a Golden Globe, the New York Film Critics' Circle Award and a Best Actress award from the National Board of Review—the last two being for her body of work throughout 1954, including her first two Hitchcock films.

Hitchcock was thrilled at all the attention that was being paid to his protégé, particularly from the critics. On each occasion, he either congratulated her in person or sent a celebratory telegram—or a witty, handwritten note accompanied by a gift. In contrast, Kelly's father Jack remained singularly unimpressed: 'I'm glad she is making a living,' was as close as the stoical Irishman came to praising his celebrity daughter.

The metamorphosis of Grace Kelly from indifferent film actress into movie star received a temporary setback from the very studio which, nominally at least, stood to gain most from her rise: MGM. Dore Schary, having been manoeuvred by Kelly and Hitch in agreeing to the loan-out of Kelly for *Rear Window*, did not have long to wait to reinforce his authority. The day after the loan-out was agreed with Patron, Schary was approached by producers William Perlberg and George Seaton, who were casting *The Bridges at Toko-Ri* (1954), a Korean war story starring William Holden. Perlberg and Seaton needed an actress for a couple of weeks, to play the role of the woman that Holden leaves behind. It was a minor part, superfluous to the main narrative, which was included only to establish that the protagonist has a family life away from the field of combat—the sort of thing that studios used to keep their contractees busy in the lean times. Schary informed Kelly's agents that she had been allocated to Messrs Perlberg and Seaton as soon as the *Rear Window* shooting wrapped.

With *Rear Window* being hailed as a return to form for the director and earning him his first Academy Award nomination since *Spellbound* in 1944, Hitchcock once again felt at the top of his game. The sheer joy of making the film was reinforced by its box-office success, and he would often identify *Rear Window*, along with *Shadow of a Doubt,* as one of his favourite films. Even before he had finished shooting, he was suggesting to close associates that Kelly represented the ideal movie heroine and, given the choice, he could think of no good reason why he would use any other actress for his future films. Hitch was even dusting down one of his most treasured projects, *Mary Rose*, and having it tailored especially for 'Miss Kelly'. His plans

Grace Kelly and James Stewart attend the premiere of Rear Window

Kelly, Hitch and designer Oleg Cassini at the premiere of Rear Window

would have to wait; Kelly was *not* a free agent and, though it was frustrating for both of them, she was left with no choice but to honour her commitment to MGM, and Perlberg and Seaton's *The Bridges at Toko-Ri.*

Not that it stopped Hitchcock from dreaming up a new project for Kelly—one that would occupy more than a few weeks on a studio sound stage. And this time, he planned not only to have the role written especially for her but to set his film in an exotic location and dress it up with action, adventure, and more than a touch of sexual larceny.

If *Rear Window* was the consummation of the relationship between Kelly and Hitch, *To Catch a Thief* was to be the full-blown love affair.

Grace Kelly

Dial M for Murder (Grace Kelly)

To Catch a Thief (Grace Kelly, Cary Grant)

PRESENTED BY WARNER BROS.

STARRING RAY MILLAND · GRACE KELLY · ROBERT CUMMINGS WARNERCOLOR

WITH JOHN WILLIAMS DIRECTED BY ALFRED HITCHCOCK WRITTEN BY FREDERICK KNOTT who wrote the International Stage Success

Theatrical poster for Dial M for Murder

PARAMOUNT presents **JAMES STEWART** in **ALFRED HITCHCOCK'S**

REAR WINDOW

co-starring
GRACE KELLY
WENDELL COREY
THELMA RITTER
with
RAYMOND BURR
Color by
TECHNICOLOR
DIRECTED BY
ALFRED HITCHCOCK
SCREENPLAY BY
JOHN MICHAEL HAYES
BASED ON THE SHORT STORY BY
CORNELL WOOLRICH
A PARAMOUNT PICTURE

Copyright 1954 Paramount Pictures Corporation COUNTRY OF ORIGIN U. S. A. 4 Property of National Screen Service Corp. Licensed for display only in connection with the exhibition of this picture at your theatre. Must be returned immediately thereafter. 54-337

Lobby card for Rear Window

Grace Kelly in an Oleg Cassini dress

Publicity shot for Rear Window (Grace Kelly, James Stewart)

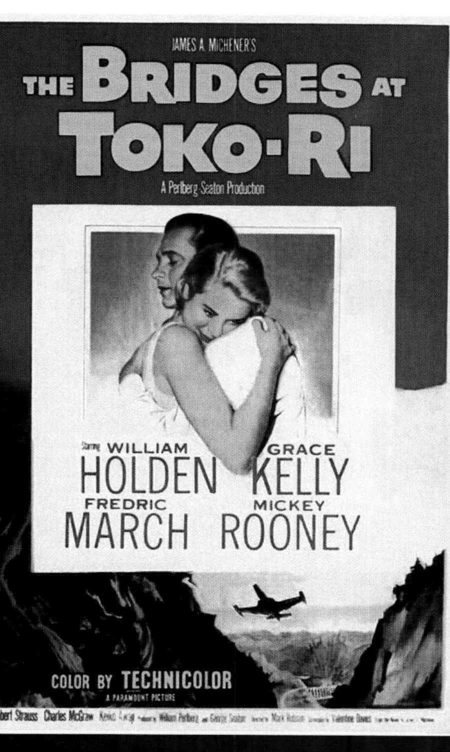

Theatrical poster for The Bridges at Toko-Ri

Kelly and Hitch on the set of To Catch a Thief

The 1955 Academy Awards (Bette Davis, Marlon Brando, Grace Kelly)

Theatrical poster for Vertigo

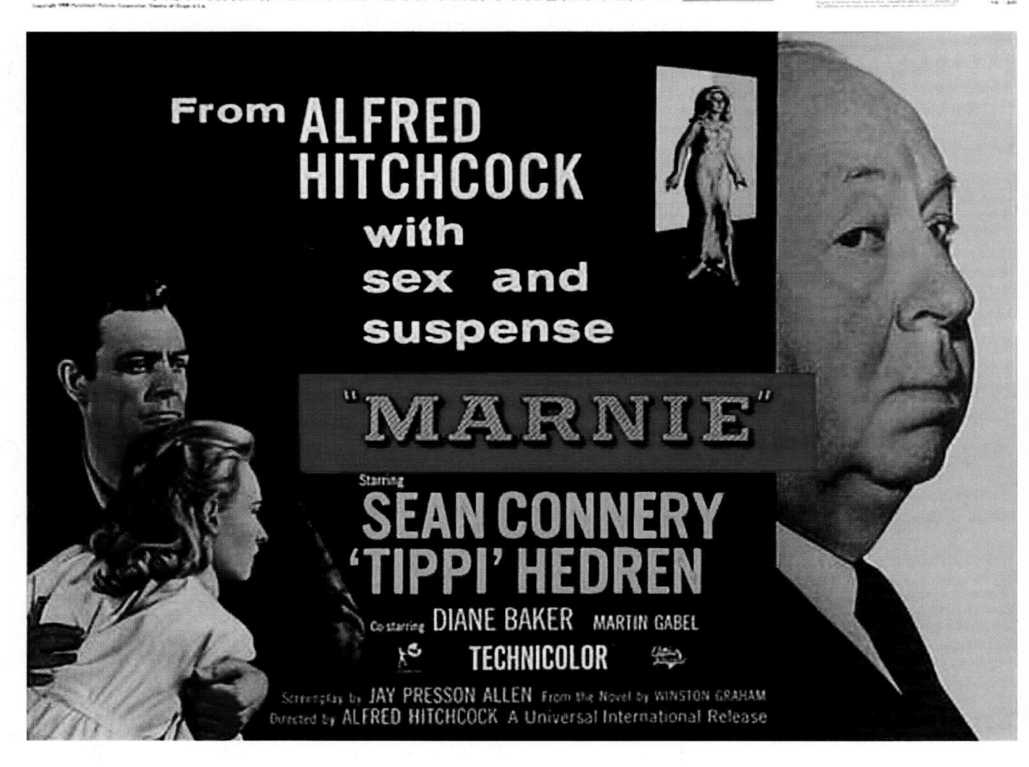

Theatrical poster for Marnie

The Grimaldi family in Monaco, circa 1972

1979 AFI Tribute Dinner—Hitch and Princess Grace

1979 AFI Tribute Dinner—Hitch and Cary Grant

Princess Grace in regal pose(s)

Chapter 5

To Catch a Thief

Kelly and Hitch on the set of To Catch a Thief

'Do I have anything to do with your going?'

'No.'

'Would you stay if I asked you to?'

'No.'

'Will you come back?'

'No.'

'I can follow you.'

'It would be a waste of time'

'I'll have to waste it then.' He pulled up a chair and sat down with his arms crossed on its back. 'Go on with your packing, if your mind is made up. Bellini says I've got a one-track mind, and I know what I want, even if I'm late in finding it out.'

'What do you want?'

'You.'

'Didn't you hear me say that you can't have me?'

–David Dodge, *To Catch a Thief* (1952)

Consciously or unconsciously, Alfred Hitchcock knew by now that the only way he could play suitor-by-proxy to Grace Kelly was to create a film that would whisk her away on a suitably exotic idyll, where they would not be subject to the day-to-day pressures of Hollywood and professional duties and personal pleasures could merge into one. The thinking behind *To Catch a Thief* was exactly that, but Hitchcock's carefully-chosen location was to lead indirectly to a new third-party involvement in Kelly's life that would threaten to end his relationship with his blonde muse once and for all. That was more than a year away; in the meantime, her tangled love-life was to undergo another test of public endurance.

Just as soon as she had finished her scenes in *Rear Window*, Kelly left Hitchcock and his crew at work on Paramount's Stage 18 and walked the short distance across the lot to where William Perlberg and George Seaton were shooting interiors for *The Bridges at Toko-Ri*. The cast was recently returned from a period of location-shooting in Japan, but she was not to be afforded the luxury of overseas travel; under instructions from MGM, she extended the lease on her tiny apartment on Sweetzer Street and settled into what she regarded from the outset as a routine and pointless role.

Both Perlberg and Seaton were aware that their film was fluff—a strictly by-the-numbers war movie designed to appeal to the widest-possible audience. They made no pretence about how peripheral Kelly's role was to the piece, though they were not above exploiting her high profile status to help sell it. Much was made in the subsequent publicity releases of the actress wearing a bathing suit on screen for the first time (a one-piece of course; American audiences were not yet ready for leading ladies in bikinis). On the same theme, *The Bridges at Toko-Ri* also marked the first time that she would be seen sharing a bed with her co-star. As the scene involved a married couple, it caused no trouble with the censors, but it too was to feature prominently in the movie's advertising campaign.

Kelly was further persuaded to pose for some cheesecake publicity shots to be circulated to the press on the release of *The Bridges at Toko-Ri*. This was something she had managed to resist at MGM, on the grounds that it would detract from her status as a 'serious' actress. But Perlberg and Seaton's track record featured some very worthy films, including *The Song of Bernadette* (1943) and *Miracle on 34th Street* (1947), so her objections were waived and her agents were delighted when a new 'pin-up' image not only helped to promote the film but made her appear more approachable to regular filmgoers. While she still showed no desire to stay in Hollywood, she at least had managed an uneasy truce with the press; she had survived *Rear Window* without a hint of scandal—other than being seen on the arm of a (very recent) widower—and she now conducted herself as well as any attractive but unattached star might. But that was to change, and the calm which had been brought about by a carefully-contrived PR campaign was soon to be shattered completely.

The Bridges at Toko-Ri starred William Holden as a navy pilot tasked with leading his squadron on a highly dangerous bombing mission over Korea. At the age of 35, Holden was one of the biggest box-office draws around; his good looks and air of world-weariness made him one of the few stars to appeal to both sexes, and he had top-lined a string of commercial and critical successes, including Billy Wilder's *Sunset Boulevard* (1950).

Dubbed 'Golden Boy' by the press after his 1939 film of the same title, Holden enjoyed all the trappings of his success: wealth, fame and casual sexual encounters—he boasted that he had bedded an actress in every location in which he had filmed. A number of affairs had dogged his twelve-year marriage to former actress Ardis Ankerson Gaines (Brenda Marshall), including a very public dalliance with Audrey

Publicity shot for The Bridges at Toko-Ri (William Holden, Grace Kelly)

Hepburn during the making of Wilder's *Sabrina*, some six months earlier. Holden's philandering was another one of Hollywood's 'open secrets', but his wife showed remarkable restraint and a futher eighteen years would pass before she finally sued for divorce.

In Kelly's eyes, Bing Crosby was suddenly yesterday's man as the handsome Holden now became the latest object of her affections. Mel Dellar, a friend of Holden's and Hitchcock's assistant director on *Dial M for Murder*, told James Spada, 'Bill was absolutely crazy about her and they had quite a fling. I was hoping they would get married, because that's what Bill wanted.' The affair quickly spilled out into Hollywood's night-spots and then to Kelly's home-life, to the extent that the 'Golden Boy' was invited to Henry Avenue to meet Jack and Ma. By all accounts, the get-together did not go well for Holden; his chosen profession and marital status ticked two of Jack's list of taboos and, to Kelly's parents, he was simply the latest

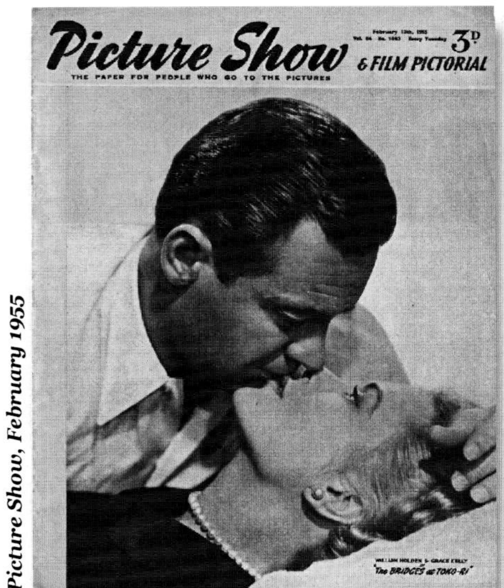

Picture Show, February 1955

in a long line of unsuitable beaux. Jack Kelly never subscribed to the view that discretion was the better part of valour; he knew a wolf when he saw one slavering and was not slow in saying so to Holden's face. Some years after the actor's death, his psychiatrist, Michael Jay Klassman, told *Weekend* magazine of the actor's version of events. 'I thought he might take a swing at me,' Holden had informed Klassman, adding that Grace had fled the room in tears. The visit was described as 'cold and hostile', and it came to a sudden end when Holden thundered out of the house, slamming the door behind him.

Soon after his first two films featuring Kelly had opened, a reporter asked Hitch if she was now a star: 'No,' he replied. 'She has yet to play the character about whom a film is built. That will be her big test.' Hitch had in mind his next project, and his dream of launching her into the major league himself; he knew that *The Bridges at Toko-Ri* would do little more for her career. But his goal of being the one to propel her onto Hollywood's 'A' list was about to be snatched away from him by his colleagues on the Paramount lot.

George Seaton, like Hitchcock, occupied his quieter moments on set by planning his next film, and he had *The Country Girl* ready to start shooting as soon as *The Bridges at Toko-Ri* wrapped. Adapted by Clifford Odets from his Broadway hit of the same name, *The Country Girl* was the heart-rending story of a burnt-out singer named Frank Elgin, who has come to rely on his wife Georgie for emotional support. The film was again to be produced by William Perlberg and was intended to reunite the pair with Jennifer Jones, whose role in *The Song of Bernadette* had won her the Oscar for Best Actress. Also attached to the production was Bing Crosby, playing against type in a rare dramatic departure as the alcoholic Elgin. But Jones found that she was pregnant shortly after the project was announced and promptly withdrew, which left Perlberg and Seaton without a leading lady.

The part of the embittered Georgie Elgin had been widely-touted as one of the hottest of the year, and it was being hailed by fan mags as a 'sure-fire bet' for an Oscar nomination; the moment that Jones withdrew, all and sundry in Hollywood lined up to be associated with *The Country Girl*. Kelly was one of the first off the mark—formally and informally. She instructed MCA to canvass on her behalf and, at the same time, asked George Seaton if she could test for the part; she even approached Bing Crosby, in the hope that he might use his influence with the producers. Crosby was less than enthusiastic, however, and he told the producers that he did not think her suitable for the role. William Holden thought otherwise, and he stepped in to the fray, pointing out that Kelly's contribution to *The Bridges at Toko-Ri* had been of such benefit that she at least deserved a screen-test.

Perlberg and Seaton were hesitant; there was little in Kelly's previous screen credits to suggest that she could play a character as complex as Georgie Elgin. But under pressure from all sides, Perlberg relented and agreed to let her test. Even in horn-rimmed glasses, with no make-up and her hair dragged back into a bun, Kelly appeared too young and pretty to make Georgie convincing and the matter might have ended there had not Holden intervened once more; he told Perlberg that he would be willing to play the supporting role of the Broadway producer who tries to entice Frank Elgin into making a comeback provided that he was cast opposite Kelly. Holden's offer too good to resist: having he and Crosby—two of the biggest names in Hollywood—in the same film was a major coup, and hiring Grace Kelly was a price worth paying; it was a question of convincing Bing Crosby. The singer was persuaded that the commercial prospects for the film would be enhanced by the casting of the younger players, but there remained the matter of the billing. Holden offered to take third-billing if it placated his co-star, and Crosby accepted the compromise. Seaton later joked that this was the only example he knew of an actor insisting on reducing his credit! He and his partner had now to convince MGM to loan out Kelly for another Paramount film.

Perlberg and Seaton had every right to feel pleased with themselves about the way that *The Country Girl* was shaping up, but Dore Schary was enraged; he had loaned out Kelly for a second-rate part in *The Bridges at Toko-Ri* to stamp his authority, not to provide her with leverage to a more significant role. Despite the tidy profit that MGM had made (Paramount had been charged $25,000 for Kelly's services), Schary was in no mood to repeat the process and declined Paramount's approach, claiming that she would be occupied for the foreseeable future on a number of 'major' projects for MGM.

MGM actually had *no* films lined up for Grace Kelly—certainly none that had been conceived with her specifically in mind. Schary's response to Paramount's offer was a reactive one, inasmuch as he figured that if she was in so much demand by others, then MGM must be missing out, somehow. He instructed his people to find something for Kelly to do in a studio programmer, in order to justify his claim of 'major' projects.

Kelly could have knuckled down and served out her time with MGM in decorative roles; Elizabeth Taylor, a contemporary at the studio, was doing exactly that and would later make the jump to more creditable parts. But this time, Kelly was not of a mind to compromise; she had decided that she was going to play Georgie Elgin, irrespective of Dore Schary's views on the matter. Battle-lines were drawn, with she and MCA insisting on better scripts than MGM could offer her, and Schary reminding her that the studio had the option of suspending her if she failed to comply—effectively preventing her from working for anyone. It was Jay Kanter who managed to break the deadlock and secure a deal which doubled MGM's previous fee for allowing Kelly to work at Paramount for Perlberg and Seaton, while Dore Schary saved face by securing her commitment to star in an as-yet undesignated MGM project, just as soon as *The Country Girl* was completed.

Now, it was Hitchcock's turn to be aggrieved. While Kelly had been slumming it through *The Bridges at Toko-Ri* and cavorting with 'inappropriate' men, Hitchcock had not been idle. John Michael Hayes had been working on the director's next project, *To Catch a Thief*, since December 1953, and Hitch had once again designed the lead role with Kelly in mind. Aside from keeping in touch with the actress on a social level, Hitchcock was alert to the buzz that was surrounding her and the war of words between MCA and MGM did not bode well for his plans. The feeling in Wasserman's office was that repercussions from the affair would impact on future loan-outs.

Hitchcock had been comfortable with the first of Kelly's Perlberg/Seaton films—he had not been in a position to start shooting *To Catch a Thief* till the spring of 1954 at the earliest, and *The Bridges at Toko-Ri* would only help to make his own next outing with Kelly the more impressive. As things now stood, he would be forced to wait through a *second* Seaton movie for Kelly, followed by another from MGM. Hitch ensured that Lew Wasserman kept him up to date with developments between MGM and Paramount; the attitude adopted by Schary was especially fascinating to him, in that the mogul had the wherewithal to decide—in theory at least—what pictures Kelly could and could not make. To Hitch, his behaviour echoed that of David Selznick when he heard that Ingrid Bergman had refused the role in *Spellbound*; it took no more than a phone call from Selznick for her to report for costume fittings.

The power-play unfolding behind the scenes presented Hitchcock with two alternatives: he could buy Kelly out of her existing contract with MGM which, despite her low salary and relatively-poor standing, would be prohibitively expensive and therefore not an option, or he could bide his time and make of her what he was able until she was free to work exclusively for him. The latter meant having to share her with MGM, but Hitch was now telling associates that he intended to make his next ten pictures with Grace Kelly, so accommodating the needs of Dore Schary would be a necessary evil. Schary's treatment of Kelly had opened Hitchcock's mind to the possibility of establishing contract-artists of his own, tied to a company under his control. He instructed his agents to look into the technicalities of contracting performers at some point in the future; in the meantime, he pressed MCA to secure Kelly's services for his next picture.

David Dodge's 1952 novel *To Catch a Thief* is a tale of an ageing jewel thief, John Robie, who is forced out of retirement in the South of France when a series of copycat crimes have the local police calling at his door. Hitch felt that Hayes's gift for narrative and crisp dialogue would bring the somewhat lightweight novel to life, and that shooting on location would offer a welcome change of pace after a run of films in Hollywood. He also thought that it presented the perfect opportunity to create a starring role for his favourite blonde. Under the terms of his agreement with Paramount, the new film was to belong to the studio in perpetuity, which afforded him more flexibility in terms of the budget but also meant that he was effectively an employee. Not that he was to lose out financially: he was on a salary of $150,000 plus 10% of the profits. But the deal was even sweeter for Hitch—he had bought the rights to the book for around $15,000 as part of his short-lived Transatlantic experiment, but he had sold them to Paramount for a substantial $150,000!

Hayes laboured on *To Catch a Thief* throughout the Christmas period and into the New Year. Hitch, with a generosity born out of a studio expense-account, sent Hayes and his wife on a 'working vacation' to the South of France to soak up the atmosphere, see the sights and sample the cuisine. When he returned, Hayes settled down to finish the script with Hitch and found that Kelly's suddenly crowded schedule afforded him the luxury of working at a more leisured pace. '[Hitch] was very easy to work with,' he recalled for Steven DeRosa. 'I learned a lot.. about gourmet food, cigars and wine, in addition to learning about screenwriting. Most of my conferences with Hitch were concerned with his reminiscing about how he had solved some cinematic or story problem.' In between the trips down memory lane, Hitch and Hayes reconstituted Dodge's story and made a number of crucial changes, including eliminating a number of subplots and minor characters. In the course of their discussions, Francie Stevens, the novel's heroine, was transformed from a brunette into an elegant and calculating blonde; even so, Kelly could still flesh out Dodge's description of her as having 'a good figure and the kind of Irish attractiveness that goes with blue eyes'.

Francie, as crafted by Hitchcock and Hayes, was Lisa Fremont with attitude—no longer content to beg for attention but going out and taking what she wants.

'You know why I favour sophisticated blondes in my films?' Hitchcock was to ask rhetorically of Truffaut. 'We're after the drawing-room types, the real ladies, who become whores once they are in the bedroom.' In *Notorious,* Ingrid Bergman's Alicia allowed herself to be used and abused in order to help the man that she loved. In *Rear Window,* Lisa pouted and preened and put herself in mortal danger in her attempts to entice Jeff into marriage. In *To Catch a Thief,* Hitchcock turned the tables and created in Francie a sexual predator—every bit as elegant and sophisticated as her predecessors but without the submissive reliance on feminine wiles to win her man. This was Hitchcock's 'drawing-room type', with the morals of an alley-cat and the appetites to match. The prospect of snaring an infamous thief not only intrigues Francie, it arouses her as well—and this time, she is not afraid to show it.

Hitchcock's interpretation of the Francie character gives the title of the picture an added subtlety: on the face of it, Robie comes out of retirement to track down and capture the bogus 'cat'—a case of it taking a thief 'to catch a thief.' But the Hayes/ Hitchcock script also offers up a scheming beauty with a fixation to capture her very own 'thief'. Expanding on his theories about female sexuality to François Truffaut, Hitchcock said, 'An English girl, looking like a school-teacher, is apt to get into a cab with you and, to your surprise, she'll probably pull a man's pants open.' In *To Catch a Thief,* Hitchcock was to provide an example of this, censor permitting: Francie allows Robie to escort her to her hotel room, having previously given him no indication that she has any interest in him—then quite without warning, she turns to him and kisses him full on the mouth. The pants stay shut onscreen, but the inference of sexual aggression is plain to see.

According to Hayes, Hitchcock was inspired by personal experience to create the scene, and the players in life were not Kelly and Cary Grant (as in the film) but Kelly and *Hitch.* In Hayes's version, which presumably took place during the shooting of *Rear Window,* Hitch escorted Kelly to her room and, as he bade her goodnight, she

To Catch a Thief (Grace Kelly, Cary Grant)

kissed him passionately on the lips. Things went no further than the kiss—Hitch was too startled to say anything and Kelly retired to her room. For the film, Hitchcock allowed his imagination to finish the evening on a more consummate note, with his cinematic alter ego acting out the dénouement. 'The kiss in the hallway is as if she had unzipped his fly,' he told Dorothy Chandler. 'The fireworks scene is the orgasm.'

Predictably, this hotel corridor scene raised some censorial eyebrows when Paramount submitted the script for approval. Hitchcock may have thought the censors unsophisticated, but they knew exactly what he was up to and insisted that he cut the scene before its 'climax'. Hitch decided to play a little game: he shot the scene as its was written, but he also filmed a running gag with two French policemen and some nude postcards; the level of innuendo was such that these vignettes were never likely to be passed for exhibition, but they enabled Hitch to volunteer to cut the 'postcard' scenes if the fireworks stayed! Breen also cautioned against some of the dialogue, which pushed at the bounds of good taste: lines like, 'What you need is something I have neither the time nor the inclination to give you—two weeks with a good man at Niagara Falls,' left little scope for innocent interpretation.

Breen's office was further concerned about the leading role being occupied by a 'thief', which could be taken to run counter to Production Code diktat that crime must not be seen to pay. Hitchcock escaped censure on a technicality; it is made clear in the film that Robie has been pardoned for his offences and is an honest, law-abiding citizen once again. And for good measure, Hayes had him make the point, 'I never stole from anyone who would go hungry.'

Aside from the requirements of the censor, Hitchcock made a number of changes to the story for dramatic purposes, and among his innovations was the addition of a lavish costume ball, intended to show off Grace Kelly to maximum effect. The traditional gala marks the end of the summer season on the Riviera—a time when the rich engage in a drunken debauch on the scale of a Roman orgy—and Dodge's book sets its climactic confrontation on the evening before the ball. But Hitchcock was not about to pass up the chance to stage his finale against a background of opulent excess.

Right from the start of the project, Hitchcock had only ever envisaged the debonair Cary Grant as John Robie, reluctant thief-catcher. The fact that the star had recently announced his retirement from films made no difference to Hitch—he was confident that Grant could be lured back into the limelight for *To Catch a Thief*.

The 50-year-old Grant had married Betsy Drake, his third wife, in 1949. Born Archibald Leach in Bristol, England, Grant had left school at fourteen to join a circus as an acrobat and mime artist and he enjoyed considerable success touring music halls. The troupe was popular enough to transfer to Broadway in 1920, where the young Leach perfected the mid-Atlantic nasal twang for which he was to become renowned. In 1931, he arrived in Hollywood and, under his new name of Cary Grant, quickly established himself as a charismatic leading man, competent in both drama and screwball comedies. Hit movies like *Bringing Up Baby* (1938) and *His Girl Friday* (1940) secured his position as a top box-office draw, while working with Hitchcock in thrillers like *Suspicion* (1941) and *Notorious* (1946) allowed him to demonstrate his abilities as an actor. Grant always maintained that he invented his own persona, telling one interviewer, 'Everyone would like to be like Cary Grant—so would I', but the attempt to broaden his range in *None But the Lonely Heart* (1944) failed. After shooting *Dream Wife* in 1953, and observing the inexorable rise of the Method school of acting (with which he had no sympathy), he had decided to devote his life to something more fulfilling than film. However, his decision to retire at the height of his fame was to prove premature.

Cary Grant turned out to be every bit as accommodating as Hitchcock predicted. 'I had left the business, or thought I had,' he told James Spada, 'when Hitch sent me a cable to call him. I did, and he told me about the idea for a script he had, to be set in the South of France. Well, both of those things were very attractive—that Hitch had glommed onto a script that he enjoyed and that we would travel to the South of France.' Grant, who was holidaying in Hong Kong when the telegram arrived, was offered the added incentive of 10% of the film's gross. (Though his name added considerably to the film's box-office appeal, Hitch resented having to pay so much money to Grant and made a conscious decision not to cast the actor in his two remaining movies for Paramount—those that he was to own himself!)

Behind the camera, Hitchcock surrounded himself with familiar faces, including Herbert Coleman as assistant director, Robert Burks as cinematographer, Clarence Erickson as production manager, and the trusty Edith Head as costume designer. *To Catch a Thief* would be the fourth time that Head had worked with Kelly and it was to be easily the most rewarding. After dressing the actress 'off the shelf' for *The Country Girl,* Head was delighted to receive detailed instructions from Hitch for a dizzying array of gowns and summer dresses, to say nothing of the budget to indulge in what she described as 'a costume designer's dream'. In all, Head was to design eleven costume changes for Kelly, including a ball-gown made of gold mesh, complete with golden wig and mask. 'That was the most expensive setup I've ever done,' Head said, 'Hitchcock told me he that he wanted her to look like a princess. She did.'

To supplement the leads, Hitchcock chose John Williams, the detective from *Dial M for Murder*, to play an insurance investigator hot on the trail of the burglar, while stage actress Jessie Royce Landis was cast as Francie's battle-axe of a mother. The remaining roles were filled by predominantly European actors, including French starlet Brigitte Auber as Danielle, who turns out to be the villain of the piece.

The decision to shoot *To Catch a Thief* was a calculated one for Hitchcock. After two studio-bound movies in quick succession, he was desperate to do something less demanding. The stunning scenery of the French Riviera offered an opportunity for self-indulgence. Hitch and Alma had holidayed on the Cote d'Azur many times; they found the climate agreeable and the people warm, and Hitch revelled in the abundance of good food and wine. The other incentive was the prospect of sharing a part of the world that he loved with his new leading lady—although at this point, he still did not have Kelly's signature on a contract.

Naturally, Kelly had been kept up to speed with progress on the screenplay while she was working on *Rear Window*, and Hitchcock had confided to her that her co-star would be Cary Grant. Despite that, she was not about to fall straight into Hitchcock's lap; in a repeat of the situation that arose after *Dial M for Murder*, when she risked *Rear Window* for a theatre production of *Cyrano de Bergerac*, she was now pushing so hard for *The Country Girl* that it risked jeopardising *To Catch a Thief.* For Kelly, however, it was a price worth paying.

The Country Girl was to become one of the highlights of Grace Kelly's screen career, but the general opinion of the film was not one that would be shared by Hitchcock. 'Not my cup of tea,' he told Kelly, with the tone of a disapproving uncle. 'But you do it if you want to, dear. You do it and find out what you can do.' Having appeared as a glamorous clothes-horse in *Rear Window*, the careworn Georgie Elgin slowly unravelling on screen could not have been more of a contrast, and it is easy to see why the role had no appeal for Hitch. Thanks to careful direction from

Grace Kelly in make-up for The Country Girl

George Seaton, Kelly would gain plaudits from all directions (including an Academy Award for Best Actress, beating hot favourite Judy Garland in *A Star is Born*).

The Country Girl was a product of its time. If it has any lasting significance, it is due to its off-screen *ménage à trois*. Crosby and Holden had both carved a notch in their bed-posts in respect of Kelly, and both had come to the set thinking to pick up where they had left off. Holden's ardour had cooled somewhat since his encounter with the Kelly clan, but 51-year-old Crosby was still in the market for a new trophy bride, though he was in no position to compete with Holden in the virility stakes. The two met for drinks, talked through their mutual attraction for their co-star, and thrashed out a compromise of sorts—Holden agreed to stand aside and let Crosby have a free hand; if the older man failed to woo her, then he would step back in.

This faintly dishonourable arrangement opened the way for Crosby to engage in some heavy-duty courtship. He and Kelly worked on their scripts together, shared barbeques, and then as the sun set on Los Angeles, they appeared together at the best tables that Hollywood star-power could muster. Since Crosby was a respectable widower, more or less, the couple had no need to hide away and newspapers and fan mags were spoiled for choice when it came to pictures of them together. Crosby, as the reporters dutifully pointed out, had only recently buried his wife but was 'smitten with the twenty-five year old starlet'. The singer denied a tryst: 'If I was fifteen or sixteen years younger,' he told the *Saturday Evening Post*, 'I'd fall willingly into the long line of limp males who are currently competing madly for her favours.' But his denials did not fool the press, and a posse of journalists continued to trail the couple from nightclub to nightclub.

Crosby finally proposed that that he and Kelly should make their relationship permanent and raised the subject of marriage; it was a step too far for Kelly, who demurred and turned to Holden to rescue her from the situation. Holden did not need to be asked twice and, while Crosby brooded over his failure to win fair maid, he waltzed in and claimed the prize—except that he was still a married man, so Kelly once again found herself adrift in the murky waters of *Confidential* magazine.

On this occasion, the allegation was that Holden's Eldorado convertible had been parked outside her apartment all night while he and Kelly canoodled within.

Holden was outraged; he demanded a retraction and engaged his lawyers. Jack Kelly, not known for his subtlety of expression, threatened to use his fists on the reporter in question—or anyone else who got in his way. Denials flew in interviews from all the parties, but the protestations of innocence did nothing to convince the press corps that Kelly was not up to her old tricks. Lack of proof and Holden's impending lawsuit forced *Confidential* to back down and it published the retraction that he had demanded. However, it was contrived to sound as bad as the original article, and it repeated its main assertion about Kelly, that 'behind that frigid exterior is a smouldering fire.. and what the older fellows go for.'

Holden felt duty-bound to try to counter *Confidential*'s salacious image of Kelly, and he told the *Ladies' Home Journal*, 'For a long time, our actresses were popular in proportion to their breastworks. Phoniness did not matter. But now I think the world wanted to go back to honesty and dignity. Grace Kelly helps us to believe in the innate dignity of man.'

Kelly may have helped others to believe in the 'dignity of man', but she herself had hit an emotional low. Speaking to *Star* in 1979, she revealed the extent of her bitterness about this period in her life: 'As an unmarried woman, I was thought to be a danger. Other women looked on me as a rival and it pained me a great deal.' But the episode presented Hitch with the opportunity that he had been waiting for and he put in a request to MGM to borrow Kelly for *To Catch a Thief*, suggesting to Schary that a spell away from Hollywood might be just the ticket for both actress and studio.

Schary was of a similar opinion, but he had a different continent in mind; MGM turned down Paramount's approach and informed MCA that its client would be required for the first of her 'major' MGM movies.

Kelly had barely the chance to catch her breath after completing *The Country Girl* before she was headed to the jungles of Columbia for *Green Fire* (1954). But MGM's intransigence had not come as much of a shock—MCA had told her to expect MGM to dismiss Hitchcock's pleading out of hand. Lew Wassermann was an old hand at this kind of corporate posturing, and he assured Kelly that the real negotiating for *To Catch a Thief* would begin when she was on location. 'No matter what anyone says,' Kelly wrote to Edith Head, 'keep right on making my clothes. I'm doing the picture.'

In the meantime, Paramount had sneaked *Rear Window* out for preview at the Academy Theatre in Pasadena, where the reaction was extremely positive, although some complained about the risqué dialogue. But the studio was confident that it had a hit on its hands, and it scheduled the world premiere for the summer. Word of mouth on Kelly had already begun to grow. The *Life* magazine feature that proclaimed the 'Year of Grace' started the bandwagon rolling—the cover had a relaxed Kelly looking remarkably like a young Ingrid Bergman, and the item predicted that she would become one of hottest box-office properties in Hollywood. But one perceptive observation in the otherwise-bland commentary noted of Kelly: *Like all of her performances her deliberately planned career has been a masterpiece of underplaying. Life* also dug up one (unnamed) Hollywood producer, who suggested that the actress was not to be taken lightly, adding that she was 'stainless steel inside'. Even MGM could not ignore the momentum that was beginning to build around its contract artiste.

All the excitement generated by the publicity largely passed Grace Kelly by. She slogged her way through *Green Fire* in April and did not return to Los Angeles until mid-May, when she had to re-dub some dialogue. More convinced than ever that MGM was mismanaging her career, she arrived back in town with a renewed

Green Fire (Grace Kelly, Stewart Granger)

contempt for the studio and for Hollywood in general. The primitive conditions that had to be endured by cast and crew in Columbia, as well as the standard of the production in general, only made her mood all the darker. To make matters worse, Schary appeared utterly indifferent to her dissatisfaction and continued to send her what she regarded as sub-standard scripts, including *The Adventures of Quentin Durward* (1955) opposite Robert Taylor, and a western, *Jeremy Rodock.*

MGM's publicity blurb for *Green Fire* promised 'a modern story of dangerous adventure' but it was just another lame-brained action movie, with Kelly stuck in a badly-written role as a plantation-owner who distracts Stewart Granger's treasure-hunter from his pursuit of the titular emeralds. The story was hackneyed and the film itself was limply directed by Andrew Marton, and she had hated every minute of it. Shortly after its opening, Kelly described it to *Red Book* as a 'wretched experience.. everybody knew it was an awful picture'. To rub salt into the wound, MGM decided to 'remodel' her for the posters, superimposing her face onto the body of an extravagantly-endowed blonde. This embarrassing effort would turn out to be that rarity in the Grace Kelly canon—a box-office flop.

Infuriated by the sheer awfulness of *Green Fire,* Kelly showed some of her much-touted 'steel' and, in so doing, she compromised MCA's negotiating position with MGM. She ignored Wasserman's advice and announced that unless Schary agreed to the loan-out for *To Catch a Thief,* he 'could forward all her correspondence on to Philadelphia'—meaning that she would call a halt to her screen career, rather than tolerate this attitude from her employers. Few in Hollywood thought that MGM would tolerate another ultimatum after all the fuss over *The Country Girl* and the first ladies of gossip, Parsons and Hopper, were quick to say so in their respective columns. Hitchcock knew that all of this was background noise, and he pressed on with the preproduction planning of *To Catch a Thief,* quietly confident that MCA could break down Schary's objections.

The hero of the hour proved once again to be William Holden. The actor had performed in a previous loan-out to MGM (for *Executive Suite*) and he made it be known that he was amenable to another stint at the studio, as a gesture of goodwill. Faced with the inevitable, Schary backed down and with a suitable hike in his studio's fee, he agreed to Kelly appearing in *To Catch a Thief*. It was a relaxed Hitch who travelled to London for the British premiere of *Dial M for Murder*, posing on the red carpet with Alma; from there, the invigorated director journeyed on to the Mediterranean, where the second unit of *To Catch a Thief* was already at work.

Grace Kelly could not get out of California quick enough, as she later recalled, 'I finished *Green Fire* one morning at eleven, I went to the dubbing-room at one—and at six o'clock, I left for France..'

The trip to Europe began with a flight to New York, where Kelly was joined by the rest of the *To Catch a Thief* crew and they flew on to Paris. At the airport, she was besieged by reporters and autograph hunters and, after five films in eight months, countless air miles and dozens of interviews, her natural reserve began to crack. The barrage of intrusive questions—'What did she wear in bed?'; 'What is the secret of her charm?'; 'What was the size of her bosom?'—was met with increasingly terse replies. Having only recently attained film stardom, she was already growing fractious with her new lifestyle, insisting, 'I am not employed to give monologues, I am hired to be an actress.'

Grace Kelly's hectic schedule was not the only factor in her impatience. In the months since the completion of *Rear Window,* her much-publicised love life had continued without pause, and in addition to her liaisons with Holden, Crosby, and then Holden again, her name had been romantically linked to that of dress designer Oleg Cassini, a 51-year-old French-born Jew of Russian extraction.

Hitch meets Kelly at Nice station en route To Catch a Thief

Oleg Cassini's profile was almost a template for that of the international playboy. His mother was an Italian countess and his father was a Russian diplomat; he was born in Paris and raised in Italy before he moved to America in 1936. A celebrated designer, he could also boast of playing tennis to Davis Cup standard but he was probably better known in the society pages for his marriage and subsequent divorce to patent medicine heiress 'Madcap' Merry Fahrney, followed a year later by his marriage (and subsequent divorce) to Hollywood film star Gene Tierney. When not rubbing shoulders with the rich and famous, Cassini was a regular at gaming tables in the US and Europe. He had a continental sophistication, a natural charm, and he sported the sort of 'old school' manners that American blue-bloods found so appealing.

In Cassini's version of his relationship with Grace Kelly, he would tell that he saw her in *Mogambo* and decided then and there that she was to be the next Mrs Cassini; his courtship of her certainly exhibited the careful planning of a man on a mission. He engineered a casual meeting with her in New York, which was not difficult as they had a number of acquaintances in common. He then contrived to be in Hollywood while she was shooting *The County Girl,* ensuring that he popped up at the same parties without actually intruding on her life. Cassini was unshakable in his belief that he and Kelly were made for each other and that it was their destiny to marry, and he wooed her in such an understated manner that, tired as she was of affairs with married men, she could not help but be quietly impressed.

But Cassini could offer Kelly more than charm. His marriage to Gene Tierney had given him good contacts in Hollywood, and when Kelly initiated her battle with MGM, he offered to use his influence to help. His intervention consisted of arranging lunch for her with his friend Ray Stark, a highly-regarded talent agent and later Columbia powerbroker, who represented stars such as Lana Turner, Ava Gardner and Kirk Douglas. It was the sort of move that was calculated to impress someone like Kelly, and it helped to turn Cassini from companion to confidant in her eyes. (Stark, a notorious exponent of the 'casting couch', evidently felt that there was nothing of value to be had by supporting Kelly and begged off: 'Sorry Oleg,' he said. 'No sex appeal.')

Upping the pace of his courtship, Cassini took to sending Kelly red roses on a daily basis, along with little notes and modest gifts. She found this approach endearing and, on the day that she left America for Europe, she left a note for him which said, simply: *'Those who love me follow me'.* Cassini was not about to pass up such an opportunity and he booked a seat on the same flight to Paris; unluckily for him, he arrived at the airport without a valid passport and he was left stranded in the departure lounge while Kelly waved goodbye to the world's media from the steps of her aeroplane.

Cassini was not one to brood about the fickleness of fate. He returned to his New York apartment and the very next day, he set about putting his affairs in order. Kelly, meanwhile, had touched down in Paris, and she sent a telegraph to Hitchcock pleading exhaustion and requesting a few days leave of absence in Paris to help her 'recuperate' and, possibly, to give Cassini time to catch her up. For once, Hitch allowed his impatience with Grace's love life to show; his crew, who had flown with Grace from New York, had been amused to see Cassini remonstrating with staff at the departure gate and had passed this tid-bit on to the director. With Alma, Cary and Betsy Grant, and the rest of the cast waiting patiently on the Riviera, Hitch was disinclined to be put in the position of staging the most lavish party ever given for an actress, only to be told that she might not turn up. His response was polite but firm; if she needed to rest, she could do it in Cannes. Ms Kelly was duly booked on the train south.

By the time Kelly's train pulled into Nice station to be greeted by a taciturn director and members of the press, she looked thoroughly refreshed and as radiant as ever. Cary Grant, who caught up with her some hours later when she checked into the Carlton Hotel recalled, 'If she was exhausted, it wasn't apparent to me. I think I would have noticed.' A week later, the tardy Cassini arrived in Cannes and joined Kelly in her hotel.

Hitchcock had been in such a hurry to start filming that he had been prepared to forego his usual meticulous preparations in part and accept a script that neither he nor Hayes felt was completely satisfactory. The story still needed work in a number of areas, including the climax, and Hitch had arrived in France knowing that he also had to accommodate the film's stricter budgetary requirements. Paramount had armed him with what it considered to be an adequate budget of $3m, but it was less than he had anticipated and he had to lose a number of scenes to balance the books—among those that were cut was an elaborate chase through Nice at carnival-time. Despite the constraints on cost, Hitch refused to compromise the ball sequence and announced that he would shoot it exactly as scripted.

Hitch and screenwriter John Michael Hayes

Changes aside, Hitchcock also felt that he needed to tighten up the characterisation, and although she received no credit in the final film, Alma helped him to straighten out a car-chase sequence, and she would later join him on set. Despite working flat-out throughout May, Hayes and Hitch still had no final draft, and the script was being worked on right up to the moment that *To Catch a Thief* started shooting on May 31, 1954.

John Robie, a former member of the French Resistance and a notorious burglar dubbed 'The Cat', is forced out of retirement when a series of daring jewel robberies shatter the peace of his Riviera hideaway. To the annoyance of the police, Robie's wartime heroics earned him a pardon for his previous misdemeanours but they are determined that he will not escape justice a second time; they are convinced that he is responsible for the spate of robberies and when they arrive to arrest him, only the intervention of Danielle, the daughter of an old friend, prevents him from being taken into custody.

Hughson, a London insurance investigator, believes Robie to be innocent, and they agree to join forces to unmask the real culprit. Hughson gives Robie a list of the most expensive jewels currently in the area, which includes those of a rich American tourist named Mrs Stevens, who is in France shopping for a husband for her daughter Francie. Robie is sure that the thief will attempt to steal the Stevens diamonds, and he intends to be there when he strikes. But he reckons without Francie recognising him and accusing him of planning to rob her mother. Far from being alarmed by the prospect that Robie might be the notorious cat-burglar, Francie is excited to have him in her power; as the Texan heiress and the ex-thief embark on a game of cat and mouse, the real 'Cat' plots his final caper.

A trap is eventually set and, at a lavish costume ball, hunter finally confronts the hunted high on the French rooftops..

Almost as soon as he started to shoot, Hitchcock fell behind on his schedule; defying the predictions of meteorological experts, rain constantly interrupted filming during the first two weeks. The crowds of onlookers who gathered whenever the crew set up shop also caused problems for the production, as well as for the actors. Hitch, who despised location-filming at the best of times, nevertheless remained

Grant and Kelly on the Riviera, and in the studio tank

pragmatic. While he waited for the right conditions, he allowed his principals time off to explore the avenues and alleyways around Cannes. But the eventual arrival of good weather presented Hitch with another problem, in that director of photography Robert Burks struggled to maintain continuity amid the cloudy skies. Burks and Hitchcock tried a variety of filters with little success; ultimately, the mismatched scenes had to be corrected in post-production. His efforts were so effective that Burks still managed to win an Oscar for Best Cinematography.

When he was filming in a studio, Hitchcock avoided early starts and late finishes, and he organised his schedules around regulated lunch and tea breaks. In the South of France, the director was required to relax his normal work-pattern to suit the seemingly-endless delays. While Hitch managed to accommodate a more *laissez-faire* approach to shooting, Cary Grant insisted on having a designated finish-time—18.00 hours—written into his contract, and to the dismay of the crew, he would walk off the set at the stroke of six, irrespective of what was being worked on at the time. Grant soon gained a reputation for himself as something of a *prima donna* and, on more than one occasion, a frustrated assistant had to ask Hitchcock to intervene with the fastidious star.

Hitchcock's relationship with Grant was complex. He appreciated Grant's 'bankability' and consequently indulged the actor; not only was Grant given the privilege of changing his lines, but he had the final word on his wardrobe and, of course, that generous percentage of the film's eventual profits. Grant, for his part, knew how vital he was to the success of *To Catch a Thief* and saw no reason to rein in his demands, most of which Hitchcock tolerated, usually with nothing more expressive than a frown. But there was another side to the two of them: if Hitchcock's work with James Stewart was a collaboration of equals, he stood in awe of Grant—the way that he dressed, his charm and, in particular, his calculated indifference to the opposite sex. Hitchcock's admiration of him did not go unnoticed by Grant; in *A Life in Darkness and Light*, Brigitte Auber told of a conversation that she had

Publicity shot for To Catch a Thief (Cary Grant, Grace Kelly)

with her co-star in the film, in which he revealed his own view of the relationship: '[Hitch] likes me a lot,' Grant told her, 'but at the same time he detests me. He would like to be in my place..'

The shooting continued at a stumbling pace throughout June but, in spite of the frustrations and now-soaring temperatures, Hitch maintained his customary propriety and insisted on wearing a formal suit and tie—even in the midday sun. More surprisingly, he remained, outwardly at least, chirpy and relaxed; he had been planning this jaunt for some time and was not about to let a few niggles spoil it for him. In preparation for the venture, he had subjected himself to one of his intermittent diets; by the time he arrived on location, he had lost nearly 100lbs and he took delight in showing off the new slim-line Hitchcock. 'It's been murder getting down to this weight, sheer masochism,' he deadpanned to the press. 'For months it has been one meal a day—a lamb chop and a few beans. And not a drop to drink!'

But being in the presence of Grace Kelly made life more than tolerable for the director. 'Hitch always made us feel that we were collaborators,' she recalled. 'Working with Hitchcock was very comfortable.' He and Kelly passed the time between setups with their word-games, on this occasion, rechristening members of the crew according to their jobs—'Otto Focus', the cameraman; 'Ward Robe', in charge of costumes..

From time to time, the levity spilled out in front of the camera—in particular, during the shooting of a picnic scene, where Hayes's scripted innuendoes were enough to set off a chain of saucier improvisations. According to John Russell Taylor, the actors were in 'a cheerful, silly mood, all mussed up with chicken feathers on their lips and hair and just began to make the dialogue up as they went along'. Hitch did three takes of the scene, each one completely different as a result.

When they were not actively engaged in the shooting of *To Catch a Thief*, Kelly, Grant and Hitchcock spent their leisure hours discussing the setting-up of a production company of their own, when Hitchcock's contract with Paramount expired and Kelly was free of MGM. The trio envisaged the making of light and witty thrillers, inspired by the likes of *Mr and Mrs Smith* (1941) or *The Thin Man* series; all three would be joint producers, with Hitch directing and Kelly and Grant trading on their star-status.

If *To Catch a Thief* was turning out to be everything that Hitchcock had hoped for it, the one disappointment in relation had been the eventual arrival in France of Oleg Cassini, who initially announced that he would only be there for the weekend but then managed to attach himself to the unit for the whole of the shoot.

Cassini had an excellent knowledge of both the cuisine and the geography of the region, and he would recommend out-of-the-way restaurants for Hitchcock's party to try. These little soirees were more than an amusing diversion for Hitch; they were part of the reason that he was in France in the first place. In his autobiography, Cassini wrote that the director 'had one of the most curious eating habits.. he would fast until evening, drinking only water during the filming. Then he would take a bath and we would gather for dinner at the restaurant of his choice, for the precise meal of his choice.. Hitchcock would review everything in advance: the wines, the soup, the fish, the meat.. he would preside over it all, like an emperor savouring every morsel.'

Oleg Cassini and Grace Kelly

Between times, Oleg Cassini was free to court Grace Kelly at his leisure, and the couple spent much of her spare time together, shopping, swimming and exploring the countryside. In the convivial atmosphere of the South of France, she and Cassini felt no need to be discreet and the ever-present reporters soon sniffed out a romance-on-film-set story. Photographs of the couple were despatched to newspapers and magazines around the globe, accompanied by the caption '..*clearly in love*'. Kelly could have denied everything (as she had in the past), but to the delight of the French media, she conceded that she and Cassini were indeed an 'item' and the news prompted an outbreak of wedding speculation. Cassini found himself button-holed by a journalist and asked if he was about to propose. 'No comment,' he replied. But his carefully-crafted campaign had slowly eroded the Kelly reserve, and after weeks of strolling along sandy beaches and wining and dining under blue skies, he states in his memoirs that she finally accepted his offer of marriage.

For Hitchcock, the Riviera adventure that was *To Catch a Thief* had now begun to turn sour in the company of the omnipresent Oleg Cassini. If he thought to recapture the memory of a stolen embrace in a hotel corridor under the light of a Mediterranean moon, then he was sorely disappointed; it was Cassini who was invited back to Kelly's hotel suite. Hitchcock has never commented on Cassini, but he had a low opinion of Kelly's lovers in general; the more that Cassini tried to impress the director, the less Hitch warmed to him. If he was tolerated, it was for Kelly's sake, and he was never accepted into Hitchcock's 'inner circle'.

The affair left the Hollywood gossip columnists unimpressed. Hedda Hopper adopted a matronly tone and offered the following: '..with all the attractive men around town, I do not understand what Grace Kelly sees in Oleg Cassini. It must be his moustache.' Cassini could give as good as he got and promptly retorted, 'Okay Hedda, I give up. I'll shave mine if you shave yours.' It was a witty riposte but hardly designed to endear him to the columnist, and his character and reputation would continue to take a pounding in the press in the following months. Hopper dismissed Cassini as 'another of Grace's Svengalis', and with her star on the rise, he increasingly was seen as an outsider, a 'foreigner'—someone clinging to the coat tails of her fame. By the time *Rear Window* opened in August, she was being feted by Hopper as 'the ethereal Miss Kelly', while Cassini was described as 'devilish'.

Reaction to her new romance among Kelly's New York friends was equally mixed. Gant Gaither, a Broadway producer whose association with the Kelly family went back to the 1940s when he had staged a version of *Craig's Wife*, telephoned the actress and asked, 'How low in the sewer can you go? How can you associate with this type of man?' Back in Henry Avenue, Jack Kelly was similarly immune to the Cassini charm; his reputation had preceded him and so far as Jack was concerned, Cassini was 'a waster, a gold digger and, worse of all, not even a Catholic!' Kelly was unrepentant; she wrote of her intended nuptials to her friend, Prudence Wise: 'My father isn't very happy at the prospect of Oleg as a son-in-law. But the plan is to be married the first part of October.'

With his Mediterranean idyll rapidly losing its appeal, Hitchcock worked with Hayes to reduce the amount of time that was still needed in France so that the unit could return to LA, where Hitch was once again in control of his environment, at the earliest opportunity. Scenes due to be filmed inside the Carlton Hotel in Cannes were among the casualties of this latest exercise in paring-down the plot, and these

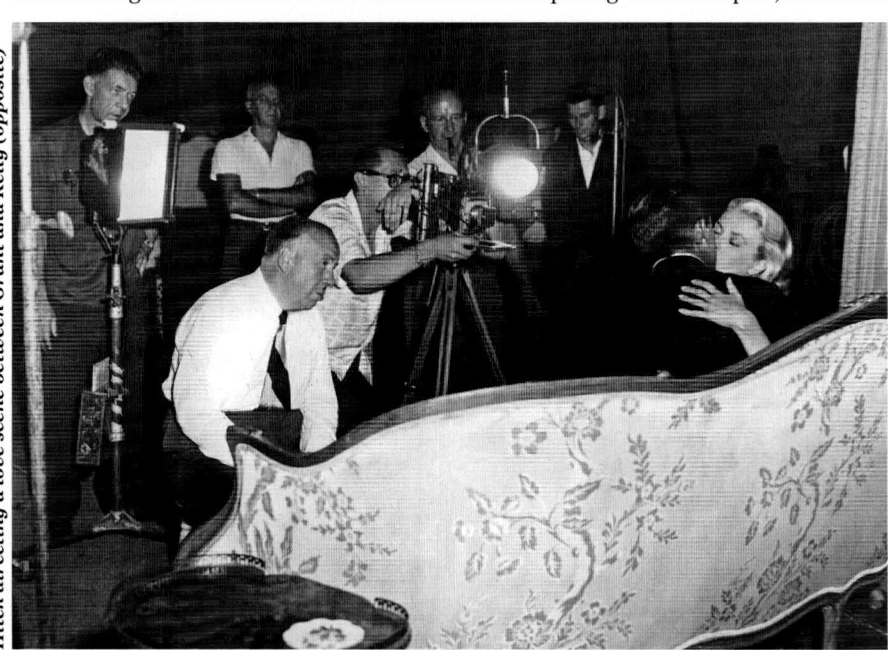

Hitch directing a love scene between Grant and Kelly (opposite)

would be recreated on a Paramount sound stage. On June 25, Hitchcock and his crew wrapped in France and prepared to return to Hollywood to resume the shooting of *To Catch a Thief* two weeks later.

Having missed the plane in New York, Oleg Cassini was now to miss the boat in France—literally. He had planned for himself and Kelly to travel to New York together, and then stage a joint news conference in Manhattan at which they would declare their love for each other and announce their upcoming wedding to the world. Kelly would have none of it; she decided that it would be more fitting if they journeyed to the US separately. Cassini did not like the idea but he was left with no choice, and while Kelly, Hitch, Alma, and Cary and Betsy Grant extended the conviviality of the Carlton in Cannes to the VIP suites of a luxury liner, Cassini was exiled to the next available flight across the Atlantic.

If Kelly thought her departure for France was hectic, then her return to New York must have seemed like a circus. Cassini's autobiography gives a rare insight into her lifestyle at the time, showing just how far removed she actually was from her public image of a shy, rich girl trying hard to avoid publicity. The press were out in force to meet the ship in Manhattan and Cassini had to fight his way to Kelly's cabin, where she was holding court before a small army of agents, publicists and studio execs, as well as couturiers, hair stylists, friends, family and numerous other hangers-on. Cassini was dismayed by what he saw as, 'fawning and flattering and nagging at her.. These gnats and mosquitoes would be a constant source of irritation in the months to come.' Kelly was now a one-woman industry—her transformation into the role of movie star almost complete—and Oleg Cassini was not popular with this particular crowd. 'They were, almost all of them, inclined to have a negative view of me,' he said. 'I was a threat to their meal ticket.' While Paramount's minders imposed a semblance of order, Cassini was reduced to skulking in a corner to await his turn.

So far as the romance was concerned, the long sea voyage, not to mention conversations on the subject with Hitchcock and Grant, seemed to have cooled Kelly's ardour and she had decided that marriage to Cassini was now well down on her list of priorities. The obligatory visit to meet the prospective in-laws did little to further Cassini's cause: 'Having dinner with Grace's father,' he said, 'was like eating a chocolate éclair filled with razor blades.' Believing that she had simply been swept off her feet by a combination of charm and circumstance, the Kellys proposed a compromise to their daughter; they would accept Cassini if she agreed to a six-month 'cooling off' period. In the manner of Holden before him, Cassini stormed out of the room, furious at being treated like a child and annoyed at Kelly for not standing up to her parents. What he failed to grasp was that she had already made up her mind and was merely using Jack and Ma to help break the bad news. Kelly and Cassini were to remain an 'item' for another few months, but with no further talk of engagement or marriage.

On his return to Hollywood, Hitchcock resumed the shooting with the corridor sequence and its 'climactic' fireworks, while a second unit under Herbert Coleman remained in France to capture helicopter shots of the car chase along Monaco's Grand Corniche. Kelly and Grant had already shot their close-ups for the scenes, in which they were to be seen careering along the very roads which almost three decades later would lead to tragedy for Grace Kelly. Kelly, who was not a confident driver, had frayed the nerves of her co-star and her director with her erratic behaviour behind the wheel, and Hitchcock had been relieved to get the sequence out of the way without mishap.

In addition to the hotel and ball scenes, Hitchcock also shot close-ups for the

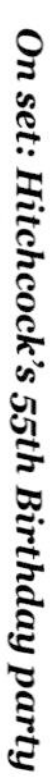
On set: Hitchcock's 55th Birthday party

film's 'raft' sequence in the giant tank at Paramount. To comply with the Production Code, he instructed costumier Edith Head to outfit Kelly in a suitably demure, one-piece, polka-dot bathing-suit for her scenes opposite Grant and the nubile Mme Auber. Hitch had thought to give the scene an understated air of sexual tension as the love-triangle between the three principals starts to develop, and Danielle Auber became an unwitting accomplice in the scheme, as John Michael Hayes told Steven De Rosa: '[Auber] had a casual way of wearing a blouse, which exposed her bosom frequently.. Hitchcock, of course, was delighted with her.'

Hitchcock maintained his humour and happily entertained the press and any other visitors who descended onto the set. The relaxed atmosphere during the final weeks of shooting was especially evident when the cast and crew of *To Catch a Thief* took a break to celebrate their director's 55th birthday. A studio secretary added to the levity by announcing, 'Would you all come into the other room, please, and have a piece of Mr Hitchcake's cock..'

The publicity photographs from this little party are telling. Hitchcock had been shooting the ballroom scene and he is standing in front of an enormous cake, wearing shirt and tie but no jacket—as casual as he ever allowed himself to be. Next to him is Grace Kelly, resplendent in all her golden glory. Hitchcock's hand is reaching out and clutching Kelly's, while she looks on—a candid gesture, underlining the bond between them. Writer Jane Ellen Wayne is in no doubt that Hitch adored his blonde star; that he and Kelly 'communicated like lovers, teased and flirted like lovers.' She adds that he sometimes seemed 'hypnotised in Grace's company, looking at her and beyond her simultaneously'. Cary Grant was aware of Hitchcock's growing obsession, but he dismissed the notion that it was of consequence: 'We were all in love with Grace for goodness sake.. Hitch may have been sexually attracted to Grace, but so were a lot of other people. So what's the big deal?'

Hitchcock's need to show Kelly off to best advantage is nowhere more apparent

To Catch a Thief (Cary Grant)

Theatrical poster for To Catch a Thief

than in the ballroom sequence in *To Catch a Thief*. The director who had once declared 'I have never been very keen on women who hang their sex around their neck like baubles' now squeezed his leading lady into a sumptuous Edith Head ball-gown, simply in order for his audience to share in his infatuation with her and gaze open-mouthed at her sleek sensuality.

Francie's gold ball-gown was Hitch's *pièce de résistance* and, having pored over and approved all of Head's sketches, he was delighted to see it fleshed out to such spectacular effect. Having been carefully stitched into it in the privacy of her changing-room, Kelly emerged onto the set to gasps of admiration. Hitch, who was seldom inclined to praise his actors, waddled across the floor to where his star waited for her master's verdict. 'I was wearing the gold evening dress that was cut really tight to show everything,' she recalled. 'Hitch walked up to me and sort of peeked down my dress and said, "There's hills in them thar gold!"'

Hitchcock had made a public display of his affection for Kelly a week earlier, when they had taken a break from filming to attend the premiere of *Rear Window* at New York's Rivoli Theatre. Alma and Oleg Cassini were also there, but both faded into the background in what had turned out to be the culmination of 'the Year of Grace'. Screen success would continue to be hers over the next twelve months, but on the Rivoli's red carpet, in front of a battery of popping flash-guns, Grace Kelly became a *bona fide* star. She invariably looked stunning at public appearances but, in New York, on August 1, there was a poise and a self-assurance that was absent before. Kelly positively radiated confidence and sheer sexual allure. And the man on her arm, bathing in all the reflected glory, was not her official date for the evening—it was Alfred Hitchcock.

Shooting wrapped on *To Catch a Thief* on September 4, 1954, 23 days over schedule. On top of that, the post-production—including the matching of exterior and interior shots—would keep a unit tied down at Paramount into the New Year, and the final result would not be ready for release until the summer of 1955.

Rear Window whetted the public's appetite for more of Kelly, and Hitchcock had designed *To Catch a Thief* with that purpose in mind. Some months earlier, she had told *Picturegoer*: 'I am too young to have taken any definite personality form. There is no "real Grace Kelly" yet. Give me time.' Hitch was ahead of her; he had discerned her personality and he put it on the screen in *To Catch a Thief*. He told François Truffaut, 'I deliberately photographed Grace Kelly ice-cold and I kept cutting to her profile, looking classically beautiful, and very distant.' This was his 'volcano covered with snow' metaphor. By first offering up the 'snow', Hitchcock lures the viewer into forming a stereotype of Kelly and the character she plays. When Francie suddenly kisses Robie—a man whom she barely knows—the 'volcano' blows.

As a film, *To Catch a Thief* plays like a huge in-joke, with Hitchcock's favourite actors running around one of his favourite locations, and all of them having a whale of a time. Hitch even encourages the audience to be in on the joke; not only is Robie described as a former acrobat, as was Grant in his salad days, but Francie says to him at one point, 'You're like an American character in an English movie.' The rapid-fire dialogue between the characters in the picnic scene could easily have been Kelly and Hitch playing word-games, as exemplified by the following exchange:

> **Francie:** I've never caught a jewel thief before. It's so stimulating. Do you want a leg or a breast?
> **Robie:** You make the choice
> **Francie:** Tell me, how long has it been?
> **Robie:** Since what?
> **Francie**: Since you were in America last?

But it is the scene in the hotel that pushes the boundaries of blue humour. 'I have a feeling that tonight you're going to see one of the Riviera's most fascinating sights,' Francie purrs. 'I am talking about the fireworks of course.' Moments later, as she poses languidly in her 'baubles', Hitchcock's camera moves in for a close-up of her chest: 'Even in this light, I can tell where your eyes are looking. Look—hold them—diamonds.. Ever had a better offer in your whole life?' she inquires of Robie. 'Kelly is an American in the film, but she wasn't frigid like the typical American woman who is a tease—dresses for sex and doesn't give it,' Hitchcock subsequently explained to Truffaut.

Kelly always maintained that Hitchcock showed her nothing but respect—'He treated me like a porcelain doll,' she said. But in the shooting of the assault scene in *Dial M for Murder*, he had demanded more realism; in the relatively-frivolous *To Catch a Thief*, the demand was repeated. When it came to a scene where Robie had to grab Francie by the wrists and push her hard against the wall, Hitchcock felt that Grant was being too gentle with his co-star and asked for a retake with more force, and then more force again. 'We went through that scene eight or nine times,' Grant said, 'but Hitchcock still wanted it again. Grace went back alone behind the door where the scene started, and just by chance I happened to catch a glimpse of her massaging her wrists and grimacing in pain.' Kelly suffered some bruising, but Hitch had pushed her further than he had before and she had remained compliant and uncomplaining. The situation was to be echoed in other of Hitchcock's films, when his insistence on 'realism' would begin to border on sadism..

If Hitchcock had brought the same edge to other elements of *To Catch a Thief*, he might have crafted a more rewarding film. Instead, he made a straightforward comedy-thriller with a welter of intricate twists and turns and a great deal of corny humour. Some of the jokes are so awful that Hitchcock cannot resist sending them up: when Francie blithely announces that she plans to join Robie on his next caper, he groans and pleads, 'Don't say it'—but she does anyway: 'The cat has a new kitten.' However, Hitch still manages some inspired touches. The opening sequence, for example, is a perfect example of his preference for visual exposition over the spoken word: a travel poster stating, *'If you love life, you'll love France'*, is followed by a cut to a screaming woman—'My jewels! I've been robbed!' It is cinematic shorthand at its best; in two short shots, the director establishes location, content and tone. It was a trick that Hitch had used in both the original *The Man Who Knew Too Much* and in *Suspicion*.

To Catch a Thief also features some nice imagery, such as a cigarette stubbed out in an egg-yolk (supposedly inspired by Hitchcock's distaste of eggs) and some of the less obvious humour works remarkably well. But there is not enough to sustain a whole film. Saddled with VistaVision, Paramount's cheaper alternative to Fox's revolutionary Cinemascope, Hitchcock had to shoot some spectacular panoramas in order to show off the system, and this tends to give the impression of a travelogue at times—a long way from film *noir*. Anyone approaching the film on the strength of, say, *Strangers on a Train* or *Rear Window,* would be perplexed and probably disappointed; in the US, the Writer's Guild probably made the right assessment when it nominated John Michael Hayes's screenplay for the category of Best Comedy.

Premiered at the Paramount Theatre in New York on August 4, 1955, *To Catch a Thief* met with a mixed reaction from critics: 'Miss Kelly is cool and exquisite and superior,' said the *New York Times*, adding that the film, 'comes off completely as a hit in the old Hitchcock style'. But *Variety* picked up on the *raison d'etre* of the piece, observing, 'Miss Kelly dresses up the sequences in more ways than one. She is a clothes-horse in some fetching Edith Head creations.. a gal who looks cold but ain't when romancing time with Grant comes up.' At its London premiere, Hitchcock decided to get his defence in first, telling the assembled media, 'It's important that filmmakers should have a sense of responsibility for the stability and continuity of their industry. And, if sometimes you have to make corn, try at least to do it well.' That plea did not stop the *Monthly Film Bulletin* from slating the film: 'Even a comedy thriller needs considerably more in the way of plain excitement and tension than *To Catch a Thief* provides.'

In later years, Hitchcock invariably seemed to be slightly embarrassed by his approach to the film; in particular, to the way that nothing startling or original is

allowed to intrude on a very basic formula. He frequently dismissed *To Catch a Thief* as 'a woman's picture'. Despite its obvious shortcomings, the film proved very popular and clocked up $4.5m in rentals on its initial North American release; that success was to be repeated across the globe.

By the time *To Catch a Thief* went into release, Grace Kelly was a major star and needed no further help from Hitchcock. However, he could barely help himself and was prone to wax lyrical about Kelly every time someone pointed a microphone in his direction. Pulling out the familiar analogy, Hitch told *Photoplay* that Kelly has 'something of Bergman's quality'. Later, he took the comparison with Bergman a step further and summarised the difference between the two as, 'Ingrid has a "muss-my-hair" quality; Grace has a "don't-muss-my-hair" attitude.' *Look* magazine liked the Bergman parallel: it had run a piece stating that Kelly had 'a quality of maturity that flatters middle-aged stars who usually shy away from too-young leading ladies, and an inner warmth and aura of sex that suggests the early Ingrid Bergman'. The middle-aged stars in question, with the exception of Clark Gable, were all on *Variety*'s list of the top box-office draws of the 1950s: Cooper, Crosby, Holden and Grant. The success of her three Hitchcock films was now to ensure that Kelly would join them.

After a short break, Hitchcock put the rigours and delights of *To Catch a Thief* behind him and started to think of his next project. It is probable that the idea of a joint-venture with Kelly and Grant was nothing more than a pipe-dream—idle conversation over a glass or two of wine. Neither does Hitch appear to have given much thought to the possibility that Kelly's status at the top of the Hollywood pecking-order could cast a shadow over his future plans. The actress was now in demand, with a number of filmmakers vying for her services on their sound stages, while Dore Schary kept a tight grip on the reins of her MGM contract.

Hitchcock, comforted by his close relationship with the negotiating powerhouse that was Lew Wasserman and MCA, remained confident that he and Kelly could work together more or less as required. On a personal level, the end of every film put some new distance between them, but it was clear that a bond of sorts existed—even if it was little more than skin-deep. Hitch was known, after one too many drinks, to hint that Kelly had pursued him after their kiss in the corridor, and that he had passed up several opportunities to put their relationship on a more physical footing. That version of events can be chalked up to alcohol and wishful thinking, but *To Catch a Thief* was still a love-letter to Grace Kelly, and it is seen as evidence by many of Hitchcock's growing obsession with the actress—or at least, his *image* of her. The coming years would test that fantasy to the limit, and they were to show just how serious this obsession of Hitchcock's had actually become.

Chapter 6

Walking the Tightrope

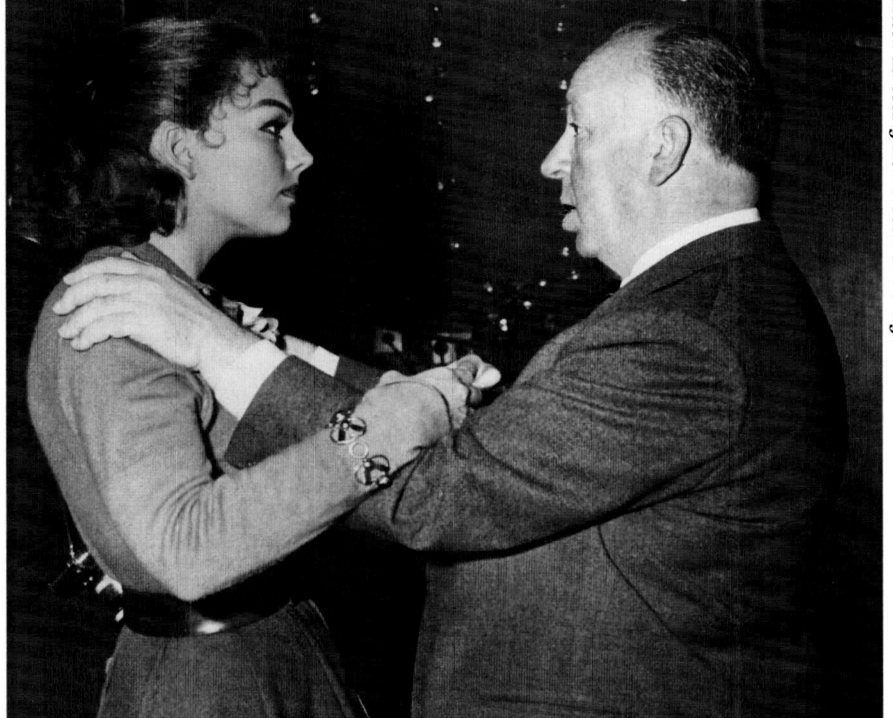

Hitch directing Kim Novak in Vertigo

'Did he train you? Did he rehearse you? Did he tell you exactly what to do and what to say?'

—Scottie (James Stewart) *Vertigo* (1958)

The young girl, dressed in black, resembled Madeleine—he was sure of it now—and had made no less an impression on him.. He had thought about her as he went to sleep and heard her footsteps in his dreams.

—Boileau & Narcejac, *The Living and the Dead* (1956)

Shortly before he arrived in Cannes to start shooting *To Catch a Thief,* Hitchcock announced that his next film would be *The Trouble with Harry* (1955), adapted from a novel by British author Jack Trevor Story. Story's book, which had been published four years before, tells the tale of a young boy in a small English community who is playing in the woods and stumbles across a corpse—that of the titular 'Harry'. Step forward a number of adults who, for various reasons, appear to be implicated in the murder, and soon a conspiracy is underway to keep the grisly discovery from the authorities. The bungling efforts and complex relationships of these conspirators form the core of a very black comedy.

Given his whimsical state of mind at the time, Story's novel was an unsurprising choice for Hitch: its humour is decidedly British and black, both of which attributes appealed to him, and the tangled plot offers plenty of scope for 'Hitchcockian' touches. He resisted the temptation to take *The Trouble with Harry* off into thriller territory, however, and rather than beef up the tension, he designed the narrative to unfold in a low-key, almost pedestrian fashion. It was an approach that alienated his supporters at Paramount, who considered the project unmarketable to American audiences, even with a switch of setting to the US. Aware that it would also be handing over the rights to him at some future point, the studio allocated Hitchcock a budget of $1m—about one-third of that for *To Catch a Thief*.

John Michael Hayes was again engaged to adapt the novel to a New England setting, and writer and director settled into their familiar routine, with Hitchcock firing off ideas and suggestions and Hayes scribbling furiously in his notepad. The plan was to shoot the film in the autumn of 1954.

Cary Grant had been Hitchcock's first choice to play the lead role, but all thought of him vanished when the economic reality of a significantly-reduced budget put his salary well beyond means. Cognisant of the fact that ownership of the film would be his in time, Hitch was keen to ensure that its longer-term value was not eroded by lavish commitments at the production stage, and Grant would not consider the role for less than a percentage; he turned his attention instead to William Holden, an actor whom he had long admired and who had already proven amenable to negotiation if the package was right—and *The Trouble with Harry* not only had Hitchcock, but Grace Kelly as well. Thanks to *Confidential*, Holden's affair with Kelly had become common knowledge, and the prospect of putting two of Hollywood's hottest and sexiest stars together again in the same film was as fascinating as it was exciting.

Since the release of *Rear Window*, the popular press had made much of Kelly and what it regarded as her 'new kind of sex appeal'. The Eisenhower years of the 1950s were a time of considerable reticence in terms of the open discussion of sexual matters, and euphemism and allusion were the order of the day. *Life* typified the general approach, when it tried to analyse the Kelly attraction: 'She has a combination of freshness, lady-like virtue and underlying sex-appeal,' the magazine said, before tempering its conclusions by adding that she nevertheless was 'not a "Lady" in the accepted sense.' There were other actresses, several of them British, who embodied many of the same qualities as Kelly: Audrey Hepburn, Deborah Kerr and Jean Simmons were all considered to be beauties, but with a certain Anglo-Saxon reserve, whereas Kelly's icy aloofness promised something more—something spoken of only in hushed tones—and Hitchcock had put on screen exactly what it was that made her brand of 'sex appeal' box-office dynamite.

Theatre exhibitors in North America had voted Grace Kelly and James Stewart the 'Top Box-office' draws of 1954; in some areas, local cinema managers had revised the billings in their foyers to promote Kelly over her co-star. In less than two years since turning her back on the stage to concentrate on movies, Grace Kelly had become the most sought-after star in Hollywood and, by March 1955, critical response to her performance in *The Country Girl* was to afford her the kind of credibility that would have been unimaginable to her when she first auditioned at AADA for its

The Trouble with Harry (John Forsythe, Shirley MacLaine)/Theatrical poster

student production of *The Philadelphia Story*. So far as Hitch was concerned, her involvement in *The Trouble with Harry* was taken as read. The only person not party to this cosy little scheme was Kelly herself.

Kelly had been pencilled in for the only suitable role in the book, that of a young mother who knows more than she makes out and whose relationship with 'Harry' is at the heart of the mystery. This was another change of pace for Hitchcock and Kelly, and it was to give Kelly the chance to create a character far removed from those in her last two Hitchcock films. MGM, as ever, presented a potential stumbling block, but Hitch had found his way around that before and he would do so again. However, as production on *To Catch a Thief* drew to a close, it had been made clear to him that he might have to rethink his plans—Kelly would not be available in the autumn; this time, it had nothing to do with her studio contract.

Kelly returned to New York in September 1954 and, in professional terms, she did little or nothing for the following six months. So far as press and public were concerned, she was 'resting' after a particularly demanding schedule that had seen her complete five films in quick succession. Fan magazines had it that she was devoting herself

Grace Kelly in New York

to the decorating of her new apartment—she had swapped Manhattan House for the more upmarket address of 988 5th Avenue. Kelly teased reporters with hints that she was considering a return to the stage, telling *Photoplay*: 'My contract gives me a year off for stage work from this month. I'd like to play in the West End of London.' There was even talk of her appearing in a play to be written by Uncle George. But nothing came of these; nor did she exert any pressure on her agents to find her work. The reason was simple, and the reporters who were scouring Manhattan for a story were only a hair's-breadth from a scandal that could easily have destroyed Grace Kelly's career. According to Kelly biographer Wendy Leigh, the actress withdrew to the seclusion of New York because she was pregnant by Oleg Cassini.

During the course of her researches, Leigh interviewed numerous sources and her claim is a provocative one, but it helps to explain Kelly's sudden decision in Cannes to marry—she instinctively followed the principles of her Catholic upbringing.

Hitchcock was certainly aware that a scandal could have destroyed everything that Kelly had achieved or was about to achieve—he had watched as Ingrid Bergman was driven out of Hollywood when *she* fell pregnant to director Roberto Rossellini. American public opinion at the time was uncompromising, and the US senate even went so far as to describe Bergman as 'a horrible example of womanhood and a powerful influence for evil.' The outcry effectively ended Bergman's ability to work in the States. Leigh claims that Kelly overcame her Catholic principles and decided that an abortion was the only solution and, to give closure to the affair, she ended her association with the designer and officially became 'unengaged'. Cassini has never commented on Kelly's possible pregnancy—his autobiography does not even hint at it. When challenged by Leigh, he said only, 'It's too delicate a matter. I don't have to answer this and I will make no comment about that.. Let people think what they want to think.' If Kelly *did* have an abortion after completing *To Catch a Thief*, it would explain why Hitchcock ruled her out of *The Trouble with Harry* without even making an approach to MGM, despite the fact that she had no other commitments with the studio.

Whatever the real reason, Hitchcock suddenly decided to push on with *The Trouble with Harry* without Grace Kelly. He briefly considered casting Brigitte Auber, with her plunging necklines and Gallic charm, in the role of the American housewife, but in the end, he opted instead for the then-unknown Shirley MacLaine. Without Kelly, Hitch lost interest in Holden also and chose to fill the remaining roles with solid, dependable, but decidedly non-'starring' performers like *Foreign Correspondent*'s Edmund Gwenn and John Forsythe.

Even with Alma and daughter Pat by his side throughout the shooting in New

England, Hitch found that without Kelly or Grant, there was little of the bonhomie that had marked *To Catch a Thief* and, while Vermont in the autumn undoubtedly had appeal, the dank weather and dreary skies matched the director's mood. By October, Hitchcock had had enough, and he was relieved to return to Hollywood to finish the film on the lot. *The Trouble with Harry* suffered as a result: even in the rushes, it looked too quirky, too dark and much too off-beat to appeal to a wide audience. Paramount set about marketing the film with little enthusiasm, sensing that it had a box-office dud on its hands.

Such was Hitchcock's speed of shooting on *The Trouble with Harry* that it arrived in the Paramount editing suite while *To Catch a Thief* was still being assembled. With no thought of slackening off on his work-rate, he announced that his next movie for Paramount would be a remake of his earlier British film, *The Man Who Knew Too Much*. Having spent a career with familiar themes, this nevertheless was to be the first time that Hitch would remake one of his own movies. He maintained it this was not an example of 'running for cover', however; on the contrary, it was motivated in part by a desire to help out an old friend, Angus MacPhail, the former caption-writer at Gaumont-British who had worked for Hitch on a number of projects including *Spellbound*. MacPhail had fallen on hard times—alcoholism had taken its toll and he was broke; Hitchcock, to his credit, wired him the plane fare and installed him in a hotel close to Bellagio Road, where he could be looked after while he worked on the script.

Hitchcock's first version of *The Man Who Knew Too Much* had a pair of British tourists caught up in a political assassination attempt, and though the new script would replace Nazis with Communists and change the couple's nationality to American, it was to retain the same basic premise. It would also enable Hitch to indulge his love of travel; apart from shooting in London, he and Hayes created a number of scenes to be filmed in Marrakech, Morocco, before cast and crew returned to Hollywood for the interiors.

On set: James Stewart and Alfred Hitchcock

James Stewart was signed for the lead, with Grace Kelly lined up in principle to play his wife, thus recreating their lucrative partnership from *Rear Window* and providing Hitchcock with an opportunity to present the Jeff and Lisa characters from that film at the next stage of their lives, engaged in the kind of adventure that Jeff had suggested would characterise their marriage. But Hitchcock had no room for manoeuvre with Kelly. Although she was available, she was so dismayed by the quality of the scripts that were being sent to her by MGM that she had embarked on another acrimonious battle of wills with the studio.

On December 15, 1954, while

Hitchcock holidayed in Europe, Paramount opened *The Country Girl* in time for the Academy Award nominations. The studio then embarked on an elaborate campaign to secure nominations for Crosby, Kelly and George Seaton in the major categories, backed by glowing reviews from some important critics and a respectable wave of public approval. The New York Drama Critics' Circle pre-empted the Academy by presenting Kelly with its own Best Actress award, which honoured her for her performances throughout the year, including Hitchcock's *Dial M for Murder* and *Rear Window*. Buoyed by this success, Kelly had felt enabled to tackle MGM on its commitment to her.

Early in 1955, MGM had decided that it was time to put Kelly back to work and Dore Schary summoned her to Hollywood to discuss projects. She had shown some interest in playing the lead in George Stevens's *Giant* (1956) opposite Rock Hudson and rising star James Dean, but that was being made at Warner Brothers and Schary had no appetite to let her wander off the lot again. Instead, he despatched Elizabeth Taylor to see Stevens and she was signed. All talk of cancelling her contract on her return from Africa was now swept under the carpet as MGM tried to take credit for her meteoric rise to fame. 'We feel Miss Kelly has certain obligations to us,' Schary advised Louella Parsons. 'After all, we were the first to give her a chance. All of her offers came after *Mogambo*.' If Kelly had been content to let MCA do the talking for her, she might have reached an accommodation with the studio; instead, its Best Actress nominee used the press-junkets for *The Country Girl* to ridicule MGM. Having already turned down *The Adventures of Quentin Durward* (1955), she was somewhat taken aback to find herself announced as the female lead in the Walter Scott romp. 'All I'd do would be to wear thirty-five different costumes, look pretty and frightened,' she complained in *Time*. 'There are eight people chasing me: the old man, robbers, the head gypsy and Durward. The stage directions on every page of the script say, "She clutches her jewel box and flees." I just thought I'd be so bored.' As she no doubt intended, MGM quietly disassociated her name from the project.

Schary raised the spectre of *Jeremy Rodock*, a western with Spencer Tracy that was due to start shooting, as well as *Something of Value* (1957), a drama set against the background of the Mau-Mau uprising in Kenya; neither of these were insignificant projects, but neither appealed and both were turned down flat. MGM also offered Kelly *The Barretts of Wimpole Street* (1957), a romantic tear-jerker, in the hope that a 'woman's picture' might be more to her liking—it was not.

In an effort to deflect some of MGM's criticism of their client, MCA adopted a new tactic and pointed out that Kelly was being unfairly remunerated for her efforts; at the time, she was earning $1250 a month, about a third of the salary of Ava Gardner, which itself was less than the going-rate elsewhere in Hollywood. Schary was reluctant to renegotiate her contract but he authorised a bonus payment of $20,000 for 1954 and said that he would have *Jeremy Rodock*, (which would be retitled *Tribute to a Bad Man*) rewritten to make it more appealing to her. Neither was enough for Kelly and she remained in New York, walking her dog 'Oliver', collecting *objects d'art* for her apartment, and granting the occasional interview.

Kelly showed no inclination to return to California, telling the *Daily Sketch*: 'Fear covers everything in Hollywood like a smog.' A few years earlier, she would have gone out of her way to have her picture in a paper but now she was insisting that she liked the anonymity of New York. 'It suits me that way,' she said. 'I like privacy.. That's something that Hollywood doesn't know anything about. In fact, I rather dislike Hollywood.'

Despite her success as an actress, MGM still saw Kelly as little more than a pretty prop for its ageing leading men, so she continued to dig in her heals: she was not prepared to make *Jeremy Rodock* with Tracy (who was bounced from the project after one drinking session too many and replaced by James Cagney). Adopting a more belligerent tone, she insisted, 'I don't want to dress up a picture with just my face; if anybody starts using me as scenery, I'll do something about it.' This was too much for Schary who, after months of trying to appease the star, was moved to take more decisive action; a telegram was sent to MCA instructing Kelly to report to the set of *Jeremy Rodock* for costume fittings. Predictably, she ignored the demand. In March 1955, Grace Kelly was given formal notice by MGM that she was suspended without pay and—crucially for Hitchcock and *The Man Who Knew Too Much*—without the option of working for any other company.

Kelly and her PR people were more at ease with the New York press than they were with scandal-hungry Hollywood reporters, and they were soon pulling out all the stops to win over public opinion. She insisted to one reporter that she was 'bewildered and disappointed' with MGM's decision and she presumably had her tongue in her cheek when telling another, 'I feel very strange not getting a salary anymore. It's going to slow down my apartment decoration considerably.' In Hollywood, the feeling was that Kelly and MCA held a winning hand in this very public game of bluff, and that with the Academy Awards only weeks away, MGM could not afford the embarrassment of suspending someone who might just walk off with an Oscar. Backed into a corner, Schary was left with little choice but to issue a statement rescinding the studio's suspension: 'We respect Grace and want to do everything possible for her during this important time in her life when she is up for an Academy Award.'

Kelly was reinstated on March 21; one week later, William Holden, who had played such an important role in her meteoric rise to fame, presented her with the Best Actress Oscar for *The Country Girl*. She was 25 years old.

Of course, all Academy Awards are the result of joint efforts between actors and crew, as well as a triumph of promotional campaigns, industry politics, public sentiment and personal influence. Kelly's victory speech made no mention of Hitchcock or Seaton, William Holden or Jack or George Kelly, or Jay Kanter or Edie Van Cleve, who had supported her throughout, or any of the dozens of others who had helped her in her short but spectacular career. Instead, holding back the tears, Kelly said, 'I will never forget this moment. All I can say is thank you.' It was the pinnacle of her professional career; this was her Olympic gold medal, her very own Henley Sculls.

Kelly had no official escort for the ceremony. Instead, she took along her favourite dress designer, Edith Head, which meant that she was a free agent when it came to the traditional post-Oscar partying. Bing Crosby was the two-time loser on the night; while George Seaton picked up Best Writer for *The Country Girl* to go alongside Kelly's Best Actress gong, Crosby lost out on Best Actor to Marlon Brando for *On the Waterfront*. Kelly's fling with Crosby was long over, but the crooner still felt that she kept a candle burning for him. Having lost out on Oscar, Crosby took solace in the fact that Kelly would be in celebratory mood when he called on her after the show. According to Brando biographer Darwin Porter, Kelly had no intention of waiting until Crosby had consoled himself at the after-parties; she had already accepted an offer from Brando and, by the time Crosby showed up at her hotel suite, she and Brando had retired for the evening. 'That must have been doubly difficult for Bing,' Edie Van Cleve told Porter. 'Earlier in the evening he'd been denied the Oscar by Marlon, his last chance. Now he finds the same young stud in Grace's bed.' Some reports told of a fracas, with a doctor being called to treat Crosby (who was probably suffering more from hurt pride than actual physical injury). But Van Cleve

Doris Day

was in no doubt about Kelly's motives: '[Crosby] wouldn't listen to her refusals of marriage, and since he kept begging her to marry him, the drama queen in Grace came up with a way to make her point.'

Hitchcock did not attend the Oscar ceremony at the RKO Pantages Theatre. Officially, he was too preoccupied with preparations for *The Man Who Knew Too Much*, although he did ensure that his office sent telegrams of congratulation to all the winners. His main concern in respect of Kelly's Oscar was whether it might take her out of his pay range for future projects.

Despite the reconciliation between MGM and Grace Kelly, Hitchcock was advised that it was unlikely to lead to more loan-outs in the immediate future, which left him with no choice but to look elsewhere for his leading lady. In order to avoid any comparisons with Kelly, he cast Doris Day, another client of MCA. The 31-year-old blonde was better known as a singer than an actress, but she had starred in a string of hit films, like *Lullaby of Broadway* (1951) and *Calamity Jane* (1953); perky and wholesome to the point of nausea, Day was about as far from Kelly as Hitch could get. With Day on board, a musical context was also appended, and to please her legions of fans, the contrived opportunity for her to sing. (The song in question, *Whatever Will Be, Will Be* [*Que Sera, Sera*] went on to become one of Doris Day's signature tunes, as well as earning an Oscar for composers Jay Livingston and Ray Evans.)

During the shooting, Hitchcock displayed his intolerance of anyone who questioned him, irrespective of personal and professional loyalty. John Michael Hayes, who had been engaged to write the script, found his working relationship with Hitch under strain when he was asked to collaborate with Angus MacPhail. Hayes very soon came to the opinion that MacPhail was not contributing enough to the script to merit a writing credit, and he submitted the finished draft under his name alone. But he misjudged Hitchcock's strength of feeling on the subject; according to his assistant, Herbert Coleman, the director took one look at the script and said, 'Call the boys [at MCA] and tell them to fire that man right now.' The dispute went eventually to arbitration, and the Writers' Guild confirmed Hayes's entitlement to sole credit. But it was a Pyrrhic victory: Hayes received his credit but his relationship with Hitchcock was damaged beyond repair; the director never spoke to him again.

The Hayes/MacPhail dispute, and Hitchcock's reaction to it, was not an isolated incident and highlights the fragility of Hitchcock's relationship with his collaborators—even those few for whom he felt some warmth and affection. Hitch seemed unable to distinguish between a professional challenge and a personal attack on his integrity; he would rid himself of a valued colleague rather than admit to being wrong. Hayes was not the first and he would not be the last of Hitchcock's associates to be frozen out over some sleight, real or imagined.

Although *The Man Who Knew Too Much* opened to solid box-office, it turned out to be a disappointing film that suffered from a number of flaws, including a

Grace Kelly receives her Best Actress Oscar at the 1955 Academy Awards ceremony

Theatrical poster for The Man Who Knew Too Much

script that showed little of the wit or polish of Hayes's previous collaborations with the director. While Stewart gave his usual reliable performance, Day was out of her depth and there was no chemistry between the leads. Hitch had once again engaged Edith Head to design Day's outfits and he had issued precise instructions on how she should be dressed, but his interest in her was non-existent: Hitch offered her no direction or encouragement; in fact, he barely spoke to her on set at all. In her autobiography, Day expressed her disappointment at his aloofness and suggested that it was inspired by the fact that she was *not* Grace Kelly. She also remarked on the fragile state of Hitchcock's mind: 'He said he was more frightened—of life, of rejection, of relationships—than anyone. He told me he was afraid to walk across the Paramount lot to the commissary because he was so afraid of people.'

Despite having been back on the MGM payroll since March, Kelly had not stepped onto a sound stage since *To Catch a Thief*, but the studio granted her permission to travel to Cannes where *The Country Girl* was to be screened as part of the annual Film Festival. MGM hoped that the glamour and excitement surrounding the trip would revive Kelly's thirst for filming and make her more amenable to their approaches. The trip was to be orchestrated by MGM's Paris bureau and Kelly would be expected to undertake a number of interviews and engage in photo-shoots; these were to include a visit to the Royal Palace in Monaco and a meeting with the tiny principality's head of state, Prince Rainier III of the House of Grimaldi. Described as a 'private visit', the tour was to be carefully staged to ensure maximum coverage in the press. Still flushed with her recent successes, Kelly boarded the plane for the South of France.

Rainier III was Monaco's absolute ruler and just happened to be in the market for a wife. He had, in the past, expressed more than passing interest in American movie stars, although his taste seemed to run to more voluptuous types, with both Marilyn Monroe and Kim Novak being suggested as potential consorts. Dressed to impress, Kelly won the Prince over, and she was afforded the rare privilege of a tour of the Royal zoo. Asked what she had thought of His Royal Highness, she gushed, 'Charming. I think he's very charming.'

The feeling was more than mutual and over the next few months, the prince conducted a clandestine courtship, conveniently removed from the prying eyes of the world's press. While Kelly and Rainier intensified their relationship in private, the newspapers continued to link the actress's name with practically every eligible man she met. In December 1955, the prince and a small delegation from Monaco (which included his doctor and his priest) descended on Henry Avenue for a 'social visit', the outcome of which was to be the formal announcement of he and Kelly's engagement. Her decision to marry Rainier came as a complete surprise to all but a select few of her close friends, while reaction from the press was one of bemusement, as the hacks scrambled for atlases so as to find out where Monaco was.

Grace Kelly and Prince Rainier III of Monaco

Jack and Margaret Kelly with Grace and Prince Rainier

'..It contains elements that are stranger than all the fiction that has gone into many of the thrillers that I've made before.'

—Alfred Hitchcock, prologue to *The Wrong Man* (1956)

Hitchcock's reaction to the wedding announcement has gone unrecorded; that Grace Kelly was engaged and would soon marry into royalty did not automatically preclude her from working for him, and she had gone out of her way to assure MCA (and thus Hitch) that she intended to continue in her career. If anything, her fractious relationship with MGM remained more of a threat to Hitchcock's future projects than her impending marriage. For his own part, he had already set in motion the train of events that were intended to replace Kelly, at least temporarily, while at the same time ensuring his own independence from the whims of studio bosses.

By 1955, Lew Wasserman had convinced Hitch of the merits of television—commercial, rather than artistic. The Hollywood establishment still held the view that television was the enemy of the big screen but MCA, alert to the opportunities presented, had positioned itself at the forefront of TV production and was actively seeking new shows. Wasserman proposed a format to Hitchcock built around his public image, arguing that he was a natural performer, had a strong brand-name and that as the 'Master of Suspense', the stamp of his authority on a drama series would find a ready market on the small screen. Hitchcock was sold on the idea of a show in his name, to which he would contribute short, specially-written introductions; after that, he could be involved as much or as little as he chose, but the scope was there for story selection and possibly even the directing of some episodes. Under Wasserman's guiding hand, Hitch set up Shamley Productions to develop the show, and he engaged Joan Harrison, previously his personal assistant, to act as his line producer.

The fruit of Shamley's labours, a series of thirty-minute shows entitled *Alfred Hitchcock Presents,* would consolidate Hitchcock's position as the foremost exponent

Publicity shot for The Wrong Man (Henry Fonda, Vera Miles)

of the 'suspense' thriller and forever associate him with a particular kind of murderous mayhem. His sardonic introductions to each show brought his self-deprecating humour into the homes of millions and made him a national celebrity, which in turn boosted the profile of his movies. Shamley Productions would eventually make Hitchcock a rich man, through his ownership of a total of 365 shows over ten years— twenty of which, he was to direct himself.

The first episode of the show aired on October 2, 1955, and starred an actress who was to become closely associated with Hitchcock: Vera Miles. Hitch had seen Miles in an episode of the Pepsi-Cola Playhouse entitled 'The House Where Time Stopped' and he claimed that both he and Alma had been struck by her resemblance to Grace Kelly; Hitch asked Wasserman to find out who she was. Hitchcock was convinced that he had made a mistake with Kelly, in that he had made a movie star out of somebody who was 'owned' by someone else. What he wanted was an actress with similar qualities but not subject to the same controls, and he thought that Miles might be the ideal candidate. With what could be seen as unseemly haste, Miles was interviewed by MCA and the 25-year-old actress was offered a five-year contract to work exclusively for Alfred Hitchcock. To protect his new protégé from exploitation, the contract prohibited Miles from appearing in advertisements for lingerie or swimsuits, or anything else that the director in his wisdom considered 'inappropriate or unladylike'. This edict extended to studio publicity photographs, and Hitchcock made it clear to Paramount what would and would not be acceptable in its promotion of the actress. He also had his staff vet interviews and press releases to ensure that the right image of Miles was portrayed at all times.

Vera Miles was told that she would be playing the leading role in Hitchcock's next movie, *The Wrong Man*, which was scheduled to start shooting early in 1956. However, her actual debut for her new employer would be in that first episode of TV's *Alfred Hitchcock Presents*: a show called 'Revenge'. Miles was cast as a young woman who moves with her husband to a trailer park, following some sort of breakdown. It soon becomes apparent that she is not all she seems but when she is supposedly assaulted in their caravan, her husband sets out to find the assailant. Despite his objections to cheesecake photographs of the actress, Hitch was not above filming her in a swimsuit for the episode and, pleased with his work, he pulled the show that had been scheduled to kick-off the series and replaced it with 'Revenge', thinking it a more suitable launch-pad both for his new business venture *and* his latest discovery.

The Swan

Hitchcock's plans for Miles went beyond her film and television work. He considered that he had a proprietorial right to shape her image in any way that might benefit her career. To that end, Edith Head was engaged to design her wardrobe—not with a specific film in mind, but for her everyday wear, 'so she wouldn't go around in slacks looking like a Van Nuys housewife,' he explained. He also gave instructions on how her hair was to be styled to suit the sophisticated 'look' that he had in mind for her.

Having unveiled his creation to the world on television, Hitchcock applied himself to the more serious business of fashioning her big-screen outing in *The Wrong Man*, which was to be made for Warners to honour a previous commitment. The film was to be based on the true story of Manny Balestrero, a jazz musician who was arrested and tried for a robbery that he did not commit; the real culprit was found before Balestrero became a victim of a miscarriage of justice, but it was all too much for his young wife, Rose, who suffered a mental breakdown and had to be institutionalised. *The Wrong Man* was the sort of gritty, down-to-earth subject that Hitchcock normally avoided. There were no slick chase scenes or elaborate set-pieces of suspense; instead, the focus was on the Balastreros' heart-breaking ordeal. Introduced to the press by Hitch as his 'first personal star', Vera Miles was to play the role of Rose.

By the time Hitchcock was gearing up for *The Wrong Man*, Grace Kelly was back at work for MGM. Schary had at last grasped the kind of projects that she was looking for and during the summer, he had announced that MGM had acquired the rights to Tennessee Williams's *Cat on a Hot Tin Roof*, specifically so that Kelly could play the role of Maggie, the titular 'cat'. Her role in *The Country Girl* may have won her plaudits, but that in *Cat on a Hot Tin Roof* had the potential to establish her as one of the leading actresses of her generation. The wheels of MGM moved exceeding slow, however, and she had first to mark time in some less worthy vehicles.

In December, Kelly completed her role in the romantic comedy *The Swan* as a European princess reluctantly engaged to a stuffy prince, played by Alec Guinness. Adapted from the play by Ferenc Molnar, the film was nowhere near as witty as it should have been, but it gave her two things which had been lacking in her career to date: top-billing, and the opportunity to carry a movie without the support of a conventional leading man. *The Swan* had an old-fashioned feel and offered nothing

Publicity shot for High Society (Bing Crosby, Kelly, Frank Sinatra)

of substance to the modern audience. Even the prospect of seeing a soon-to-be-real life princess on the screen did not entice many into theatres.

Straight after Christmas 1955, Grace Kelly, now officially engaged, started work on her second MGM film in a row—a feat that would have seemed unimaginable only twelve months earlier. *High Society* (1956) was to be a musical version of old favourite *The Philadelphia Story,* with Kelly playing the same role that she had in the AADA production—that of the spoiled society heiress who is unable to decide between suitors; Kelly accepted a reduction in her billing on this occasion, in order to share the screen with Frank Sinatra and Bing Crosby—the latter clearly prepared to forgive (or at least forget) the Brando incident. *High Society* saw Kelly sing on screen for the first time, and she pouted and posed in a fetching way, but she was not required to do a great deal of acting. Nevertheless, the combination of likeable leads, memorable tunes and top-notch production values assured MGM of its first bona fide Grace Kelly hit (if one were to count *Mogambo* as a 'Clark Gable film'). Off-set, Kelly was now being chaperoned by Prince Rainier, who had rented a house nearby to keep an eye on his new fiancée and who reportedly found the whole filmmaking process 'incredibly boring'.

The subject-matter of Kelly's two MGM movies had no appeal for Hitchcock and, deep in preparation for *The Wrong Man,* he was giving every indication that he could replace Grace Kelly as easily as he had created her. Part of the process had been to ensure that Vera Miles had the right kind of press coverage, such as a feature in *McCall's* magazine which christened her 'the latest in a famous line of cool beauties'—the description *du jour* being 'the *next* Grace Kelly.' In an interview for *Look,* Hitchcock was asked what qualities his new star had to offer and he gleefully replied, 'She is an attractive, intelligent and sexy woman. That rolls it up.' In case anyone were to fail to notice the connection with his previous leading lady, he spelled it out, 'I feel the same way directing Vera that I did with Grace. She has a style, intelligence, and a quality of understatement.'

Despite the implication in Hitchcock's response, Vera Miles was not being groomed for a glamorous role; instead, the director had decided to adopt a documentary approach for *The Wrong Man*, shooting in black-and-white and in actual locations. Not only did he insist on using the real names of those involved, but he met with the Balestreros in order to hear their side of the story, and he interviewed many of the police officers and lawyers involved. What fascinated Hitch was how sincere everyone appeared to be in *their* version of the truth; this was a story without villains—witnesses were mistaken and the police acted according to their brief. So as not to undermine the sense of realism, he thought to forego his customary cameo and instead appear in a prologue—a nod to his new TV show— to assure the audience of the film's basis in real events.

Henry Fonda, a major box-office star and an actor, like James Stewart, who was possessed of a popular 'everyman' screen persona, was cast as the hapless Manny. However, Hitchcock had decided that he was less interested in an innocent man's fight with the legal system and more taken with the tribulations faced by his wife. Angus MacPhail and Maxwell Anderson's script presents Manny as a passive figure, facing his ordeal with stoicism and dignity, but Rose gets to display the full range of human emotions. In keeping with past practice, Hitch left Fonda to his own devices to prepare for the role as he thought best; Vera Miles, on the other hand, was to have the director's undivided attention.

The realistic approach negated the need for Edith Head and elaborate costume-fittings, so Hitch and Miles spent the first weeks of March 1956 in New York, shopping. Hitch insisted that Miles be dressed 'off the peg' and deliberately took her to the sort of bargain basement stores that the real Rose Balestrero used. With

Thw Wrong Man (Henry Fonda)

shooting not scheduled till the end of March, Hitch also used the time to rehearse his star. Miles had made a number of film appearances, including *The Searchers* (1956) for director John Ford, but Hitchcock took the view that *The Wrong Man* would be her first major role and she would need additional support.

When filming began, the crew noticed that Hitchcock's treatment of Miles went beyond anything that they had witnessed before. In the past, he had bullied or cajoled performances from his leading ladies—teased them or flirted with them to achieve some effect or simply for amusement—but this was the first time that they had seen the director lavish so much time and attention on an actress, to the exclusion of all other members of the cast. Miles was taken aside each day for 'story conferences' in the privacy of her dressing-room, where Hitch would run through her scenes, again and again, while directing her from the sidelines—an attention to detail that pushed the actress to the point of exhaustion..

In the meantime, the eyes of the world were on the lavish preparations that were being made in Monaco for the wedding of the century. But in New York, Hitchcock was pouring his heart and soul into launching Vera Miles as a bigger and better version of Grace Kelly. The call-sheets for *The Wrong Man* during April show that Henry Fonda was required on set for only a few hours each day; Miles, by contrast, was in constant attendance, frequently working well past the director's much-treasured office hours.

Beyond the needs of the camera, Hitchcock flirted openly with Miles, albeit it innocently, and in those early weeks of production, he went out of his way to ensure that she was made to feel special. Roses were delivered to her dressing room every day, along with cards and gifts. Herbert Coleman, Hitch's assistant, told Patrick McGilligan, 'Hitch had an obsession with her but it never went beyond imagining. Anyone would want to be a lover of Vera Miles.' Alfred Hitchcock was not anyone, however; as both the director of the film and Miles's employer, he was in a position of power that he had never held with Grace Kelly, Ingrid Bergman, or any of his other female leads. And he was taking advantage of it. As the shooting progressed, Miles found Hitchcock's constant attention suffocating, and she began to protest.

Away from the studio, Hitchcock was showing the usual signs of stress. He had started to overeat again—particularly ice cream which he seemed unable to resist—and he was drinking heavily, putting on the weight that he had worked so diligently to lose. One of the factors that may have preyed on his mind was that Grace Kelly's wedding was scheduled for April 18; the actress had already made what would prove to be her last public appearance as an unmarried woman when she presented the Best Actor Award at the 1956 Oscars. From Hollywood, Kelly flew to New York, where she was to travel by liner to Monaco. Opinions about the wedding were mixed in the US, but xenophobically-biased in Kelly's favour—a tribute to how well her PR team had sold their client as 'royalty' in herself. The *Chicago Tribune* said that Kelly was 'too well bred a girl to marry the silent partner in a gambling parlour', while the *Denver Post* thought that the heir to the oldest royal family in Europe was 'beneath her station'. But there was no stopping the bandwagon once it began to roll, and the papers were soon full of what dress she would be wearing, what 'unnamed insiders' thought of her prince, how she would spend her honeymoon, and so on and so forth.

With the world's media about to descend on Monaco, the Royal Palace's tiny press office was soon overwhelmed and it accepted an offer from MGM to help stage-manage the public relations—in exchange for the rights to film the wedding. Two thousand reporters arrived in a country smaller than New York's Central Park, accompanied by MGM's movie cameras and the outside broadcast units of NBC,

CBS and the BBC, among many others. There were over four hundred guests on the official list, including, ex-King Farouk of Egypt, Aristotle Onassis, Randolph Churchill and the Shah of Iran. Kelly's close friends Jay Kanter and Rita Gam were there, as was the Aga Khan and hotelier Conrad Hilton, and the cream of Hollywood turned out in force—Ava Gardner (Frank Sinatra cried off at the last minute for fear of upstaging the bride) and Bing Crosby, as well as Cary Grant, David Niven, and their respective wives. But one face was missing: Alfred Hitchcock was notable by his absence.

Hitchcock had declined the wedding invitation, claiming that he could not spare the time away from *The Wrong Man*. If his feelings of rejection were not already plain enough from his non-attendance at the nuptials, Hitch underlined the point by choosing not to present the happy couple with a conventional wedding present. The new Princess Grace instead received a chain leash for her dog, decorated with carnations and bows and complete with a card that read, *You'll love Monte Carlo. Happy Barking!* It was signed 'Phillip', Hitchcock's dog. Kelly seemed to accept the snub for what it was: a childish gesture from a man who was incapable of expressing his emotions in any other way. But Hitch would come round quickly; Kelly was too important for him to let her slip away because of a little thing like marriage.

But the royal wedding in Monaco was not the only cause of Hitchcock's heartache. Three days before Grace Kelly and Prince Rainier III exchanged vows in the full glare of the media spotlight, a far more low-key ceremony had taken place closer to home: Vera Miles had wed her long-term partner, actor Gordon Scott, who had also been her co-star in *Tarzan's Hidden Jungle* (1955). Hitchcock had known about Miles's relationship with the 'Tarzan' actor since the start, but it had seemed irrelevant to the professional 'accord' that they shared together. No longer. By the time Miles returned to work on *The Wrong Man*, the relationship between she and Hitch had been put onto a more a more formal footing; the daily rehearsal sessions were gradually phased out.

Hitchcock had made two miscalculations in his rush to bind Vera Miles to him. She was a strong-willed woman who knew her own mind and was not afraid to stand up for what she wanted, a quality that he found disconcerting; secondly, she was an excellent actress who had already developed a unique screen persona. Try as he might, Hitch found that he was unable to mould her into something—or some*one*—else. Miles also had less ambition than Kelly; she was certainly not driven to succeed. While Kelly would instinctively adopt a pose designed to ingratiate her with those that she admired or needed, Miles steadfastly refused to be anything other than Vera Miles. She had the looks but not the inclination, and she resented attempts by Hitchcock to put her on a road that she did not wish to travel.

But even while he attempted to shape a worthy successor, Hitchcock was convinced that Grace Kelly's absence from movie screens would only be temporary. Just before the wedding, Ma Kelly had informed *American Weekly* that acting, for her daughter, was 'her triumph as a human being, her victory over all the doubts and insecurities that have haunted her life'. And she added that to turn her back on acting 'would be a terrible defeat for her. It would be like cutting the heart out of herself.' It was a view that Kelly reiterated in her own declarations to the press: 'My contract has four years to run. I have always been faithful to any agreement I have made,' she insisted. Privately, the actress assured MCA that she would continue to look at scripts. There seemed to be no ambiguity about her position, and Hitchcock's approach to her marital status would be the same as his approach to MGM—it was an obstacle that he had to work around.

Dore Schary also expected Grace Kelly to report back for work after her

Grace Kelly on her wedding day

honeymoon, and plans were advancing for her to star in *Designing Women* opposite James Stewart, with *Cat on a Hot Tin Roof* still in the drawer marked 'pending'. By the early summer, Kelly had still not returned for duty and Schary sent a missive to MCA confirming that their agreed twelve-week leave of absence was now well and truly over and that he expected her in Hollywood to discuss the forthcoming movie.

The matter of Kelly's career was not so clear cut for Rainier. He had been brought up to believe that a wife's duty was to her husband and family (and in this case, the Grimaldi royal household also), and he made it clear to her that she had a responsibility to her new subjects which she would not be able to discharge in either New York or California. It did not help her cause that Rainier had a very low opinion of Hollywood and its denizens, whom he thought superficial and tacky, and whom he felt had treated him discourteously. The ultimate affront had occurred during the filming of *High Society*, when he attended a formal dinner at MGM and was asked the size of Monaco; when Dore Schary heard the reply, he scoffed, 'That is not as big as our back lot!' Rainier, already annoyed by the attitude of the American press, had no intention of becoming 'Mr Grace Kelly', and he was already telling anyone who would listen that there was no debate over his wife's future: she would be giving up her Hollywood career to take on a new and far more worthwhile role as Princess Grace of Monaco.

If Hitchcock was aware of what was going on between MGM and the Palace at Monaco, he chose to ignore it and press on instead with his preparations for *Flamingo Feather*, based on a story by Laurens Van der Post; the film was to shot in Africa, and it would star James Stewart and Grace Kelly, he told the press. After the dourness of *The Wrong Man*, *Flamingo Feather* represented a return to action/adventure, and the book's premise is similar in many ways to *The 39 Steps*, with a white hunter caught up in a Russian plot to destabilise an Africa country. To make a role for Kelly, Hitchcock had added a love interest—something that Van der Post had thought unnecessary, and he planned to downplay the political angle in order to steer Her Royal Highness clear of anything controversial.

By the first week in July, Hitch, Alma and the ever-reliable Herbert Coleman had arrived in South Africa to scout locations and talk to the author. The trip went well, but the country proved to be a disappointment so far as the prospective film was concerned. Studio facilities were basic, there were insufficient numbers of technicians, and locations were less exciting than Hitchcock envisaged. To make matters worse, by the time he returned to LA, there were murmurings at Paramount about the budget and the politics. Hitchcock looked on the project as a challenge and continued to develop the idea, convinced that an 'unnamed foreign power' could be employed instead to take the sting out of any complaints from the Soviet Union and sure that he could find cheaper and better alternatives to shooting in Africa.

The final blow came on August 2, when a communiqué from the Royal Palace announced that Her Serene Highness Princess Grace was pregnant. Kelly then went on record with *Look* and confirmed that a new stage in her life had begun—one that did not include films: 'My career was the central focus of everything I did,' she stated. 'Now my life centres around my husband..' Hitchcock remained unimpressed and said only, 'Grace has bounced around with the ease of a girl on the trapeze. Whether the platform on which she has landed is too narrow, I don't know.' *Flamingo Feather* was always going to be an uphill struggle for Hitchcock, but without Kelly on board, he felt it did not merit any further effort. The script went into a filing cabinet from which it never emerged.

At this point in time, Alfred Hitchcock was only days away from his 57th birthday. Love stories and impulses of the heart had been at the centre of so many of his films, and yet his orderly, methodical, largely mundane and, by his own admission, celibate existence had left him little scope to indulge the passionate side of his nature. When Grace Kelly came into his life, Hitch had felt a pang of longing that he thought would never be his—he had experienced an emotion that he thought he had put behind him in his youth, sure in the knowledge of his ungainly physique that he was not to be one of the lucky ones in the romantic stakes. Now, in middle age, his life had started to close in around him; he faced health problems for himself and for Alma (who was diagnosed with cervical cancer but managed to make a full recovery), was fighting a losing battle to control his intake of food and alcohol, and he had to endure the pain and humiliation of not only losing Kelly but her surrogate, Vera Miles. The anxiety and disappointment that he felt were to spill over into his work. There would still be the humour, but increasingly his films were to move away from escapist fantasy and begin to confront his inner demons. It would be more than a vicarious venting of spleen, played out in the safety of a cinema screen; if author Patrick McGilligan is to be believed, Hitchcock was no longer able to separate self-delusion from bitter reality.

In *A Life in Darkness and Light,* McGilligan tells of an incident which took place around this time, concerning French actress Brigitte Auber, with whom Hitchcock had maintained a friendship after they worked together on *To Catch a Thief.* Auber considered the relationship to be one of 'father and daughter', and the two met up whenever the director was in France to share a meal and indulge in a little *bonhomie.* One evening, Auber gave Hitchcock a lift to his hotel; they sat in her car and talked, and Hitch related the oft-told story of the famous actress (unnamed on this occasion) who had thrown herself at him while they were filming. Without warning, he tried to kiss Auber on the lips. She resisted, and he immediately apologised and left the car. According to Auber, Hitch contacted her several times over the next few years in the hope that they might rekindle their friendship, but she had felt 'betrayed' and had ended their association that night. The man who valued the virtues of good manners and restraint had allowed the mask to slip for an instant to reveal the desires that bubbled away beneath the surface. From now on, Hitchcock's films would increasingly reveal the emotional turmoil in the man was to create them.

'There is a devil in every one of us.'

—Alfred Hitchcock

With Grace Kelly now removed—perhaps permanently—from his plans, Hitch turned his attention back to Vera Miles, believing she could yet be transformed into the kind of star that he was looking for if he could only find the right vehicle. 'Romantic obsession has always obsessed me,' Hitch once said. 'Obsessions of all kinds are interesting, but for me, romantic obsession is the most fascinating.' The concept of romantic, or sexual, obsession had opened up a rich vein for the director over the years, but in October 1956, he began to contemplate a project which would blur the distinction between what appeared on the screen and what was actually happening behind the scenes..

Hitchcock announced that his new movie would be an adaptation of *D'entre les Morts* by Pierre Boileau and Thomas Narcejac (Pierre Ayraud), which was published in the UK as *The Living and the Dead.* A previous novel by the two French authors (*Celle qui n'était plus*) had been adapted by Henri-Georges Clouzet as *Les Diaboliques* (The Devils; 1955), which Clouzot had turned into a chilling murder mystery that Hitchcock admired enormously. *D'entre les Morts* was imbued with the same dark, disturbing qualities; it also featured a premise that seemed to mirror, in part at least, his own preoccupations. More curiously still, the book had been written by the pair with a rights purchase by Hitchcock in mind, after he had tried, and failed, to secure their earlier *Celle qui n'était plus* (aka *The Woman Who Was No More*).

The central character in the novel is a Paris detective during the Second World War, who is forced to retire from the police when his fear of heights leads to the death of a colleague. Unable to find alternative work, he agrees to help out an old friend who believes that his wife, Madeleine, may be predestined to commit suicide. The detective settles into what seems to be a routine surveillance job, following the wife to ensure that no harm comes to her—but he has reckoned without falling madly in love with his charge; fate intervenes and he fails to prevent her from taking her life. Some years later, he sees a woman in a newsreel who bears a striking resemblance to Madeleine. He tracks her down and obsesses about transforming her into the

***Vertigo* (James Stewart)**

Publicity shot for Vertigo (Kim Novak, James Stewart)

Publicity shot for Vertigo (Kim Novak, James Stewart)

image of the dead woman. The detective's love for the dead Madeleine drives him to the edge of sanity, and when he finds out that it was all a plot engineered by her husband, and that his 'new' love and Madeleine were actually one and the same from the start, he strangles her.

Hitchcock initially engaged *The Wrong Man*'s Maxwell Anderson to adapt the book into a treatment called *From Amongst the Dead*, later *Vertigo*, in which the setting was switched from war-torn France to present-day San Francisco. Alec Coppel, another client of MCA, was then hired to work with Hitch on the characters and dialogue. Hitch always maintained that any relationship between the events depicted in *Vertigo* and real-life was purely coincidental, but he felt a strong affinity with the project—probably for the first time since *Rear Window*; how much thought Hitchcock had invested in the film became clear during his first meeting with Coppel, when he dictated a total of 23 scenes to the writer that he had been carrying around in his head!

Hitchcock announced Vera Miles as his leading lady, with James Stewart as detective Scottie Ferguson. As with *Rear Window*, Stewart was crucial to the project from the outset, but the actor insisted on taking a break after finishing his current assignment, a western called *Night Passage*, and rather than lose the marquee value of Stewart's name, Paramount agreed to postpone production and the crew were retained on salary pending Stewart's return to work. Hitchcock filled the time by shooting wardrobe tests with Miles, while the second unit started work in San Francisco. But in January 1957, as *Vertigo* was gearing up to begin again, Hitch underwent surgery for a hernia which had been bothering him for some time; a little later, he was admitted for a second operation, this time for gallstones. Forced into an extensive period of recuperation, he thought to further refine the script, but the additional delays were to have dire consequences for his relationship with Vera Miles.

Vertigo (Kim Novak, James Stewart)

It was April before Hitch felt fit enough to return to the studio, only to be met by Herbert Coleman with some bad news: Vera Miles was pregnant. Hitchcock was furious—to his mind, she had picked the worst possible moment to conceive. (Five years later, his bitterness was still apparent in an interview with journalist Oriana Fallaci: 'I was offering her a big part, the chance to become a beautiful sophisticated blonde, a real actress,' he said. 'We'd have spent a heap of dollars on it and she has the bad taste to get pregnant.') He was not a man to throw tantrums—he kept his anger and frustrations bottled up inside—but the moment he put a line through Miles's name on the *Vertigo* call-sheets, he was effectively ending their relationship. She and Hitch would work together again in *Psycho* (1960), where she would be allocated a supporting role, but that was purely to extract some value from her contract; Hitchcock had lost interest in turning Vera Miles into a star, and he freely admitted that he 'couldn't get the rhythm going with her again.'

Lew Wasserman hosted a crisis lunch with Hitchcock and Stewart to find a replacement for Miles, at which the name of MCA client Kim Novak came up. The 24-year-old actress was under contract to Columbia Pictures, where Harry Cohn had been trying, with some success, to build her up as a replacement for Rita Hayworth. Novak was no wide-eyed, impressionable *ingénue*; she was opinionated and forthright, and her battles with Cohn were legendary on the Columbia lot—as was a string of highly-publicised affairs. There was no denying Novak's sex-appeal: she had statuesque good looks and an eye-catching figure that she was happy to show to advantage, but she was hardly on a par with Hitchcock's taste in women. Novak was a Nordic blonde, but she was a long way from the 'drawing room type'. However, with time against him, Hitch was prepared to compromise in order to get *Vertigo* off the ground.

A new start-date was set for June. Wasserman then brokered a loan-out with

Cohn, with Stewart agreeing to star in a Columbia film in return. But Novak had other ideas and refused the loan-out on the basis that her salary would be a fraction of what the studio was to receive. Neither she nor Cohn was prepared to give ground and they were still in dispute as *Vertigo*'s intended start-date came and went; the project was postponed once again. By the time Novak and Cohn had settled their differences and a new date was agreed for the autumn, Vera Miles was available for work. Hitchcock nevertheless refused to reconsider his position, and he left Miles to languish until he could think of something to keep her occupied.

Over the twelve months of delays and rewrites, the screenplay to *Vertigo* had developed a bleak and fatalistic edge that was absent in the original draft. Its leading lady is portrayed as a duplicitous and treacherous vixen, who seduces the fragile Scottie when he is at his most vulnerable and then abandons him in shocking circumstances. Morbidly obsessed, Scottie is depicted as being out of control—sick, and possibly even dangerous. The distorted love story at the heart of the piece is made more unsettling by the casting: there is something distinctly uncomfortable in the middle-aged James Stewart lusting after a woman half his age, and his aberrant behaviour as Scottie leaves no room for doubt, as he pleads with his new lover, Judy, to dress exactly as her dead predecessor did before he can make love to her. 'If I let you change me, will that do it? If I do what you tell me, will you love me?' she asks. 'All right then, I'll do it. I don't care any more about me.'

Vertigo's themes of sexual dominance and romantic obsession are only too obvious, and it is significant that the Madeleine of the novel was changed in the film from brunette to blonde on Hitchcock's instructions. In a 1975 interview quoted by Donald Spoto, he gave away more than he probably intended when he said, 'I was very much intrigued by the basic situation of *Vertigo*—of changing the woman's hair colour—because it contained so much analogy to sex'; he had earlier stated that Scottie's pleasure was one of 'dressing rather than undressing his love. Dressing Judy was really undressing her. But Scottie can't really possess the woman in his mind because she is only in his mind..'

Hitchcock and Novak did not hit it off; he had been lukewarm about her from the start, and he soon began to rue his decision when she objected to the styles that he had in mind for the characters of Madeleine and her alter ego, 'Judy'. Hitch wanted a grey business-suit and a plain, unfussy hair-do for Madeleine and to have her transform into something more radiant and *alive* as the story progressed. Novak, who was not accustomed to her directors telling her what she should wear, insisted that her public expected glamour and that was what they were entitled to. Tired of explaining himself to his head-strong star, Hitch adopted a different tack. 'Listen. You do whatever you like; there's always the cutting-room floor,' he said.

On another occasion, Hitch argued with Novak over her decision not to wear a brassiere in the film—a blatant display of sex that flew in the face of all of his theories on the subject. Rather than fight her on every point, he gave in on this one, convincing himself that it might help to give the 'Judy' character an 'animal-like sensuality'. A year after *Vertigo* was released, he would change his mind: in an interview for *Films and Filming*, he was to launch a thinly-veiled attack on Novak, insisting, 'the conventional big-bosomed blonde is not mysterious. A woman of mystery is one who also has a certain maturity and whose actions speak louder than words. Any woman can be one, if she keeps those two points in mind. She should grow-up and shut up.'

During the months of waiting for *Vertigo* to be given a green light, Hitchcock had pored over every tiny detail of the script. Always meticulous in his preparations, he now took this fastidiousness a stage further, going so far as to describe the arrangement of the flowers in a florist's shop. Hitchcock felt closer to *Vertigo* than he had to his previous films, and he was very protective of it. Samuel Taylor, who joined the production to help with the script, said, 'Hitchcock knew exactly what he wanted to do in this film.. and anyone who saw him during the making of the film could see, as I did, that he felt very deeply indeed.' The atmosphere on the set, which Hitchcock's biographer John Russell Taylor described as 'strange and intense', seemed to affect everyone, and it made the sixteen days of location shooting in San Francisco awkward and uncomfortable for cast and crew alike. It was little different in the studio, with Hitch pushing for retake after retake in an effort to capture shots exactly as he had imagined them in the months leading up to the shooting.

Principal photography on *Vertigo* was finished just before Christmas, 1957, and the film was ready for release the following May. In keeping with the film's location, the premiere was held in San Francisco. Reaction from the critics was negative; many found the subject, and the way that Hitch had handled it, too dark and too Freudian. Audiences agreed, and *Vertigo* was designated one of the director's failures. The muted reception handed out to such a personal project affected Hitchcock deeply, and when the rights to the film reverted to him under the terms of his Paramount contract, he had it buried in the vaults; it was not to surface in public again during his lifetime.

In the attempt to put *Vertigo* behind him, Hitchcock decided on a change of pace and a change of studio. Having honoured his commitment to Paramount, he moved to MGM to work on an adaptation of *The Wreck of the Mary Deare* but when that proved unwieldy, he turned his attention on to an original idea that he had carried in the back of his mind for some time. *North by Northwest* (1959) was planned as another romantic suspense-thriller, a chase movie to end all chase movies, which would end up containing so many 'Hitchcockian' elements that it could almost be seen as pastiche. Cary Grant, now six more films on from his proposed 'retirement', was engaged to play an advertising executive named Roger Thornhill, who is mistaken for a CIA operative by agents of a foreign power intent on smuggling secrets out of America. Unbeknown to the villains, the real agent is already in their midst: a beautiful blonde, who has been masquerading as the heavy's mistress. Hitchcock's flair for high-octane adventure was to be on display with some imaginative and iconic set-pieces, but the film was never intended to be anything more than light entertainment, and the director approached it very much with that idea in mind.

James Stewart had been Hitchcock's original choice for the role of Thornhill, but he was soon superseded by Cary Grant, when MGM showed itself to be less squeamish about Grant's salary demands than Hitchcock was. Less clear-cut was the casting of the female lead. Dore Schary had long since exited MGM, a victim of its declining fortunes, but his spirit remained and Hitch was asked to draw on the studio's pool of contract artists for the role of the sultry blonde. Four years earlier, he could only have dreamt of such a request—but that was then; the best that MGM could come up with now was Cyd Charisse. Technically, Grace Kelly was still under contract, and Hitch had maintained social contact with her after her marriage, but she was not yet ready to contemplate a return to the screen. And Vera Miles was still *persona non grata* with Hitchcock, despite separating from her husband in the interim. 'She cost me several hundred thousand dollars,' he told *Cosmopolitan's* Jon Whitcomb. 'I don't know what I'm going to do with her. Movie careers have a rhythm you know. She broke the rhythm and it means making a whole new start.'

Casting his net wider, Hitchcock failed to land anyone that appealed to him and, with the start-date approaching rapidly, he agreed to meet Method actress Eva

Maria Saint, the New Jersey-born star who had won an Oscar for her film debut in *On the Waterfront*—in the role that was offered to Grace Kelly. Saint, true to her Actor's Studio roots, was better known for down-to-earth performances in 'kitchen sink' dramas, but over dinner at Bellagio Road, she charmed Hitchcock and his wife with her wit and intelligence and they both agreed that she would make an ideal choice. Saint remembers Hitch telling her that audiences did not like to see their leading ladies looking dowdy and offering her the chance get away from roles where she had to 'do the dishes and wear an apron'; he promised that she would appear on screen as 'sensual, sophisticated and witty'—in short, as Grace Kelly.

Hitchcock paid Eva Marie Saint the same level of attention as he had Vera Miles; he took her shopping for clothes and jewellery, selecting the items personally and

***North by Northwest* (Cary Grant, Eva Marie Saint)**

Hitch and screenwriter Ernest Lehman

charging the whole amounts to studio expenses. He was only too conscious of the real-life parallels with his last film and even commented upon them, 'I took a lot of trouble with Eva Marie Saint, grooming her and making her appear sleek and sophisticated.. I acted just like a rich man keeping a woman: I supervised the choice of her wardrobe in every detail—just as Stewart did with Kim Novak in *Vertigo*.' Even on a project intended from the start as a piece of froth, Grace Kelly was never far from his thoughts, and when asked about Saint, he said, 'I watched every hair on her head.. I went along to Bergdorf Goodman's myself and sat with her as the mannequins paraded by. I chose the dress for her. I did the same for Grace Kelly.' Grace Kelly had become the yardstick by which Hitch now measured every actress with whom he worked.

But Hitchcock's relationship with Eva Marie Saint was never going to draw comparison with that of Kelly; Saint was an experienced actress, with a strong track record behind her, and she had no reason to feel grateful to or be dependent upon Hitch. She also gave birth to a second child a month before shooting started, and the baby naturally occupied her time when she was not on call. Much as Hitchcock respected her abilities as an actress, he found himself unable to compete with a newborn baby for Saint's attention, and their relationship remained strictly that of employer/employee. Even so, when the film was launched, Hitchcock spoke of Saint in the same terms that he had of Kelly after *Dial M for Murder*, telling the press that she was no longer a 'drab, mousy little girl'. 'I have given her vitality and sparkle. Now she's a beautiful actress,' he proclaimed.

North by Northwest was slick, stylish and witty, but altogether undemanding entertainment. Grant and Saint had been set up to mirror the chemistry of Grant and Kelly in *To Catch a Thief*, and they made an attractive couple; the chases were exciting, the villains—led by James Mason—were suitably villainous, and the jokes came in all the right places (thanks to a clever script by Ernest Lehman). After the reaction that was meted out to *Vertigo*, the popularity of *North by Northwest* came as a welcome bonus for Hitchcock. But his own thoughts were once again on darker subjects. In April, 1958, shortly after shooting on *North by Northwest* had wrapped, Hitch returned to Paramount and took Samuel Taylor and Herbert Coleman off to London to scout locations for a film that was intended to shock audiences, rather than exhilarate them, and which would push the boundaries of sexual violence further than ever before.

> **The little hole was just a crack in the plaster on the other side, but he could see through it. See through it into the lighted bathroom. Sometimes he'd catch a person standing right in front of it. Sometimes he'd catch their reflection on the door mirror beyond. But he could see. He could see plenty. Let the bitches laugh at him. He knew more about them than they ever dreamed.**
>
> —Robert Bloch, *Psycho* (1959)

No Bail for the Judge was the story of an Old Bailey judge who is arrested for the murder of a prostitute. But he is suffering from amnesia and is unable to convince even himself of his innocence. His daughter, a barrister, sets out to find the real killer and plunges into a murky world of crime and prostitution.. Hitchcock wanted Audrey Hepburn to star in the film, and Hepburn welcomed the approach, saying that she was keen to work with the director—it was when she read the script that she began to get cold feet. In one scene, while masquerading as a streetwalker, her character was to be dragged into bushes and sexually assaulted. Hitch felt that Hepburn's delicate, waif-like appearance and natural air of vulnerability would make the indignities heaped upon her character all the more real and threatening. But Hepburn stalled on committing; she had just appeared in *The Nun's Story* (1959), and she thought that going from Holy Orders to rape victim was too much of a jump. Alarm bells had also started to ring at the studio, when it was realised that Hitch had inserted a sex attack into what had been a straightforward thriller. Ignoring all this, Hitch and Samuel Taylor pressed on with shaping their storyline, confident that Hepburn could be won over by a strong script. *Dial M*'s John Williams was lined up to play the judge, with new young star Laurence Harvey pegged for the role of a thief who befriends the barrister.

By the time the script was finished, Audrey Hepburn's nervousness had turned to indecision; she continued to put off committing to the project until it reached the point where Hitchcock had to start preparing for the production. She then cabled the studio to say that she was pregnant and would be withdrawing from the film as a result. Hitchcock was now of the view that it was either Hepburn in the role or no-one, and he briefly considered flying out to her home in Switzerland to persuade her to change her mind. In the end, he decided to abandon the idea, writing off some $200,000 of Paramount's money in the process.

Lew Wasserman and Alfred Hitchcock

Hitchcock was keen to move swiftly on from *No Bail for the Judge* and, by mid-summer, he thought he had identified a suitable project to carry the Hitchcock brand into the new decade. His choice of material was curious to say the least: *Psycho* was a 'pulp' novel written by short horror story specialist Robert Bloch and based loosely on the career of Wisconsin serial killer Ed Gein. It had no pretensions to be other than a sensationalistic shocker, and it had already been read and rejected by Paramount as unsuitable for filming. But Hitchcock and the executives at the studio were on divergent paths; Paramount wanted glossy entertainments like *North by Northwest*, whereas Hitchcock was minded to move into much darker territory.

Psycho, with its graphic violence and overt sexual perversion, was a long way away from the inoffensive thrillers at which Hitchcock excelled; it was in territory which was considered to be the exclusive preserve of horror and exploitation filmmakers. Hitchcock's decision to option Bloch's novel was one that his closest collaborators warned could backfire and tarnish the reputation that he had worked so exhaustively to build.

With Paramount regarding *Psycho* with some distaste, Wasserman persuaded Hitchcock to finance the film through his own company, Shamley Productions, with Paramount taking a reduced share in exchange for the distribution rights. For once, Wasserman's advice was less than altruistic; in December 1958, MCA had extended its interests into film production and it had bought ailing giant Universal-International. The deal was finalised in February 1959, and it transformed Lew Wasserman from the most powerful agent in Hollywood into one of the most powerful film moguls of the new age. Wasserman was now keen for Hitchcock to make the move from Paramount to Universal, and *Psycho* presented an opportunity for him to ease Hitch into MCA's new set up. By November, Hitchcock had moved his production office into a purpose-built bungalow on the Universal lot, with adjuncts for his assistants, his secretaries and his writers, as well as facilities to edit and screen movies. It gave Hitch an empire, where his word would be law.

Hitchcock's approach to the material was in keeping with the risky nature of the project. The rights to the novel had been acquired for a mere $9000, with MCA driving so hard a bargain that Bloch was excluded from any share of the film's profits. Even so, Hitchcock felt that he needed to keep costs low, and he allocated a modest $800,000 to the project and a shooting schedule of only five weeks; he was back in 'B' movie territory again and to reduce costs still further, he engaged his television crew, who already worked cheaply and quickly, and opted for black and white film stock.

This policy of thrift extended to the casting of the movie. Anthony Perkins was offered the leading role. Perkins was to be the highest-paid member of the cast, but as a Paramount contractee, he could still be obtained relatively cheaply. Janet Leigh, who was under contract to Universal, was signed as the film's nominal leading lady; she was a friend of Wasserman's, who had guided her career since she first arrived in Hollywood. Vera Miles, who was already on salary, was given a major supporting role, as was MCA client John Gavin.

Hitchcock set James Cavanagh onto adapting *Psycho* while he attended to the casting, but he soon dispensed with Cavanagh's services when early drafts did not meet his requirements. Acting on the recommendation of Lew Wasserman, he handed the project to Joseph Stefano, whose only previous credit of note was a 'weepie' for Sophia Loren and Anthony Quinn (*The Black Orchid*). Stefano worked with Hitchcock to restructure much of Bloch's book, including changing killer Norman Bates from a middle-aged, overweight misfit with a drink problem into a younger, good-looking youth, whose worst vice *seems* to be an addiction to candy. Abandoning the more grisly of the real Gein's traits, Stefano's script presented the audience with an isolated motel in which lurked a transvestite murderer. Into this searing glimpse of American Gothic steps Marion Crane, a secretary on the run with $40,000 of her employer's money and looking for somewhere to rest for the night while she works out her next move. The rest, as they say, is now movie history.

Hitchcock's relationship with Janet Leigh, who played Marion Crane, was the model of professionalism. An experienced screen actress and the wife of Tony Curtis, Leigh had none of the lithe sophistication of Grace Kelly or even Eva Maria Saint, but she had an easy-going manner that suited Hitchcock and complemented the pace at which the crew were working. 'I hired you because you are a talented actress. You are free to do whatever you wish with the role of Marion,' he told her when she arrived on set. 'I won't interfere unless you are having trouble and require my guidance.' That edict set the pattern for the shoot and extended to the other

Publicity shot for Psycho (Vera Miles, John Gavin, Janet Leigh)

members of the cast, including Vera Miles, who expressed her annoyance at being cast as Marion's frumpy older sister. Hitchcock laughed off suggestions that he was punishing her.

If *Psycho* was a next step, then it was a journey that had begun long before Grace Kelly, and changing attitudes towards what was acceptable on the screen enabled the darker side of Hitch to emerge from behind the camera. The decision to finance the film through Shamley Productions neatly side-stepped the moral strictures of a major studio, and the explicitness of the film was almost a celebration of Hitchcock's freedom as a result. *Psycho* opens with a love scene between a semi-naked, unmarried couple in the middle of the day—an act with a clear connotation of sleaze; there is a further scene of Leigh in her underwear (complete with flash of breast as she strips for the shower), followed by a graphic murder-scene, the like of which had never been seen before in terms of its sheer brutality.

The Production Code is further flaunted by a script that wallows in transvestism, incest, voyeurism and the repeated use of 'profane' language. Even the sight of a toilet being flushed was considered to be beyond the pale in mainstream American cinema. The Breen Office was so outraged by the script that Hitchcock was warned that his film could be uncertifiable, and therefore unreleasable in the States. When *Psycho* was submitted to the censors, Hitch made a number of concessions over the shower-sequence, which allowed him to keep other scenes intact. In the UK, British censor John Trevelyan thought the shower-sequence less offensive because it was black and white, but he still insisted on cuts 'to lessen the sadism'.

Psycho's famous 'shower scene' was the highlight of the film, as Hitchcock had intended it to be. He had shot it over seven days, lavishing the same care and attention to detail upon it that he had on the attempted slaying of Grace Kelly in *Dial M for Murder*; title-designer Saul Bass had 'storyboarded' the montage to Hitchcock's designs, and Janet Leigh's frantic attempts to fend off her attacker were accomplished with the aid of body-double Marli Renfro. So shocking was the end-result that when the film was released in June 1960 as 'Alfred Hitchcock's *Psycho*', the pun was probably intentional.

Publicity shot from Psycho (Janet Leigh)

Hitchcock threw himself into the promotion of *Psycho* with gusto—he had a lot to gain if the film was a success. In the absence of box-office stars, the publicity was built around his name and image, and he conceived the ideas of allowing no-one into theatres after the show had begun and asking critics not to give the game away—both of which intrigued the public. He also shot an extended trailer in which he took viewers on a whistle-stop tour of the Bates Motel, making droll observations and hinting at dark deeds behind the sunny facade.

For his efforts, Hitchcock was rewarded with a film that turned out to be his biggest box-office success and one of his most enduring and iconic movies, though many critics reacted in horror at what they regarded as its tawdry and deliberately-exploitative quality. If Hitchcock had had his way, it would have been more explicit still; the opening lovemaking, for example, had Leigh in a brassiere, but Hitchcock said, 'I can see nothing immoral about that scene and I get no special kick out of it. But the scene would have been more interesting if the girl's bare breasts had been rubbing against the man..'

Psycho was to change forever the public's perception of a 'Hitchcock film'. No longer was he to be associated with glossy thrillers set in exotic locations; now, he had to scare the pants off his audience and push the boundaries of taste to ever further extremes. It was a path that Hitchcock would be only too willing to follow in the years ahead.

Chapter 7

Marnie

Hitch directs 'Tippi' Hedren in Marnie

'Had any trouble with the birds?' asked Nat.
'Birds? What birds?'
'We got them up our place last night. Scores of them, came in the children's bedroom. Quite savage they were.'
'Oh?' It took time for anything to penetrate Jim's head. 'Never heard of birds acting savage,' he said at length. 'They get tame, like, sometimes. I've seen them come to the windows for crumbs.'
'These birds last night weren't tame.'

– Daphne du Maurier, *The Birds* (1952)

Having honoured his commitment to the promotion of *Psycho*, Hitchcock settled back in his bungalow office on the Universal lot to consider his next project. His relationship with his old ally Lew Wasserman had changed from the moment that Hitchcock moved from his film-by-film deal with Paramount and signed a new contract with Universal. While Hitch was a client of MCA, Wasserman effectively worked for him, but with Wasserman running the studio, he found himself in a position as employee to his former advisor—albeit one of Universal's most important assets. Aware of the sensitive nature of their change of roles, Wasserman went out of his way to ensure that Hitch was comfortable with the arrangement; installing a layer of management between Hitch and the studio executives meant that Wasserman could drop by his bungalow for lunch or a drink, or simply to discuss the latest gossip. If Wasserman did need to talk business with Hitchcock, he would still make the trip across the lot rather than summoning Hitch to him. To all intents and purposes, Hitchcock squatted in his office suite at Universal like a potentate, while the head of studio paid homage. But the truth was that Lew Wasserman was now in the driving seat.

Hitchcock's already-considerable wealth was further enhanced when he decided to sell Shamley Productions to Universal for a cash sum and stock options. The studio acquired the rights to the television series as well as Hitchcock's share of *Psycho* and, in return, he became the third-largest shareholder in Universal. This made Wasserman's diplomatic balancing-act all the more delicate, but as head of Universal, he had the right of veto over Hitchcock's projects and it was a power that he would not be afraid to use.

Hitchcock had a number of projects on file that he could have enacted to inaugurate his new relationship with Universal, including a more explicit revision of *No Bail for the Judge*; he also considered an idea about a blind jazz singer whose sight is restored when he is given the eyes of a murdered man during a transplant operation. But Wasserman had urged him to think along the lines of *To Catch a Thief* and *North by Northwest*, and Hitch decided to meet the studio halfway. What he sought was a project that would be suitable for a screen partnership like that of Grant and Kelly, but he also wanted it to have the dark and subversive tone of *No Bail for the Judge* and the graphic shock-element of *Psycho*. Inspiration came in the form of a short story by Daphne du Maurier, called *The Birds*.

The Birds tells of an isolated community whose inhabitants are subjected to unprovoked assaults by birds. What at first appear to be random attacks quickly increase in ferocity and number, and the story takes on the bleak, apocalyptic tone of an end-of-the-world scenario, if not a political parable. Either way, it made a strange, almost surreal choice.

Hitchcock nevertheless liked the basic premise, and the allusive nature of the slim work provided a perfect template on which he could build. The first of his alterations was the now- obligatory relocation to America, in this case the California coast. Du Maurier's characters, a local farmer and his family, had only a passing interest for Hitch; he wanted more colourful protagonists to face the feathered onslaught. After considering a number of possible writers (Joseph Stefano, his first choice, was busy on TV sci-fi series *The Outer Limits*), Hitchcock picked up on a suggestion from Joan Harrison and hired Evan Hunter, the acclaimed author of *The Blackboard Jungle*, as well as a number of crime thrillers under his pen-name of Ed McBain. It was Hunter who came up with the idea of having a schoolteacher visit the town at the time of the initial attacks; the teacher would become a target for the anger and frustrations of the locals, who would believe her somehow to be the instigator of the violence. Hitchcock liked the concept of the 'stranger in our midst', but he did not like the fact of his leading lady being a schoolma'am. He wanted someone more refined, more sophisticated.. Someone more like—Grace Kelly, perhaps.

If Hitchcock had felt any bitterness or rejection when Kelly married Rainier, he never let it show. To the contrary, he had gone to great pains to cultivate a close personal relationship with the prince, often sending him amusing notes and other personal messages. The reason was simple: staying on good terms with Rainier was a key factor in securing Kelly's return to the screen, and Hitch remained determined to do just that as soon as circumstances allowed. The time was not yet right, but it would not be long in coming.

With the prototypical 'Hitchcock blonde' still unavailable for any duty other than that of royal princess, Hitch searched through a number of possible alternatives, including Sandra Dee and Carol Lynley, without coming upon the elusive qualities that he was looking for. The exercise might have been simply to placate the studio; Hitch already had a fall-back position in place for just such an eventuality, but it

'Tippi' Hedren

meant returning to an idea that had seemed to be dead in the water. Just as Vera Miles was hired as the 'next Grace Kelly', Hitchcock had been acquiring actresses to be the 'next' Vera Miles.

The first starlet whom Hitch had put under contract after Miles was 28-year-old Joanna Moore, a Southern beauty queen who had appeared in *Touch of Evil* (1958) with Janet Leigh. Moore was blonde, and with the striking looks of a model, but she was no pushover; she did not like the hairstyles or the clothes that Hitch foisted onto her and was not slow in saying so. Try as he might, Hitchcock could not persuade her that the best course of action to further her career was to pay obeisance to him and Moore stubbornly refused to be transformed. She appeared in a handful of episodes of his TV show, none of which he directed himself, until he finally tired of her attitude and wanted nothing more to do with her. Moore's contract was allowed to lapse.

Hitchcock found Claire Griswold more amenable. Griswold had a small part in 'I Saw the Whole Thing', a television episode that he directed in 1962, and he picked up her contract and submitted her to the regulatory 'star treatment': hair, clothes and lifestyle all came under the Hitchcock spotlight. Hitch also shot a series of test-reels of the actress while holding out the carrot of a leading role in his next movie. Griswold had the beauty and the physique that Hitchcock admired, but she lacked the drive and ambition that had singled out Grace Kelly; she was also married to acting coach and future film director Sidney Lumet, and it gradually became obvious to Hitch that Griswold merely wanted to play the role of wife and mother; After a second outing for him on television, she retired from acting to do just that. By then, it hardly mattered to Hitch: he had started to groom another actress whom he would put under contract—one, more than any other, who would come to personify all the hopes and dreams that he had for his protégés. She would also become the cause of his most damaging personal failure. Her name was Tippi Hedren.

Hitch and Alma were at home watching TV when their attention was drawn to a young woman in a commercial who had turned round in response to a wolf-whistle and flashed an engaging smile at the camera. Something about that smile struck a chord, and the Hitchcocks agreed that the girl in question bore a striking similarity to Grace Kelly. The next day, Hitch instructed MCA to track her down and bring her in for interview, with a view to signing her to an exclusive contract.

Tippi Hedren was a native of Minnesota, but she had relocated to New York to pursue a career as a model; she then moved to California with her daughter Melanie (later to become a successful actress in her own right under the name of Melanie Griffiths) in the hope of more lucrative work in television. When Hedren was summoned to

MCA, she assumed that it was for an audition for a commercial, and she brought a portfolio of photographs and a show-reel of her other work. Hitchcock's name was never mentioned, nor was there any suggestion of a contract. The following week, she was called to another meeting and, subsequent to that, she was offered an exclusive seven-year contract. Although he had kept a close eye on the whole process, poring over the photos and quizzing the MCA interviewers, Hedren never met Hitchcock until she signed on the dotted line—at which point, she was paraded in front of her new employer, who toasted her good fortune with a bottle of very expensive champagne.

Hitchcock's characteristic thriftiness soon kicked in and, when it came to the terms of her contract, Hedren found her future employer less than generous. Hitch offered her a paltry $500 a week for the first year, with modest annual increases thereafter. It was substantially less than she could earn as a model but it offered her the kind of security that modelling never could—an important consideration for a single mother. In addition, she would enjoy the prestige of having Alfred Hitchcock mentor her career, even if accepting his terms meant that his authority would extend beyond the roles she played to the way that she looked, dressed and behaved.

The transformation of Hedren began immediately, and the remit was wide-ranging. She was to report to Bellagio Road, where Hitch and Alma were to conduct master-classes to drill her in the fundamentals of being an actress; she was also introduced to Edith Head, who was to design her wardrobe, as well as make-up artists and hairdressers who would ensure that she attained the standards required of a 'Hitchcock blonde'. When he was satisfied with her progress, Hitch arranged what subsequently has been described as 'the most expensive screen test in the history of Hollywood'. Actor Martin Balsam, who had starred in *Psycho*, was flown from New York to play opposite Hedren in a number of scenes from *Notorious* and *Rebecca*; these were not mere dialogue tests—they were conducted in full costume and shot on real sets. As Hitch did not own the rights to either film, the footage was viewed and ultimately destroyed. Hitch also had Balsam play the Cary Grant character in a re-enactment of the picnic scene from *To Catch a Thief* with its double-entendres and erotic undercurrent; these tests, which were shot in colour, were preserved.

Content with what he had seen through the lens of his camera, Hitchcock performed one final refinement: Hedren had been christened Natalie, but she had adopted her father's pet-name for her when she started to model; Hitch, for reasons known only to himself, decided to add single 'quotes' to the name and she became 'Tippi' Hedren from that point on.

From the outset, Hitchcock took a paternal interest in his new protégé; after remarking that he thought her too thin, he had several sacks of potatoes delivered to her apartment! Throughout this period of induction, Hedren displayed nothing but a willingness to please her employer and, more importantly for a man who sought to avoid conflict at all cost, she showed no signs of resistance to Hitchcock's views—his word was final. If 'Tippi' had any reservations, she did not confide them to him. That is not to say that she was weak-willed—quite the reverse: she was fully committed to the task and determined to prove herself as an actress and therefore worthy of the time and effort that was being expended upon her. For the first time, Hitch had found himself a willing pupil. More than that, he had found another Grace Kelly.

As the process of turning Hedren into a star continued, Hitchcock's largesse shifted from the practical to the decorative; flowers, jewellery and other tokens of his esteem appeared at 'Tippi's' apartment with some regularity—which were interpreted by Hedren as signs that she was pleasing her benefactor. But despite the attention that was lavished upon her, Hitchcock remained tight-lipped about

***The Birds* ('Tippi' Hedren, Rod Taylor)**

the project for which he had wanted 'Tippi' in the first place, and it was not until she was asked to dinner at *Chasen's* with the Hitchcocks and the Wassermans that the director revealed to her what he had in mind. In a typically dramatic gesture, 'Tippi' was handed a jewellery box containing a gold pin in the shape of three birds in flight, inlaid with seed-pearls: the former model, who had never acted in a film before, had done enough to earn herself the leading role in what would be Hitchcock's most expensive film to date, *The Birds*.

Lew Wasserman's presence at *Chasen's* was not the wholehearted support of Hitchcock's choice that it was intended to be; the Universal studio boss expressed concern about 'Tippi's' inexperience, but he was reassured by Hitch that it was not a problem and that he personally would ensure that she acquitted herself appropriately. After all, had he not done the same for Grace Kelly, whose early performances gave no indication of star quality? Wasserman agreed that Hedren certainly had the looks to be a star, and he accepted the director's word that he could make her into an actress; *The Birds* was given the green light.

With Evan Hunter and Hitchcock jokingly referring to the main characters in *The Birds* as 'Grace' and 'Cary', they set about constructing their story around the female lead. 'Tippi's' character of Melanie Daniels was put at the centre of the action, in a role especially designed to showcase her looks and shine the best possible light on her acting abilities. Melanie was a bored socialite with a slightly dubious reputation and an impulsive nature—a perfect role for an actress whom Hitch assured the press, possessed 'a faster tempo, city glibness and more humour' than Grace Kelly. And he told reporters that his new star had 'assuredness, pertness, and an attractive throw of the head'.

With the Hitchcock name enough to assure the film of marquee value, there was no need to break the budget and hire an 'A'-lister as a leading man—even if they could find one willing to play second-fiddle to an unknown blonde. After some

The Birds ('Tippi' Hedren)

consideration, Hitch settled on Rod Taylor, a physical Australian actor with a passing resemblance to Cary Grant, who had played second-fiddle to a veritable army of unknown blondes (in the shape of the Eloi and the Morlocks) in George Pal's sci-fi spectacular *The Time Machine* (1960). Taylor was cast as Mitch, a charismatic, big-city lawyer, who makes an immediate impression on Melanie when she bumps into him during a shopping expedition. Melanie is so taken that she is prepared to resort to some playful subterfuge to find out more about him; in so doing, she follows in the footsteps of Lisa Fremont and Francie Stevens and determines to get her man, pursuing him to his family home in the remote costal community of Bodega Bay—where the titular 'birds' are poised to strike..

The film started shooting on March 22, 1962, and would eventually take over a year to complete—largely due to the complex special effects. Hitchcock's schedule required Hedren for twenty weeks work, including eight days on location at California's Bodega Bay; in all that time, she was to be afforded only one day off. Once again, Hitch went through the routine of overseeing the wardrobe for 'Melanie Daniels', giving Edith Head detailed instructions on how she should look on film. It was a familiar pattern for those who worked with Hitch, but his interest in Hedren seemed to go beyond the mere shaping of a character—he appeared to want the actress by his side throughout the whole of the filmmaking process: Hedren sat in on the daily production meetings, and she became a fixture at conferences with his heads of department, as though Hitch were intent on educating her in every aspect of the business—or, conversely, as though he were trying to make her fall in love with him.. When shooting started, his mentoring took on a more proprietorial edge, and he had members of the crew follow her around and report to him on where she had been and who she had seen.

The director who told Janet Leigh he would not direct every nuance unless she needed it, was suddenly giving the most precise instructions to his new leading lady and the greatest of care was taken over the slightest detail—the turn of a head, the casting of an eye. 'I brought her to Hollywood, I changed everything about her. "Svengali Hitchcock" rides again,' he was later to confide to David Lewin of the *Sunday Express*. During a press junket in London, he went further. 'You know she had never acted before.. she had nothing to unlearn. I controlled every movement on her face. She did purely cinematic acting of very fine shadings all the time. She wasn't allowed to do anything beyond what I gave her. It was my control entirely.'

Hitchcock's 'control' over 'Tippi' Hedren was never more apparent than when he came to shoot a scene in which Melanie was to be trapped in a room and viciously attacked by birds. Hitchcock told Hedren that they would be using model birds, with effects added afterwards, but the tests were so unconvincing that he had decided to use real birds instead. 'I always believe in following the advice of the playwright Sardou,' Hitchcock had claimed once, his tongue firmly in his cheek. 'He said, "Torture the women!"' It was a quote that would come back to haunt him over his treatment of Hedren when it came to filming the scene.

Hedren was not told that she would be acting opposite real birds until she arrived on the set, by which time the crew had worked out how it could be done but not what the impact was going to be. Shooting started with two men in protective suits literally throwing live birds at the actress, who was outfitted in normal clothes and told (unnecessarily, as it happened) to wave her arms about 'as if to protect herself'. Not only was the scene physically exhausting, it was gruelling and unpleasant for Hedren, and the assumption among the crew was that the required shots would be captured as quickly as possible. As the morning passed, Hitchcock expressed himself dissatisfied with the results and shooting continued for the rest of the day, and for two days following. On the fourth day, Hitch decided that enough was enough; the birds simply did not look as though they were attacking Hedren—if anything, they looked as though they were intent on getting out of her way.

It was then someone suggested that the desired effect might be achieved if the birds were tied to Hedren's clothes with elastic bands—at least they would not be able to exit the scene as soon as the camera started to roll. Hitchcock ignored signs of fatigue from Hedren, as well as her growing unease with the situation, and resumed shooting. The birds, unable to escape, reacted in alarm and turned on Hedren in their panic, and she found herself acting 'for real' in her frantic attempts to ward them away from her face. Cary Grant, who was visiting the set as the scene unfolded, was appalled at Hedren's ordeal and called her 'one of the bravest girls I have ever seen'. By day five, Hedren was close to physical and mental exhaustion; when one of the birds scratched her face, narrowly missing an eye, she became hysterical and collapsed. Hitch had no choice but to call a halt, but he saw no reason not to continue from where he was forced to leave off after the weekend break. On the following Monday, Hedren returned to the set, but she was in such a state that filming could not resume; she was sent home and told to rest for at least a week.

Despite the sufferings of Hedren and the best endeavours of cast and crew, the finished film fell a long way short of Hitchcock's expectations for it. He would later deliver that most damning of verdicts: 'Alma had never liked the original idea of doing *The Birds*. She didn't think there was enough story there. Well, she was right. Not enough story, too many birds,' he said. Putting on a braver face at the time of the film's release, he boasted to the press that *The Birds* would herald a new 'golden age' for himself and his work. Audiences on the whole were lukewarm; too much ambiguity in relation to the bird attacks and the deliberate lack of a satisfactory conclusion annoyed and frustrated them in equal measure. *The Birds* returned a profit but it fell a long way short of *Psycho*. The critics had mixed views on the merits

Hitch and Hedren in promotional mode for The Birds

of the film, but they were uniform in their low opinion of 'Tippi' Hedren—though *Time Out* thought her 'pleasant, and ladylike.. *as Grace Kelly was*.'

> **He put his hand on my shoulder and then to my disgust suddenly brushed the nylon down and put his hand right over my breast. He put his hand right round it. It was just as if he held something that belonged to him.**
> **'Let me go,' I said.**
>
> —Winston Graham, *Marnie* (1961)

For a man who was normally placid and reserved, Hitchcock had suffered mood-swings during the filming of *The Birds*. Part of this was due to the technical rigours of making a film that turned out to be so heavily-reliant on special effects, but some of it was down to the fact that after years of patience and gentle cajoling, he had come excruciatingly close to tempting Grace Kelly back in front of his cameras.

Since last appearing on screen in *High Society*, Kelly had settled into her role as Princess Grace of Monaco with quiet fortitude. Aside from the usual household duties, she had been required to tour orphanages and day care centres, become the president of Monaco's leading charity, The Red Cross, and look glamorous and serene at state functions. She had no formal role to play in her husband's business affairs, however, and the general administration and government of Monaco was left to its head of state, Prince Rainier.

Hollywood, or at least the more socially-acceptable parts of it, had nevertheless remained in the background. Hitchcock and his wife would visit the principality whenever they contrived to be in the area, and Kelly could always rely on old friends like Cary Grant, David Niven, Ava Gardner or Frank Sinatra to drop in occasionally, or lend a touch of razzmatazz to any fund-raising activities; among the other regular visitors were Jay Kanter and his wife Judy, both of whom she counted as personal friends. The former, in his professional capacity, was still her agent and, as well as keeping her up to date with news from California, he would ensure that any script enquiries were forwarded on to the Palace. Offers still came Kelly's way, such as the role of the mother of Christ in the Samuel Bronston/Nicholas Ray biblical epic, *King of Kings* (1961). Producers seemed to think that a film with a religious theme was the most reverent way to entice Her Royal Highness out of retirement, and she was also to be offered George Stevens's *The Greatest Story Ever Told* (1965). Whenever a studio felt the need to generate some column inches in the press, Kelly's name would be 'associated' with a project—whether she was aware of it or not. Kelly respectfully declined all offers, and she would shake her head politely when the question of her acting again arose in interview. But despite her stance in public, she never instructed her agents to stop sending scripts, which only fuelled speculation at MCA that she would one day return to the screen.

Rainier was aware that Kelly's air of detachment was in part a façade, and that there was a vacuum in her life that royal duties were insufficient to fill. He offered some insight into his wife's state of mind to his biographer, Peter Hawkins: 'There were times.. when the Princess [was] a little melancholic—which I quite understand—about having performed a form of art very successfully, only to be cut away from it completely.' He claimed that it was geography, rather than her new vocation, which kept Kelly from the screen: 'Let's imagine that we had gone on living in New York, or London or Paris,' he said. 'She would have been able to keep up with acting activities.'

Grace Kelly's emotional world had been in a state of some flux since the birth of her son Albert. Her disquiet had been compounded by two miscarriages which had followed the birth and plunged the Palace into a state of near-mourning. In

Princess Grace and Prince Rainier celebrate their 4th wedding anniversary in 1960, and attend the 1st International Television Awards in 1961

June 1960, Jack Kelly died and she lost one of the rocks on which she had built her life. His financial support had given her the means to succeed at AADA, as well as sustaining her through the early years in New York and Hollywood; more than money, he had gifted his daughter with ambition, drive and the guile to achieve her goals. By elevating the Kelly bloodline into true-blue royalty, she had repaid him with the one thing that he could not acquire on his own: she had put him on a par with the top echelons of society. When she exchanged vows with Rainier in Monaco's cathedral, Kelly became part of the aristocracy, and none of *her* children would ever be barred from Henley Regatta or excluded from a debutante's ball.

Insiders at the Palace intimated that after her father's death, Kelly had become surly and lackadaisical, showing little concern for royal duties. According to those closest to the couple, a gulf was opening between then; they were quarrelling over the slightest things and seemed to go out of their respective ways to avoid each other's company. When a member of Kelly's staff was dismissed without explanation, rumours of extra-martial liaisons on Rainier's part darkened the mood still further.

Hitchcock had remained an avid observer of events in Monaco, maintaining both casual contacts with the royal couple and appraising himself of news through the channel of MCA, and the signs that he might revisit the scene of his greatest personal triumph were becoming more positive by the day. In 1961, on his return from a trip to the South of France, Cary Grant had informed Hitch that he thought Kelly was ready to make her screen comeback; this view would later be verified by actress Rita Gam, who had stopped by to see her old friend on her way back from the Berlin Film Festival, where she had been given a Best Actress award for *Sinners Go to Hell* (1962). It was the news that Hitchcock had been waiting for since 1956: having toyed with a number of ideas over the years, he was confident that he had the perfect project with which to lure his princess back to Hollywood.

Marnie was a psychological crime-thriller by Winston Graham, a Mancunian author who was best-known for his series of 'Poldark' historical novels set in the Cornwall of the 1780s. The story told of a beautiful but psychologically-disturbed female kleptomaniac, who is forced into marrying a millionaire industrialist who has become besotted with her, despite falling victim to one of her habitual scams. Hitchcock had been sent the manuscript before the book was published, and he was immediately attracted to the complex character of Marnie Edgar and her twilight world of theft and deception: Marnie is a confident and alluring woman on the surface, but she has been so traumatised by an incident in her childhood that she has become frigid and incapable of forming normal human relationships. Evan Hunter, who was to work on the script, described the character as 'a clever and witty woman. But she is also afraid and mysteriously remote—and terrified of men. If a man touches her she becomes violent.'

In January 1961, MCA offered Graham's agent the sum of $25,000 for the film rights, the recipient of which was to remain anonymous. Its offer was declined, but MCA persisted and the price was raised to $50,000—enough to indicate a major movie in prospect. Only after a deal was struck was the identity of the interested party revealed, and agreement was reached with the publishers for Hitchcock's name to be used to promote the book, as well as the mooted film version. The Bodley Head promotional campaign to launch *Marnie* hailed it as a forthcoming *Alfred J Hitchcock Production*, with Hitch's image on the book-jacket and a full-page advertisement in *Publisher's Weekly*, which attempted to explain the connection in a teasing headline: *Why is Marnie the perfect Hitchcock heroine?* Describing the character as 'an accomplished liar, forger and embezzler,' the ad carried a quote from Hitchcock in which he nominated Marnie, 'one of the most unusual heroines I've encountered'.

Lew Wasserman did not agree; he disliked the book and thought the title-character and lurid subject-matter unappealing. Like Paramount before it, Universal had assumed that its association with Hitchcock would yield big, prestigious pictures with international stars and, *Psycho* notwithstanding, it was looking to him to come up with another *North by Northwest*. (*The Prize*, a more typical 'Hitchcock picture' made around the same time and scripted by *North by Northwest*'s Ernest Lehman, was made by MGM and directed by Mark Robson.) To counter Wasserman's distaste of the project, Hitchcock produced his trump card: he told Wasserman he was now confident that he could get Grace Kelly's signature onto a contract to play the lead role in *Marnie*. The Universal boss was convinced, and Hitch was sanctioned to begin the courting process.

With his predilection for reinventing his own history, Hitchcock later insisted that he did nothing to persuade Kelly to the film. 'I never went after Grace, you know. I saw her and the Prince several times over dinner in Paris but I am too much of a gentleman to mention work to a princess. That would be most uncouth,' he explained to Peter Evans of the *Daily Express*. 'I waited, and finally she came to me.' It was Hitchcock portraying himself as the irresistible flame that attracts the moth—the cinematic genius with the power to lure the most beautiful women in the world to his productions. Romantic it may be, but Hitchcock's version jars with that put forward by Kelly's sister Lizanne, who would tell of him whispering in the princess's ear for some time: 'They want you back, he kept repeating like a scratched record,' she said, and declared that he made a special trip to Monaco to pitch the idea personally to Kelly.

Hitchcock, with Universal's endorsement, outlined the story in broad terms to Kelly and Rainier but specifically asked them not to read the book before they had seen his treatment; he assured them that he was intending to make 'substantial changes' to it. It was Joseph Stefano, the screenwriter of *Psycho*, who initially was entrusted to carry out Hitchcock's revisions.

In February 1961, just as soon as he had acquired the rights, Hitchcock had handed the book to Stefano and asked him to do a treatment. Stefano reshaped the narrative and tightened the characterisation, and he was particularly interested in the psychological aspects of the story—he was seeing an analyst at the time and he brought some of his own experiences to bear on the script. Throughout the process, it was an open secret between Hitch and Stefano that the film was intended for Kelly, and Hitchcock often referred to the character of Marnie as 'HSH' (Her Serene Highness); to make the project even more appealing to his target, the action was switched to the nostalgically-familiar locales of Philadelphia and Maryland.

Stefano worked on his treatment through the summer, but not until November did Hitch feel confident enough in the material to submit it to Universal for approval. This draft, which had no dialogue, was the one that was given the green-light and, from there, Hitchcock and MCA initiated negotiations with Kelly to secure her commitment. The treatment had none of the detail of a screenplay but it was enough to excite the interest of the princess. Rainier, who often spoke of Hitchcock as being 'family friend' and a 'filmmaker that we both could trust', took the director at his word that there would be nothing in the completed script that would compromise his wife's regal standing or personal dignity. Throughout this time, Hitchcock's public pronouncements about the film were deliberately vague as to his eventual intentions and Marnie was described merely as a 'lady robber'—an innocuous expression, designed to conjure vague images of a female version of Cary

Grant's Raffles-like persona in *To Catch a Thief*. Privately, Hitch confided to friends that he was making a 'sex mystery'.

Aside from the appeal of working with Hitchcock again, it is not difficult to understand why the actress in Grace Kelly would have been attracted to the role of Marnie; it is harder to fathom why Princess Grace, wife of the head of the oldest royal family in Europe, might have wanted to make such a film. According to Stefano, Hitchcock had the idea that the Grimaldis were short of cash and that Kelly's considerable salary—which he estimated would be in six figures—would be used to swell the Palace's depleted coffers. But it seems unlikely that their financial position was such that Kelly needed to return to work in order to balance the books; her family had paid a $2m dowry to Rainier in order to sanction the wedding. Jack Kelly's will had not been over-generous to his daughter, but Prince Rainier was still a man of means on his own account. Hitchcock would revisit his version of events later, when the project was on the brink of floundering.

> *'Her Serene Highness, Princess Grace, is returning to Hollywood to appear during her summer vacation in a motion picture for Mr Alfred Hitchcock, to be made in the United States. The Princess has previously starred in three films for Mr Hitchcock. The film to start in late summer is based on a suspense novel by the English writer Winston Graham. It is understood that Prince Rainier will most likely be present during part of the filmmaking depending on his schedule and that Princess Grace will return to Monaco with her family in November...'*

By the time the news emerged from Monaco that Grace Kelly was to make time available for filming during the summer of 1962, Stefano had left the project; as usual, there had been no confrontation with Hitch—the writer merely found himself 'uninvolved'. Hitch handed the task of scripting *Marnie* to Evan Hunter, fresh from his chores on *The Birds*.

Hunter was not shown Stefano's treatment, but Hitch made it clear to him that there was only one actress in the running for the character of Marnie. Hunter told *Sight and Sound* that the director's mind was fixed from the outset: 'Who better to play a compulsive thief who also happens to be frigid because of a childhood trauma? Grace Kelly committing burglaries? Grace Kelly riding a horse after each theft? Grace Kelly being blonde and elegant and glacial and elusive? Grace Kelly being Grace Kelly.' When interviewed by the *Daily Express*, Hunter confessed to keeping a photograph of Kelly on his desk while he was writing the film.

Hitchcock now instructed Hunter to make a number of other enhancements to the story, including the merging of two of the men in Marnie's life, her analyst and her lover, into one character, with Mark Rutland emerging (courtesy of some late night reading) as something of an amateur psychiatrist. Next to Marnie, it was Mark who was to receive the most attention from Hitchcock: Mark was made younger and more virile than in the book—and a good deal more controlling; as Hitchcock explained, 'He has the fetish of a man wanting to go to bed with a thief, like going to bed with a coloured woman or a Chinese girl.' He subsequently told biographer Charlotte Chandler that he had seen Mark as a 'a late-Victorian, Edwardian type of hero,' and Hitchcock himself was born during the final years of Queen Victoria's reign and raised in the values of the Edwardian age. With the leading character having been remodelled as Grace Kelly, it became increasingly obvious to his various collaborators that Mark could be seen as an embodiment of Hitchcock's alter ego of a suave 'Svengali' figure whose power over women unleashes their 'inner fire'.

Marnie screenwriters Joseph Stefano (right) and Jay Presson Allen

Stefano had suggested that Mark's 'sadism' towards Marnie in forcing her into marriage and bedding her against her will is matched by a parallel masochism in her, and that captor and captive are equally attracted, but for different reasons; this was a mirror-image of the relationship between Francie and Robie in *To Catch a Thief*, but there the situation had been played largely for laughs. A more relaxed censorship regime now allowed Hitch the freedom to explore the deviant nature of this kind of sexual attraction more fully and, at one stage, he considered the idea of having Mark spy on Marnie as she commits one of her robberies and, unable to contain himself as a result, 'jumping at her and raping her on the spot.'

Hitchcock adopted his usual approach to the scripting process with Hunter, offering his thoughts on both story and characters during informal sessions. While Hitch worked on *The Birds*, Hunter was left to translate his ideas into a workable screenplay. On the whole, it was a straightforward and productive arrangement—but there was one scene in particular which troubled the writer. When Marnie and Mark embark on their honeymoon, Mark finds that he can no longer contain his pent-up desires and he strips and rapes the frigid Marnie. Hunter felt that the sudden switch in Mark's persona from that of sympathetic saviour to unthinking violator of a vulnerable woman was too extreme and would alienate audiences and threaten the integrity of the entire film. Hitchcock casually dismissed his writer's concerns, telling him that they could cross that bridge when they came to it. Hitch left for Bodega Bay to put 'Tippi' Hedren though her paces in *The Birds*, and Hunter returned to New York to put the finishing touches to *Marnie*.

Hitchcock was in Bodega Bay when the news of Kelly's casting was formally announced. He had accepted that royal protocol demanded the Palace be the first to make the statement, but he appeared to be caught off-guard with the suddenness of it. Hitchcock feigned surprise and was studiedly droll on his indifference to the idea. When reporters descended on the set of *The Birds* to quiz him about the coup, he quipped, 'I was told she would do it, just like that. I have not even spoken to her about it, not even a wire. I suppose I should send a wire, congratulations or something..'

Given the subject-matter of the novel in question, the press was determined to find out more and when Hitch was asked if Kelly's screen comeback would involve love scenes, he let the mask of disinterest slip for a moment. 'Passionate and most unusual love scenes,' he said, 'but I am afraid I cannot tell you anything beyond that. It is a state secret.' Hitch continued to tease the press, insisting that the public had totally the wrong impression of his leading lady. 'They think she is a cold fish; remote like Alcatraz out there,' he notioned. 'But she has sex appeal, believe me. She has subtle sex appeal of the English woman and that is the finest in the world. It is ice that will burn your hands, and that is surprising and exciting too.' For all his banter with the media, Hitchcock was giving nothing away and neither Kelly nor her royal spouse had any real inkling of how the script to *Marnie* was being shaped to play.

Across the Atlantic, the tiny press office in Monaco was suddenly swamped by a deluge of reporters trying to spirit out some hard facts. Kelly's private secretary, Phyllis Blum, could add little to the official announcement beyond the aside that 'Prince Rainier would probably be present during part of the filmmaking, depending on his schedule.' But the statement was enough to encourage the less reputable among those who heard it to speculate that Kelly's return to the screen was actually due to a reluctant prince indulging a petulant wife, a trial separation, an impending abdication and return to America for Rainier, or that preferred by Hitchcock—the need for a contribution towards the principality's balance of payments.

When the British press got in on the act, Winston Graham, who had no contact with Hitch and was not involved in the filmmaking process in any way, found himself mobbed at the airport on his return home from a trip abroad by frenzied journalists who wanted to know if Kelly was really going to make the film or if it was all a publicity stunt. There was no respite for him at his East Sussex cottage either, which was put under a state of siege by reporters who appeared to expect that Princess Grace, or Hitchcock, or both would be dropping in for tea at any moment.

The papers continued to make capital out of the story and managed to find a number of unnamed sources close to the princess who were only too pleased to confirm how 'happy she was now that she was going back to work' and how much she 'wanted to revive her career.' At first, even Rainier adopted a positive stance and told the *Daily Mail*, 'I am delighted. This is a friendly enterprise with a director we all like.' As reporters searched for a more interesting angle and began to dig deeper, his tone changed and he grew more defensive. When stories surfaced questioning the state of his marriage, Rainier flew into a rage and insisted, 'It's the most ridiculous nonsense to suggest that my wife is making a film because our marriage is breaking up or because Monaco is on the rocks. How stupid can people be?' But the more that Rainier denied it, the more he inadvertently fanned the flames. Gossip columnist Shelia Graham, writing for the *New York Mirror* sniped, 'I don't care what Prince Rainier says, the fact that his wife Grace Kelly is returning to her movie career—no matter what the reason—is indicative that something in some way has gone wrong with their marriage.'

Rainier and his princess could pretend to shrug off the criticisms of the press but, as the rulers of a Catholic state, it was harder to ignore the Pope, and John XXIII was reportedly unhappy at the example that was now being set by the mother of two young children. (Their daughter Caroline had been born in 1957.) However, the most damaging rumour was that Monaco itself was on the verge of bankruptcy and Kelly was bailing out its stagnant economy. Repeated denials by prince and

Grace Kelly in Monaco, circa 1961

princess seemed to have little effect, so Hitch was drafted in to lend moral support. Despite his comments to the contrary to Joseph Stefano, Hitchcock made a point of challenging one reporter with a terse, 'I don't think the money she makes will take care of the financial needs of a country.'

Hollywood 'sources' were soon confirming to the press that Kelly was being paid a salary of $1m, plus a percentage of the profits—a staggering sum, which would have put her in an exclusive club inhabited only by stars of the magnitude of Taylor and Brando. The figure was even more extraordinary when one considered that the actress had not made a film for seven years. The heavyweight newspapers found their own sources, who confirmed that Kelly was taking no money up front but was instead settling for a percentage of the gross. Inevitably, with that amount of money involved, the MGM management took a proprietary interest in its erstwhile employee and, noting the four-and-a-half years that remained on a contract which had never been rescinded, Joseph Vogel, MGM's head of production, wrote to Hitchcock and Universal in the strongest terms. The letter pointed out that the unexpired portion of Kelly's contract *'represented and represents an important and unused asset of this company.'* Vogel then went on to propose a compromise, that *'in all sense of fairness and equity, her return to the screen should be made with the participation of Metro-Goldwyn-Mayer.'*

MCA's legal team had over a year to prepare for exactly this challenge, and it reassured Hitch that he and the studio were on safe ground. Always happy to spare time for reporters, he interrupted filming on *The Birds* to insist that MGM's contract was not worth the paper it was written on: 'By the Statute of Limitations, it can last no more than seven years.'

The debate over Kelly's remuneration refused to die down, and it was becoming acutely embarrassing for the Palace. The royal couple were backed into a corner and belatedly they authorised a fresh announcement, delivered by Kelly's press secretary, which 'quoted' her as saying, 'In the same way as some priests or nuns perform common artistic, musical or sporting tasks for example, with the aim of raising funds for their work, I feel I am able to return to cinema for a film with the charitable aim of aiding needy children and young sportsmen.' By evoking a sanctimonious image for the cinematic endeavours of Her Serene Highness, the Vatican was placated and MGM effectively outmanoeuvred—the studio could hardly be seen to be taking money out of the pockets of 'needy children'—and the suggestion that it was a ruse to raise money for the Monacan treasury was quashed. The statement was worded to suggest that such had always been the intention, and that it was the press which had gotten hold of the wrong end of the stick.

To the outside world, the whole episode was something of a circus. But the

Marnie affair could not have come at a worse time for Rainier, who was facing a crisis which threatened the long-term future of himself and his line.

Relations between Rainier and France's President De Gaulle, barely cordial at the best of times, had grown distinctly frosty. The French had watched their tiny neighbour grow from a sleepy coastal anomaly with quaint royal pretensions into an exotic playground for the idle rich, complete with generous personal and corporate tax allowances and a relaxed attitude to gambling. The French state felt that it was entitled to a share of the cake and openly criticised the prince for his refusal to sanction foreign (that is, French) investment. Matters came to a head when Rainier expelled the French ambassador, and on April 11, De Gaulle served notice that he intended to end all French support for Monaco, including the provision of essential services such as power, water and phone—the move was destined to bring the principality to its knees within days.

Rainier and his cabinet went into eleventh-hour negotiations with the French in an effort to stave off financial ruin. He would ultimately have to back down completely and accept an humiliating *'compromis'* that acceded to all of De Gaulle's demands, but in the meantime, the fallout from the debacle was to have implications for Hitchcock and *Marnie*.

The French saw nothing glamorous or exciting in Kelly's supposed return to Hollywood; instead, it was viewed as an example of the self-serving decadence of an outdated aristocracy. The French press was openly hostile to the idea; *Le Monde*, for instance, told its readers, 'The Princess's place is not in Hollywood, but in Monaco beside her husband and children and among the people who have adopted her.' It added that the citizens of Monaco were similarly opposed, and it quoted the disbelief and dismay expressed by Her Serene Highness's subjects for good measure.

Added to the clamour that was emanating from Monaco, Hitchcock was facing frustrating delays on *The Birds*, where it had now become obvious that the complex special effects were to take far longer than was originally estimated and a deferment of *Marnie* was inevitable. Putting a brave face on impending disaster, Hitchcock told reporters, 'Grace and I have agreed to push back the picture definitely, not indefinitely, until next spring,' before retiring to brood in the quiet confines of his bungalow.

The postponement was indeed to be indefinite. The pressure on Kelly to withdraw from the project intensified, and Rainier felt duty-bound to review the options: his wife had made a verbal commitment to Universal, but no contract had been signed and she had not seen a script—certainly not Hitchcock's version of the script. Public opinion in Monaco and France was well and truly against Kelly making more films, and *Marnie* was being touted as betrayal of her subjects. Equally as important, the princess who had played such a significant part in Monaco's recent rise to prominence in the global community, to say nothing of its glamorous international image, was seen to be in danger of undoing all her good work and dragging the principality's reputation through the mud.

As 'Grace Kelly', Her Serene Highness Princess Grace had managed her career with the assurance of 'a tightrope walker,' in Hitchcock's view; now, she had been put in a position in which she had to re-evaluate her life and future goals, and it came down to a choice between remaining in Monaco and renouncing Hollywood, or return to Hollywood and turn her back on Monaco. The deciding factor for Kelly was the same as any mother: it was not the chance to work with Hitchcock, nor the opportunity to resurrect her career—it was altogether closer to home. Whatever the state of the royal marriage (and despite the speculation, no-one really knew for sure), if she had decided to return to America, she would have done so without her children. Caroline and Albert were an integral part of the Grimaldi bloodline, and they would remain in Europe with their father. Opinion may be divided on how much Grace Kelly did or did not love Prince Rainier, but there is no question as to where her loyalties lay; in a private letter published posthumously, she wrote: '*We have to sacrifice for our children. I am afraid it is necessary.*'

On June 18, 1962, Grace Kelly formulated a letter to Alfred Hitchcock:

'*Dear Hitch,*' she wrote.

'It was heartbreaking for me to have to leave the picture. I was so excited about doing it, and particularly about working with you again...

When we meet I would like to explain to you myself all of the reasons, which is difficult to do by letter or through a third party. It is unfortunate that it had to happen this way, and I am deeply sorry.

Thank you dear Hitch for being so understanding and helpful. I hate disappointing you. I also hate the fact that there are probably many other 'cattle' who could play the part equally well. Despite that I hope to remain one of your 'sacred cows'.

With deep affection,
Grace.'

Then, in another move calculated to win over the European audience, Kelly deliberately chose not to broadcast the news to the world's media and instead granted an interview to the French magazine, *Nice-Martin*: 'I am not going to do the movie after all,' she said, 'I have been influenced by the reaction which the announcement provoked in Monaco.' She went on to explain that the re-scheduling of the production would not allow her to spend the time that she needed to in Monaco, attending to her royal duties.

Hitchcock remained true to his character and upbringing: he held his feelings in check and penned a sympathetic response that was intended to leave the door open, if not for any further projects, then at least for a continuation of his friendship with Kelly. His handwritten note said merely—

'Yes it was sad, wasn't it. I was looking forward so much to the fun and pleasure of our doing a picture again.

Without a doubt, I think you made not only the best decision, but the only decision, to put the project aside at this time. After all, it was only a movie..'

Marnie was 'only a movie' because of Grace Kelly, and Hitch had laboured long and hard to make his dream-project a reality. Thus it was not to be consigned to the dustbin; there was too great an emotional investment for that. As soon as was practical after he had finished on *The Birds*, Hitchcock dusted down the script for *Marnie* and began to modify it for an actress who had shown that, unlike the others, she was prepared to go to extraordinary lengths for the director: 'Tippi' Hedren.

'You don't love me. I'm just something you've caught!'

—Marnie Edgar ('Tippi' Hedren), *Marnie* (1964)

When Hitchcock and Evan Hunter resumed work on *Marnie*, Hitch decided to tape their conversations, possibly with a view to creating a permanent record for future film students to pore over. He and Hunter then continued their conversations

June 18th 1962

Dear Hitch -

It was heart-breaking for me to have to leave the picture - I was so excited about doing it and particularly about working with you again -

When we meet I would like to explain to you myself all of the reasons which is difficult to do by letter or through a third party - It is unfortunate that it had to happen this way and I am deeply sorry - Thank you dear Hitch, for being so understanding and helpful - I hate disappointing you - I also hate the fact that there are probably many other "cattle" who could play the part equally as well - Despite that I hope to remain one of your "sacred cows" -

With deep affection -

Grace -

Hitchcock on set; (inset) the June 18 note from Princess Grace in relation, unperturbed by the eaves-dropping. It was when they came to discuss the rape scene that Hitchcock asked for the machine to be switched off.

The rape of Marnie by Mark Rutland has its basis in Graham's novel. After several tense days of 'honeymooning' in Spain, a drunk Marnie finally succumbs to Mark's advances with the words, 'One minute I felt I'd let him get on with his lovemaking and be like a cold statue to every feeling except hate, and just see what he made of that. But the next I was ready to fight him.. In the half dark he tried to show me what love was, but I was stiff with repulsion and horror, and when at last he took me there seemed to come from my lips a cry of defeat that was nothing to do with physical pain.' Evan Hunter remained convinced that the rape as Hitchcock wanted it would shatter audience sympathy with Mark's plight as a husband who has to deal with an unresponsive wife. Dismissing Hunter's concerns, Hitchcock described to the writer how he planned to shoot the scene. 'Hitch held up his hands,' Hunter recalled, 'the way directors do when they are framing a shot; palms out, fingers together, thumbs extended and touching to form a perfect square. Moving his hands towards my face, like a camera coming in for a close shot, he said, "Evan, when he sticks it in her, I want the camera right on her face."' Hunter was taken aback by what he regarded as a significant error of judgement but when he protested, he was told to write the scene as Hitchcock had outlined.

Hunter was convinced that when Hitch saw the damage that the rape did to the structure of the film, he would agree that it was a step too far; when he delivered the finished script, he included his own alternative version of the rape scene. In a covering note, he again explained his reasoning and urged Hitch to shoot the amended scene, 'for the good of the film'. Instead, he received a letter from Hitchcock, pointing out that there was 'still a lot of work to be done on it' and suggesting that they put it aside for a while and then approach it with a fresh mind. A few weeks later, Hunter's agent was informed that he had been removed from the project. There was no contact from Hitchcock, and the two men never spoke again.

Evan Hunter's replacement on *Marnie* was Jay (Jacqueline) Presson Allen, a hard-nosed Texans-born ex-actress and screenwriter, who had written a number of television scripts but only one film, the as-yet unproduced *The Prime of Miss Jean Brodie*. Many years after the release of *Marnie*, Hunter met Allen and told her that

he had argued vociferously against the rape scene, to which she replied, 'You just got bothered by the scene that was his reason for making the movie.'

Allen was far less squeamish than Hunter had been about the rape, and she laboured to transcribe Hitchcock's vision exactly as he had articulated it. Much of that work was done at Hitchcock's home in Bellagio Road, and Alma would chip in from time to time with ideas and observations. Freed from the encumbrance of *The Birds,* and with Grace Kelly now out of the running, Hitchcock devoted his energies to recasting the role of Marnie Edgar. For a time, he pretended that it was a close race between the two actresses who still remained in his private 'stable', Claire Griswold and 'Tippi' Hedren. Despite the teasing, Griswold was not interested, and Hedren's compliance on *The Birds* had already ensured that she was to be the preferred choice. Griswold was to announce that she was pregnant in the event, and her contract with Hitchcock was cancelled the following year.

Having played a character in *The Birds* who was created using the image of Grace Kelly, 'Tippi' Hedren was now shoehorned into a role which had also been devised with the princess in mind, and Hitchcock approached the shooting of *Marnie* with the idea that Hedren would not merely replace Kelly, she would *be* her.

The previous May, while Kelly was still attached to the project, the *Hollywood Reporter* announced that Rock Hudson had been lined up to play Mark Rutland. But due to the delays, Hitchcock had lost his option on the actor. In Hudson's place, Hitch made the unlikely choice of Scots-born Sean Connery, riding the crest of a wave as the screen's suave new secret agent James Bond 007 and currently one of the hottest leading men in films. Connery was to bring Bond's animal magnetism and distinctly dangerous edge to the role, which neither Graham's novel or Hitchcock's script envisaged in their leading man. Hitchcock liked Connery, but his casting was fuelled by the need to appease Lew Wasserman, still smarting at the loss of

On set: Hitch and 'Tippi' Hedren

Hitch directs Sean Connery in Marnie

Grace Kelly from the project. Connery, now a global superstar, was keen not to be typecast as Bond, and he agreed to accept second billing to Hedren in the US for the opportunity to work with Hitchcock and broaden his range (his contract still afforded him top billing in Britain).

Even when casting the supporting roles, Hitchcock seemed incapable of seeing beyond Kelly. Brunette Diane Baker had been a Fox contract artist, known only for her work in cheap programme-fillers like *Strait-Jacket* (1964), written by *Psycho* novelist Robert Bloch. Baker was awarded the role of Marnie's jealous sister-in-law and was invited to dinner at Bellagio Road to celebrate; amid the customary hospitality, she had to endure a misty-eyed Hitchcock poring over photographs of Kelly in her prime and telling her how alike he thought she and Baker looked. Baker had many of the qualities that Hitchcock admired in the actresses whom he placed under contract, and she was to become something of a confidante for the director during the troubled shoot.

Princess Grace may have been offered a six-figure salary for *Marnie*, but 'Tippi' Hedren was not about to receive anything remotely close. When shooting started in November 1963, Hedren's second leading role in a Hitchcock film was rewarded with a modest $100 a week pay-rise. There were other benefits, however, such as a purpose-built trailer for her exclusive use, stocked with fine wines and personalised stationery. Hedren's caravan was installed next to Hitchcock's bungalow on the Universal lot and to ensure that the actress felt suitably feted, he had champagne and flowers delivered to her on a daily basis. Hitchcock's generosity did not end with gifts; he was already talking about his next project, the long-cherished romantic ghost story *Mary Rose*, and the role in it that he had in mind for 'Tippi'. 'He was an old Turk,' Jay Presson Allen confided to writer Tony Lee Moral. 'He liked to control them.. He did have a Pygmalion complex about 'Tippi'.'

While still willingly submitting to Hitchcock's directorial demands, Hedren had

Marnie ('Tippi' Hedren, Sean Connery)

detected a subtle and unsettling change in their relationship—one which suggested to her that he was engaged in more than just the creation of a star. On Valentine's Day, Hitchcock had sent her a rambling telegram couched in romantic terms, which he had signed *Alfredus*. He later took Hedren aside and told her of a passionate dream which he had had about her, before ending with, 'If it wasn't for Alma..' He did not stop there; he constantly asked after her whereabouts and spoke openly with the crew about his feelings for 'Tippi', despite the fact that she was now engaged to her agent, Noel Marshall—a side-issue that Hitch chose to ignore.

Years after she finished with *Marnie*, Hedren would reflect on how suffocating she found Hitchcock's attention to be, insisting that she did nothing to encourage him or give him the idea that she was anything other than an actress working on a film. If she was uncomfortable, she never let it show either to Hitchcock or his crew—it was a price worth paying for stardom. By not protesting his over-weaning attitude, Hedren may inadvertently have fed Hitchcock's delusions with regard to her; in any event, a misunderstanding grew, and it was to have dire consequences for both parties.

From the first day of shooting on *Marnie*, Hitchcock gave 'Tippi' Hedren his full attention while he left Sean Connery, as was customary with his male leads, largely to his own devices. When she was not required in front of the camera, she was to be found resting in her trailer or sitting with Hitchcock in his office, being appraised of his latest ideas; they lunched together and they took tea together every afternoon. Hitch told anyone who questioned his behaviour that keeping Hedren isolated from the rest of the cast was essential to the performance that he was after. There was bemusement from the crew when Hitch told visitors to the set that he was fashioning an 'Oscar winning performance', and the murmurings set alarm bells ringing in Lew Wasserman's suite. The Universal head could hardly be seen to be checking up on an old friend, so he took to despatching minions on goodwill visits and then quizzing them on how Hitchcock was doing and what they thought of his current frame of mind.

After the usual break in filming during Christmas 1963, Hedren was invited to an awards ceremony for the 'Star of Tomorrow' in New York and requested a few days off to attend. This was a big moment for a woman who had stumbled into films almost by accident and was still being referred to in some newspapers by the derogatory designation of 'actress/model'. Hitch either underestimated the importance that his leading lady attached to the event or he simply did not care—his answer was an emphatic 'No'.

To his surprise, Hedren *did* protest Hitchcock's decision on this occasion and the debate which followed quickly escalated into an ugly row. Reports differ on the detail of what was said but all who were present on set agree that tempers flared and insults were exchanged. In Hitchcock's version, Hedren 'did what no one is permitted to do. She referred to my weight.' The exact phrase, according to one source, was 'fat pig'.

Given the months of unquestioning obedience to Hitchcock that she had been forced to endure, not to mention the physical torment which she had been put through on *The Birds*, Hedren's outburst was perhaps understandable. But she had

struck at the heart of a man who spent his entire life feeling trapped in a bloated body; it was more than he could bear. When the actress demanded to be released from her contract, Hitchcock testily refused, saying that he would rather destroy her career first. From then on, he stopped talking to Hedren directly and would not even speak her name, referring to her only as 'that girl'. Gone was all talk of an Oscar, and Hitchcock would not comment on her performance other than in scathing terms. The gifts dried up, and the lunches and afternoon teas were ended.

In a move that seemed designed only to provoke 'Tippi' Hedren, Hitchcock made a show of turning his attention to Diane Baker, who was suddenly promoted to the inner circle. 'He was becoming very solicitous of my interests, talking with me, and he spent a lot of time ignoring 'Tippi' and paying attention to me,' Baker told Dorothy Chandler, adding, 'I noticed he would always begin talking to me in front of her or around her dressing room.' Despite being invited to join Hitch for lunch, Baker was uncomfortable at being caught in the middle of a feud and when he began to tease her about her love life in front of the crew, she made her position clear. Hitch backed off—at least to the extent that he stopped using Baker to get at Hedren, but he nevertheless continued with his war of silence against his star.

While it was clearly not in the best interests of *Marnie* to have its director and star not talking to one another, they could still have crafted a satisfactory film together had Hitchcock only chosen to let matters rest. But there was to be a further confrontation, and this one not only had repercussions for *Marnie*, it was also to end the relationship between Hitchcock and his last blonde 'star'.

In his 1988 book *The Dark Side of Genius*, Donald Spoto claims that Hitchcock asked to see Hedren in her trailer after filming and when most of the crew were gone, and there made her a sexual proposition; according to Spoto, Hitchcock told her that unless she complied, he would cancel *Mary Rose*, which could effectively end her career. One of the crew alleged that the approach was more physical than verbal, but Jay Presson Allen, who was not on set at the time, dismisses the idea that Hitch would have made a crude pass at the actress. 'He would never in one million years do anything to embarrass himself,' she insists. 'He possibly got a little carried away by 'Tippi', how attractive she was, but that was all there was to it."

'Tippi' Hedren herself has always remained coy about what happened that night, but her reticence on the subject has left room for much speculation. She is on record as stating that the incident which ended her association with Hitchcock was something 'said not something done', and when asked in *The Times* in 2005 if the truth would damage Hitch's reputation, even after all the intervening years, she said, 'Yes, I think it would and, you know, it's over and I don't think it's anybody's business.' In the same interview, she discussed his attitude towards her early in their relationship: 'I don't know whether he did this with other actresses, I have no idea, but there certainly was an obsession there and it's difficult to be the object of someone's obsession if you're not interested in being that object.'

Whatever it was that happened in 'Tippi' Hedren's trailer, it represented the moment that the film ended for Alfred Hitchcock. He told Diane Baker, somewhat melodramatically, that he felt he had lost Grace Kelly 'for the second time', and it was clear to everyone involved that he was no longer interested in *Marnie*—he wanted to get out of the studio as fast as possible and go home. The film has all the hall-marks of this disinterest; it has the feel of a rushed job and it displays a catalogue of errors that are in marked contrast to the fastidiousness exhibited in the rest of Hitchcock's work.

When *Marnie* opened in July 1964, Hitchcock's disappointment with the film was compounded by its tepid reception from critics and public alike. The film simply did not work, partly due to the difficulties in its storyline and its rather downbeat ending, but mostly because the characters are stubbornly unconvincing—Hedren is particularly weak in a complex role that was beyond her range and experience. Hitchcock was in no doubt that Grace Kelly would have been much better, but he also claimed that his 'bad judgement with the script' cost him the opportunity ever to work with her again. Kelly always maintained that Hitch's impeccable handling of her decision to withdraw meant that they could remain on friendly terms but, behind his show of fortitude and good manners, Hitch was broken-hearted.

Universal did what it could to rescue *Marnie*, at least as far as its commercial prospects were concerned, but even its unsubtle stressing of the sexual content ('On Marnie's wedding night he discovered every secret about her.. except one!') was not enough to tempt audiences. 'Tippi' Hedren honoured her contractual commitment to promote the movie and embarked on a tour of North America, making a number of personal appearances alongside a smiling Hitchcock. They also crossed the Atlantic together and appeared on the red carpet at Cannes to give the impression of a happy and mutually-beneficial relationship. Privately Hitchcock blamed Hedren for the failure of the film: 'It's a very intriguing yarn, very meaty stuff. It had wonderful possibilities, or so I thought,' he told Dorothy Chandler, 'I thought I could mould Miss Hedren into the heroine of my imagination. I was wrong. She couldn't live up to her character.' In press interviews, he avoided referring to her as much as he could.

Hedren was kept on Hitchcock's payroll until 1967, but he had no intention of ever using her again. Whether this was a deliberate attempt to destroy her career, as he had threatened, or whether it was simply too painful for him to have direct contact with her is open to debate. They did meet up on one further occasion, in London, when Hedren was filming a small role in Charlie Chaplin's *A Countess from Hong Kong*. The Hitchcocks happened to be in town and Alma insisted that they invite 'Tippi' to tea at Claridge's; Hedren said later that it was an awkward, unpleasant experience, and uncomfortable for all three of them.

When eventually she was freed from her Universal contract, Hedren would go on to appear in over forty films without ever managing to achieve the status that she had briefly enjoyed with Alfred Hitchcock. She was among those who gathered to honour the director at an American Film Institute dinner in the 1970s, along with other stars from his films, but the organisers were at pains to ensure that Hedren and their guest of honour did not cross paths during the event.

If *Marnie* was a traumatic experience for 'Tippi' Hedren, it was tantamount to a disaster for the 'screen comeback' ambitions of Grace Kelly. Any prospect that she might be one day be allowed to take an occasional sabbatical in Hollywood vanished when she withdrew from the film. The remaining years of her life would be devoted to her family and to her royal duties, and although she would flirt on the periphery of show business (more so in the 1970s, when her [three] children were grown up), she never again sought to star in a major movie or even entertain the notion that she could. After *Marnie,* Grace Kelly truly became Princess Grace of Monaco, finally and forever.

Prior to *Marnie*, Hitchcock had occasionally taken solace in a fantasy world of his own imaginings, where Ingrid Bergman had begged him for sex and Grace Kelly had kissed him passionately on the lips in a hotel corridor—episodes which almost certainly had occurred only in his mind. Hitchcock the dreamer, the forlorn romantic, was constrained by nurture to observe the rules of civilised behaviour at all times, a situation which was reinforced by his own feelings of insecurity with regard to his appearance, and an unwavering sense of duty towards his long-suffering wife.

Marnie

Marnie

In a single moment, on the back-lot at Universal studios, he had crossed the line and tried to merge dream with reality. 'I felt very sorry for Alfred Hitchcock,' Hedren remarked, 'for what it was like *being* him.'

'Tippi' Hedren had seen a side to the director that had been kept repressed for decades, and which had crept up on him in the most inappropriate of circumstances. *Marnie* changed everything for Alfred Hitchcock, and it was to be the beginning of the end of an illustrious career in the movies.

Chapter 8

Growing Old Dis-Gracefully

'I always take care in my own films to use the best possible taste.'
—Alfred Hitchcock to *The New York Times* (1972)

She made a final, gasping effort to writhe away from him but realised it was useless. Looking into his eyes, she knew that this man was the worst kind of sex maniac. He had lost all control. He would not only rape. He would mutilate. He would kill. She was at his mercy.
—Arthur La Bern, *Goodbye Piccadilly, Farewell Leicester Square* (1966)

French director and *auteur* critic François Truffaut, who first met Hitchcock at the height of his powers and who remained one of the Englishman's most fervent admirers throughout the 1960s and 1970s, concedes that his idol was never the same again after *Marnie* and that 'its failure cost him a considerable amount of his self-confidence.'

In the case of *Marnie*, Truffaut's definition of failure did not only refer to the film's box-office take—it was hardly the first flop in Hitchcock's long career—but to the director's judgement as well. *Marnie*'s standing as a movie has risen over the years, as new audiences find hidden meaning in its visual contrivance. But its own reappraisal in critical circles has been in sharp contrast to the reputation of its creator, with those who worked on the film offering their own versions of what did or did not occur during the shooting. Some of these revelations call into question Hitchcock's status as a man of impeccable character, but Hollywood was used to the transgressions of its gilded citizenry and such things only mattered when they got in the way of business. More damaging to Hitchcock's confidence in 1964 was the inference that he was washed up as a commercial force.

Lew Wasserman was steadfast in his support of Hitchcock and Universal still provided the director with a safe-harbour—but there was a price to be paid. Hitchcock's contract gave him the freedom to develop projects with budgets of less than $3m, but he had no latitude on anything above that threshold. The disappointing returns from *The Birds* and outright failure of *Marnie* had raised serious doubts about his continuing ability to choose bankable subjects; contract notwithstanding, Universal's front office was now intent on playing a far more active role in Hitchcock's pictures from here on in.

Wasserman and Hitchcock remained close, but the views of the Universal president were increasingly to influence Hitchcock's films—subject-matter, casts and presentation; all would bear the stamp of concessions to big studio requirements. Despite the bonhomie between the two old friends, there would be no doubting who was the decision-maker in the relationship as Wasserman opted to take a less advisory and more instructive approach with Hitch.

The first project to fall victim to this new Universal regime was *Mary Rose*, Hitchcock's long-cherished fantasy about a woman who disappears for decades only to return unchanged to her now-aged husband. Soon after *Marnie* opened, Hitchcock informed Universal that he intended to revamp the script as a vehicle for 'Tippi' Hedren—despite the fact that everyone knew he could barely stand to be in the same room with her. Wasserman determined that the studio would not be stuck with another *Marnie*, and he told Hitch that he would not sanction the film, with or without Hedren; the director was asked to find another subject.

The cancellation of *Mary Rose* left Hitch temporarily high and dry. He had a number of projects at various stages of development, including *The Three Hostages* from the novel by John Buchan and an original screenplay for a crime movie provisionally titled *R.R.R.R.*, but he could find nothing to generate much enthusiasm at Universal. In an attempt to energise him, Wasserman again urged Hitch to think in terms of big stars and international settings, pointing out that films like Stanley Donen's *Charade* (1963)—another espionage caper in the Hitchcock mould, featuring Cary Grant and Audrey Hepburn—had shown that there was still much mileage to be had from comedy-thrillers and it was Hitchcock who practically invented the genre. If he had been at the top of his game, Hitch might have resisted the pressure to reinvent himself but instead, he was pushed into what was to become *Torn Curtain* (1966), a Cold War thriller loosely based on Britain's Burgess-Maclean spy scandal of the 1950s.

By now, filmmaking had lost some of its comfortable familiarity for Hitchcock. George Tomasini, his favoured editor for over a decade, had passed away, and Robert Burks, his trusted cinematographer since *Strangers on a Train*, was unavailable. (Burks would later die in a house fire without working for Hitch again.) Things had changed in front of the camera as well. The two actors whom he had entrusted with his self-image for almost two decades were now thought passé: James Stewart seemed happy to age into character roles, while Cary Grant, despite the success of *Charade*, was again ambivalent about his screen career and was looking for an out. (Grant would complete only two more films before retiring permanently.) Of the actresses in his private stable, only 'Tippi' Hedren remained, and her name was

Torn Curtain (David Opatoshu, Julie Andrews, Paul Newman)

never spoken; Grace Kelly was beyond his reach and, as Hitch remarked sadly, Ingrid Bergman had 'turned into an old woman'.

Casting *Torn Curtain* was a problem that Hitch did not have to solve. Universal provided him with two box-office stars—both of whom would be *mis*cast—and told him to modify the script to fit their personalities. Hitchcock's new leading lady was Julie Andrews, best-known for the saccharine *Mary Poppins* (1964) and the super-successful *The Sound of Music* (1965). Despite her popularity with the public, the casting of Andrews evoked memories of Doris Day in *The Man Who Knew Too Much*, and Hitch remarked with dismay that audiences would be 'expecting her to break into song'. He found his male lead just as unsuitable. Method actor Paul Newman was one of the biggest and most respected stars in Hollywood, and Universal insisted that his participation would enable Hitch to reach the youthful audience that had queued to see him in *The Hustler* (1961) and, most recently, *Hud* (1963)—but the blue-eyed, boyish Newman was a unlikely choice for a nuclear physicist.

Hitchcock steeled himself and invited his young stars to the customary dinner at Bellagio Road. But sixties iconoclasm and the generation gap saw Newman throw his jacket over the back of his chair and decline the fine wine that Hitch had procured from his cellar in favour of beer; Newman was not intimidated by the director's reputation, but Hitch took his attitude as a sign of disrespect. He would work with Newman on set, but he made no further attempt to develop a relationship with the young actor.

Accommodating two stars in whom he had no interest, as well as catering for the studio's requirement of an international feel to the film, proved a challenge too far for Hitchcock. He fired the first writer assigned to the project and hired two more. By the time shooting started, Andrews and Newman were both only too aware that their director had not wanted them in the first place, Brian Moore's script was below par, and Hitchcock himself lacked the necessary enthusiasm to make anything worthwhile out of *Torn Curtain*. A lacklustre showing at the box-office followed suit.

If Hitchcock found adapting to the new Hollywood difficult, Grace Kelly had no problem in making the transition to public figure. William Holden had said of her that she had 'the best calculated career in the history of motion pictures'; it seemed that by the mid-1960s, she had carried that management ability over into her new role as a head of state. Her decision to withdraw from *Marnie* may have disappointed her fans, but it had kept her reputation intact. Kelly's decision to host

The Monacan royal family: Prince Rainier, Princess Grace and their children, Albert, Caroline and Stephanie

Her Serene Highness Princess Grace of Monaco

a bland documentary for CBS entitled *A Look at Monaco* in 1963 had signposted the way that her life was now to progress, dedicated to public service—though Ava Gardner revealed, 'Give her a couple of dry martinis and Her Serene Highness Princess Grace becomes just another one of the girls.' And after visiting the South of France, Hitchcock had dubbed his favourite blonde 'Princess Dis-Grace', hinting that the erstwhile screen queen had not given herself entirely to the world of sainthood.

After the birth of her third and last child, Stephanie, in 1965, the princess sanctioned the release of endless snapshots of the royal family at rest and play—a move reminiscent of Jack Kelly's political campaigning. In an interview in *Playboy* in 1966, Kelly said of her life in the Royal Palace, 'I have never seen anything fairytale about it', but in relation to the prospect of her returning to the screen, she added, 'I don't think I'd like to go back to that again.. my life is much fuller now in every sense.'

The determination and energy that Kelly had poured into her film career was directed instead towards charity-work, in particular to her role as President of the Red Cross, with its annual fund-raising ball—invariably enlivened by a generous helping of Hollywood glitterati, like Frank Sinatra and Sammy Davis Jr. The princess's progress from actress to icon in the eyes of her subjects was encouraged by her active endorsement of a growing number of good causes, including the honorary presidency of l'AMADE (Association Mondiale des Amis de l'Enfance), a Monaco-based organisation devoted to furthering the cause of underprivileged children throughout the world. Hitchcock had expressed his view that the Monaco stage was 'too small' for someone of Kelly's *joie de vivre*, but having made her bed, she was determined to lie in it to the very best of her abilities. In a letter to journalist Barbara Walters, she wrote, 'I've had happy moments in my life but I don't think that happiness.. is a perpetual state that anyone can be in.. My children give me a great deal of satisfaction. And my life here has given me many satisfactions in the last ten years.'

As the former Grace Kelly slipped effortlessly into middle-aged respectability as Princess Grace of the Principality of Monaco, so Alfred Hitchcock was having to content himself with becoming an elder statesman of the film industry. His long-running TV series had come to an end, and although he liked to claim that he had little day-to-day involvement in it, he missed the constant buzz of production. Not that he was short of things to do; in 1965, the Screen Producers Guild had presented him with a 'Milestone Award' for his 'historic contribution to the American Motion Picture', and among those who gathered to sing his praises were David Selznick, Jack Warner and MGM's Sam Goldwyn. Selznick was particularly magnanimous in tribute, describing Hitchcock as 'cool and imperturbable—undisturbed even by memos—of which he received many.' (Hitchcock attended the former mogul's funeral only a few months later.) And that was only the start. Michael Balcon hosted a gala lunch in London sponsored by the ACTT (Association of Cinematograph, Television and Allied Technicians) and, in 1968, the American Motion Picture Academy was to give Hitchcock its Irving G Thalberg Memorial Award, in consolation for all those years that he had been overlooked at the Oscars. He would have honours bestowed on him on a regular basis for the rest of the decade, and all the way through to the last months of his life.

But the constant feting did little to counter Hitchcock's need to make films, and he badly wanted another box-office success to show that he had not lost his touch. He toyed with the idea of returning to the world of serial killers, contemplating scenarios based on the exploits of real-life murderers John Haigh and Neville Heath; impressed with the filmmaking techniques of European directors like Michelangelo

Antonioni, the result was *Kaleidoscope*, which Hitch and writer Benn Levy planned as a cinema vérité-style offering about a deformed, homosexual killer, in an attempt to recapture some of the excitement of *Psycho* and the many imitators which had followed it into theatres in the intervening years. Hitchcock asked Truffaut for his opinion on the script, but the French director was concerned by the level of graphic violence and said so. In the end, Hitchcock hired *Spartacus* author and left-wing radical Howard Fast to rework Levy's script under a new title of *Frenzy*, but when it was put to Universal, Lew Wasserman viewed the nudity and violence with similar distaste and instead urged Hitch to create an espionage adventure to rival James Bond. Elements from *Kaleidoscope/Frenzy*, including its title, were to resurface in Hitchcock's subsequent *Frenzy*, though that film would bear no other relation to the aborted original idea.

(Hitchcock never forgot Universal's dismissal of a project that he thought would burnish his reputation anew through its innovative approach to the subject-matter of serial killers; when filming *Family Plot* some years later, he and actor Bruce Dern were debating what kind of graffiti should adorn a garage door in a particular scene: 'Fuck MCA', Hitchcock suggested.)

In the spring of 1968, with some $4m of Universal's money, Hitchcock started work on *Topaz*, based on a spy novel by *Exodus*'s Leon Uris. Uris was engaged to adapt his own book, but Hitch disliked his approach and brought *Vertigo* writer Sam Taylor onto the project, with a specific brief to turn out an exciting adventure film. But Taylor found little of substance on which to hang a suitable storyline, and Hitch was pushed by Universal into shooting the film before Taylor could deliver a satisfactory script. 'One of the tragedies of *Topaz* was that Hitch was trying to make something as if he had Ingrid Bergman and Cary Grant,' the writer said later. 'But he didn't have the story for it, and he certainly didn't have the cast.'

The leading role in *Topaz* went to Frederick Stafford (Friedrich Strobel von Stein), an undistinguished Czech actor who had appeared in a number of European

Topaz (Frederick Stafford, Dany Robin)

Karin Dor

films, including a Franco-German spy yarn entitled *Agent 505-Todesfalle Beirut* (1966). Hitchcock entertained a notion that Stafford could also be turned into a major star; he was just as mistaken over his choice of leading lady. He had accepted Universal's suggestion of Karin Dor, a statuesque German blonde with glacial good looks, who had played a small role in the latest 007 outing, *You Only Live Twice* (1967). On the face of it, Dor was the ideal 'Hitchcock type', but she soon proved that under the icy exterior.. was an icy interior. She had the distinction of being the last 'Hitchcock blonde', however—though given the fact that she played a brunette and wore a wig throughout, she was also the most forgettable.

Hitchcock approached the shooting of *Topaz* with an air of resignation, and his spirits were not helped by his leading lady's stubborn refusal to strip for a nude scene. The gloom was alleviated only by a short spell of location filming in France, which afforded him a chance to dine with Princess Grace in her Paris apartment. His health was also becoming a cause for concern, both to him and to Universal, and a doctor was kept on standby throughout. *Topaz* came and went without anyone noticing—a shoddy and unappealing exercise, badly structured, poorly edited, and not worthy of its illustrious director's name above the title. Hitchcock called *Topaz* a 'complete disaster'.

'Do I look like a sex murderer to you?'

—Richard Blaney (Jon Finch), *Frenzy* (1972)

Despite his declining health and the lack of suitable subjects, Hitchcock was determined to keep working. His search for something to fire his imagination finally paid off in a novel by Arthur La Bern, called *Goodbye Piccadilly, Farewell Leicester Square*. The story involved a serial killer at large in contemporary London, and a man falsely accused of the crimes who is forced to prove his innocence; in these and other ways, it reminded Hitchcock of *The Lodger*. In the autumn of his life, Hitchcock was increasingly inclined to reminisce about the London of his youth; the prospect of returning to the place of his birth to shoot a film was appealing, and playwright Anthony Shaffer was engaged to turn the book into a script. The lower budget required meant that Hitchcock did not have to ask the permission of Lew Wasserman, but he did anyway—Wasserman again thought the whole idea distasteful, but recognising that Hitch was in need of another success, he gave it his approval. Reaching into his file of dormant projects, Hitchcock found the title *Frenzy* and appended it to Shaffer's script.

The relaxations in film censorship that had been instituted on both sides of the Atlantic since Hitchcock directed *Psycho*, or even *Marnie*, presented him with the opportunity to put the kind of sexual violence which featured on the periphery of

No Bail for the Judge right in the centre of the action. To drum up press interest in the project, he described it as 'the story of a man who is impotent and therefore expresses himself through murder.' The thought of a new cinematic freedom with which to explore themes that hitherto he had dealt with covertly sparked some of the old fire; Anthony Shaffer noticed the change and told Donald Spoto that Hitch 'seemed to have this excited interest in bizarre sexual crimes.'

Hitch arrived in England with renewed vigour. Whenever a microphone was put in front of him, he waxed lyrical about how good it was to be working with British technicians again and said how much he was looking forward to working at Pinewood Studios. He said that he would be filming scenes at Covent Garden's fruit and vegetable market, where his father had shopped for groceries a lifetime earlier, and he claimed to be thrilled at the prospect of using British actors; he told the press that he had avoided star-names and had deliberately sought out 'good theatre actors'. In fact, he had offered the leading role in the film to Michael Caine, who had turned it down, saying he thought it 'loathsome'. (Caine reports in his memoirs that he saw Hitch many times subsequently in *Chasen's* but the director never once acknowledged him.) The role of Rusk, the 'necktie murderer', was originally intended for David Hemmings, star of *Blowup* (1966) and *Barbarella* (1968); he too had declined. It seemed that star-names were also avoiding Hitchcock—if not, they were certainly avoiding *Frenzy*.

Jon Finch, star of Roman Polanski's *Macbeth* (1971), was finally signed to play Richard Blaney, a Hitchcock cliché of a man who is wrongly accused of murder and forced to go on the run with a girlfriend in tow. Unlike other Hitchcock thrillers on a similar theme, however, there was to be nothing light-hearted about *Frenzy*. Hitchcock's film was a story of violence and betrayal, centring on a particularly sadistic rape-murder. Blaney is a thoroughly dislikeable character, moody and taciturn, who despite his 'war hero' past is portrayed as narrow-minded and self-serving, whereas the real killer (played by Barry Foster) is possessed of a roguish charm and a ready smile, his repugnant nature only being revealed as events unfold.

In casting Rusk's victims, Hitch avoided the temptation to hire 'busty blondes' and went for theatrical quality: Anna Massey and Barbara Leigh-Hunt were cast as Blaney's girlfriend and ex-wife respectively. Both characters were to appear naked on screen and body doubles were used to preserve the actresses' modesty, but for Leigh-Hunt, who had to bear the brunt of the killer's ire in a graphically-explicit sex-and-strangulation sequence designed to top *Psycho* in sheer brutality, the filming was a particularly unsettling experience. Trapped in her office by Rusk, Brenda tries desperately to talk him out of assaulting her. Rusk seems hurt by Brenda's rejection: 'I have my good points,' he says. 'I like flowers, fruit. People like me. I've got things to give.' The violence erupts and he tears off Brenda's blouse and rapes her; 'Lovely—lovely,' he groans, as she first begs for mercy, then prays for salvation and finally, when she realises that her rapist is now to become her murderer, screams for help. Under the unflinching gaze of Hitchcock's camera, it is a difficult scene to watch.

In 1967, Hitchcock had criticised the growing trend for nudity on the screen: 'It seems we are all waiting for a zoom-in to a close-up of a sexual act,' he complained. With *Frenzy*, it was Hitch who was leading the permissive charge, but the sexual act concerned was a sickening rape—nasty, brutal and gloating. The scene, which took three days to shoot, ends with murder and a close-up of the victim's face, again in echo of *Psycho*: lifeless eyes bulge in their sockets and a distended tongue lolls out of Brenda's mouth. Some years earlier, Hitchcock had told his audience at London's National Film Theatre that murder was 'a messy business.' It seemed he was now intent on having that audience share in the experience.

Frenzy (Barry Foster, Barbara Leigh-Hunt)

(Another scene of dubious merit comes after the murder of Babs [Massey], when Rusk hides her naked body in a lorry loaded with sacks of potatoes; realising that an incriminating tie-pin is clutched in her dead hand, Rusk returns to the scene, where he is forced to break the fingers of the mortified corpse in order to retrieve it. Hitchcock teased his critics by calling his film a 'comedy'—a defence that he had used for *Psycho*: 'You don't find the idea of a body hidden in potatoes funny?' he asked one reporter.)

Cinematographer Gil Taylor, who was a clapper boy for Hitchcock forty years before, on *Number 17*, remembers a director who still had something of his old powers: 'He was old and he was tired, so the pace was slower. But he was still in charge and he seemed to be enjoying the experience.' Taylor recalls that one of the highlights of the film for Hitch was a visit to the set of HSH Princess Grace. 'You could tell there was something special going on between them,' Taylor said. 'He was like a little boy again.' Rainer accompanied his wife, and the royal couple quickly retired to Hitchcock's trailer. The princess declined to chat with the press and described her brief return to a film set as merely 'a private visit.'

Hitchcock's humour was infectious, but he treated his two leading men very differently. He was warm and friendly with Foster, with whom he shared a tipple at 'tea break', and they formed a friendship that lasted beyond the shooting of the film—which was more than could be said for Finch. Before filming began, Jon Finch was tempted by an interviewer to describe Hitchcock as 'past his prime'; the director was furious and considered firing him from the film. Instead, he exacted a more subtle revenge. Finch's arrival on set was met with sarcasm; Hitch would then interrupt his performance if he strayed a fraction off his marks or deviated from the script, and when he was not in front of the camera, Hitch ignored him completely.

Notwithstanding the pleasure of working in England and hosting a visit from Her Serene Highness, *Frenzy* finished on a sour note for Hitchcock: Alma suffered a stroke and had to be rushed to hospital. It was not life-threatening, but Hitch was beside himself with worry. She was eventually flown home to LA to recuperate, and

Frenzy (Anna Massey)

Wasserman offered to replace Hitch for the final weeks of shooting. Hitch refused, determined to see things through to the end, but his focus was only on finishing the film as quickly and efficiently as he could.

By the time *Frenzy* was ready for release, Alma had recovered sufficiently to accompany Hitch on the promotional tour. Universal's publicity department was certain that this would be the last 'hurrah' for the veteran director and it pulled out all the stops to ensure him a fond farewell. The highlight of the tour was an appearance at the Cannes festival, where the film was screened before a predictably enthusiastic audience. The ovation that greeted Hitchcock on his arrival reflected the critics' respect for his career as a whole, if not the particular film on show. Among the assembled guests was a certain royal princess, who was less shy about posing for the press on this occasion and who accompanied Hitch on the red carpet to watch the movie with him. Princess Grace did not share her view on *Frenzy* with the media, but no doubt it was a subject of conversation when Hitch and Alma accompanied she and Rainier to the Palace to spend the evening. The Hitchcocks then made their way to Paris for yet another premiere in front of another rapturous crowd.

If *Frenzy* was enjoyed by Hitchcock aficionados, it met with a mixed reception from the critics; in Britain, *Time Out* saw in it a 'series of variations on themes of excess, surplus and waste from the most fastidious of directors,' while others thought it old-fashioned, both in its content and approach; they were particularly irritated by the outdated depiction of London, which was not as it actually was in

Theatrical poster for Frenzy

the 1970s but as Hitchcock remembered it to have been in his youth. This became a common theme, and it surfaced again in an article written for *The Guardian* by Jonathan Jones, who felt that Hitchcock's film was 'a pastiche and reprise of his work, especially his British films, and a coded autobiography.. [his] most insidiously personal film, the Catholic director's final confession.'

Hitchcock on the set of Frenzy

More damning was a letter to *The Times* from Arthur La Bern, the author of the novel on which the film had been based. 'I wish I could share [*Times* critic] John Russell Taylor's enthusiasm for Hitchcock's distasteful film, *Frenzy*,' he wrote. 'The result on the screen is appalling. The dialogue is a curious amalgam of an old Aldwych farce, 'Dixon of Dock Green' and that almost forgotten 'No Hiding Place'. I would like to ask Mr Hitchcock and Mr Shaffer what happened between book and script to the authentic London characters I created..'

In America, where *Frenzy* would be the first Hitchcock film to receive an 'R' (Restricted) certificate, Roger Ebert of Chicago's *Sun-Times* thought it a return to his classic work, with 'macabre details, incongruous humour, and the desperation of a man convicted of a crime he didn't commit.' Ebert went on to describe the director's full-frontal way with sexual violence as a 'grisly abandon that has us imaging *Psycho* without the shower curtain.' The *New York Times* was less sanguine and enquired of its readers, 'Does *Frenzy* Degrade Women?'

Whatever the rights or wrongs of graphically-depicting rape and murder, Hitch had calculated correctly: *Frenzy* gave him his biggest hit since *Psycho* and removed all thought of retirement. 'If I can still put as much vitality into a movie as I've put into *Frenzy*,' he said, 'what's the point of retiring? I used to be called the "boy director", and I still am.'

'You kiss me and I'm supposed to melt.. Your ego is astonishing.'

—David Freeman, from his screenplay for *The Short Night*

'Vitality' was not a word that many would have associated with Hitchcock at this stage in his career, despite the impression he liked to give. Back in Hollywood, he settled down to find a new subject while moaning to Truffaut that he was allowed only to 'make what is expected of me; that is, a thriller, or a suspense story, and that I find hard to do'. Opting for another change of pace, he settled for an adaptation of

Hitch directs Bruce Dern in Family Plot

The Rainbird Pattern, a 1972 novel by Victor Canning, which pleased Universal but generated little enthusiasm elsewhere. The plot, about a phoney clairvoyant who sets out to find a missing heiress but falls foul of a kidnapping ring (and which *Time* magazine had likened to 'James Bond in the 19th Century'), was typical of the comedy thrillers that Hitchcock had made decades before, and *North by Northwest* screenwriter Ernest Lehman was hired to turn his thoughts into a workable script.

In April 1974, Hitchcock was invited to New York's Lincoln Centre for another tribute evening. This one involved a montage of film clips, introduced by some of his leading ladies, and presented to an audience of 2800 paying guests. Among the actresses who turned out to honour Hitch were Janet Leigh, Teresa Wright, Joan Fontaine—and Grace Kelly.

Hitchcock enjoyed the show from a box-seat, sandwiched between Kelly and Alma, and looking more than ever like a jolly Buddha lording it over his flock. He grinned broadly when Kelly climbed onto the stage and told the audience of his reaction when he first saw her in the gold dress on *To Catch a Thief*: 'There's hills in them thar gold.' But he was stony-faced when the scene from *Vertigo* in which James Stewart urged Kim Novak to put her hair up in a bun flashed onto the screen. Called on to make the obligatory speech, he appeared to forget the controversy which had raged over *Frenzy* and informed his audience, 'I do not approve of the current wave of violence that we see on our screens, I have always felt that murder should be treated delicately.' He used as his example the assault on Kelly in *Dial M for Murder* and said in closing, 'As you can see, the best way to do it is with scissors'—a reference to both the art of murder and the filmmaker's art of montage.

Despite having had a pacemaker inserted and a kidney-stone removed, the 74-year-old director continued to assure friends and colleagues that he would be shooting a new film, his 53rd, in the very near future. Against all expectations, he and Lehman somehow managed to extract a completed screenplay out of *The Rainbird Pattern* and Universal announced that it was to begin production on the latest Hitchcock: *Deceit*.

The omens were never good for what would turn out to be Hitchcock's final film and the end result, eventually titled *Family Plot* (1976), was a triumph of stamina over art. Universal had turned a blind eye (or deaf ear) to stories from the studio floor about Hitch falling asleep halfway through scenes or letting his crew stand idle because he was too drunk to leave his bungalow; rather than reprimand or replace the ageing director, Wasserman had him propped up—literally— to ensure that the film was finished with Hitch at the helm.

Theatrical poster for Family plot

Unsurprisingly, the listless film that emerged was a disappointment to everyone and met with little interest. Starring Karen Black and Bruce Dern, *Family Plot* was a comedy thriller with neither comedy nor thrills. It showed no evidence of the old Hitchcock style, and its sunny exteriors and bland, contemporary sets made it look like any run-of-the-mill TV movie. At the press launch, its director distracted attention from the film by promising a 54th 'Hitchcock picture'.

Soon after *Family Plot* opened, Alma suffered a second stroke, more severe than the first, which left her confined to the house and requiring round-the-clock medical attention. The couple had to forego their weekly outing to *Chasen's* and Hitchcock, for the first time in his married life, found himself in charge of domestic arrangements. During the day, he left Alma in the care of a nurse while he struggled on at Universal. He was determined not to go out on a damp squib like *Family Plot* and he decided to take a fresh look at Ronald Kirkbride's *The Short Night,* a novel based loosely on the real-life escape from Wandsworth prison of British double-agent George Blake and his subsequent defection to the USSR, which Hitch had originally optioned on publication in 1968.

American playwright James Costigan was hired to work on the treatment and Hitchcock adopted his usual tack of indulging in casual meanderings around the subject while Costigan sat pen-in-hand. It was not a work-pattern that suited the writer, and he soon annoyed Hitch by insisting on a more structured approach; Costigan was side-stepped and replaced with the more amenable Ernest Lehman. But this new-found harmony was not to last for long. Hitch and Lehman found themselves arguing over plot-points—in particular, Hitchcock's desire to introduce a rape and murder sequence into the story.

By now, Hitchcock's grip on reality was being questioned by many at Universal. He sent a crew to scout for locations in Finland—as he had with Alma nine years earlier, when he first bought the rights to the book—even though his wife was effectively housebound and in need of constant attention and Hitch himself had trouble walking the short distance from his office to his car. His ideas on casting were equally bizarre and would have stretched any potential budget to breaking-point: he lunched with superstar Clint Eastwood, and he asked the studio to check on the availability and cost of Sean Connery. French actress Catherine Denueve was pencilled in for a possible role, as was Scandinavian Liv Ullmann..

In the winter of 1977, Grace Kelly paid a visit to Hitch in his Universal bungalow. His former 'blonde', at 48, was now a middle-aged, matronly figure, drinking heavily and putting on weight to the extent that she referred to herself as the 'Blimposaurus

Rex'. But she retained enough of the qualities which had inspired Hitchcock in the first place to bathe him in a golden glow of nostalgia and have him talk excitedly of how they would soon have another premiere to attend together.

Kelly's priority had been her children. Now that they were of an age when they were no longer dependent on her, she, like other mothers, had striven to find a new purpose in life. She had founded the Monaco International Arts Festival, celebrating all branches of the performing arts from theatre to ballet to classical music, but as Hitchcock had predicted, the lure of Tinsletown had never left her.

Previously, Kelly had confided to *Photoplay*, 'There will be no more movies. I was an actress for quite long enough and I loved it. At the time I thought of nothing else but my work. It was everything to me. But marriage proved to me I was wrong. Most women need marriage and a family and I discovered I was the same.' It was a line that she had repeated many times in interviews after her withdrawal from *Marnie*, and Hitchcock had never believed it to be entirely true. Kelly biographer Gwen Robyns shared his view: 'She operated on adulation,' Robyns said of her. 'It was her fuel. She had got used to it in Hollywood.' The rarified atmosphere in Monaco could not compete with the glitz and glamour of show business forever, and Hitch was never in any doubt that Kelly would eventually hanker after that 'fuel' once more. While Hitch had been distracted with *Family Plot*, Grace Kelly had indeed returned to Hollywood, though not in the capacity that he had always imagined.

Old friend Jay Kanter, who had since moved on from MCA to run 20th Century Fox, had invited Kelly to join him in an official capacity and she had become the first woman to serve on the board of the company where she had made screen debut in 1951. The princess was at pains to point out that filmmaking was only a part of the multinational's global activities, but her new post allowed her to visit the US on a regular basis and attend board meetings in New York and LA. In 1976, she had met a 30-year-old Romanian-born filmmaker named Robert Dornhelm and had agreed to provide the intro for his documentary, *The Children of Theatre Street*. She and Dornhelm had struck up a rapport and, for the first time in a long time, Kelly had started to think seriously about a return to filmmaking—not in front of the cameras, but on the production side—and she and Dornhelm had begun to discuss projects. Kelly optioned Gore Vidal's novel *A Search for the King* and told friends that she and Dorhelm would make it as a rock opera; another proposal was for a film about Raoul Wallenberg, the humanitarian Swede who rescued thousands of Jews from the Nazi Holocaust. Kelly was so enthused by the prospect of a return to work that she even wrote her own treatment, which she described as a 'satire on filmmaking in the Sixties'. In the end, the collaboration between she and Dornhelm came down to a disappointingly-slight comedy built around the princess's interest in flowers, which eventually surfaced in 1982 and featured Kelly in a brief cameo as herself. It was called *Rearranged*.

But Robert Dornhelm was not the princess's sole distraction away from the goldfish bowl of Monaco. With the passing of time, the former Grace Kelly had been enabled to wander the global stage largely unnoticed and she had used her new found anonymity to see a number of men, often many years her junior. Swedish actor Per Mattsson was one, and he recalled that he spent an evening with her in New York, 'singing duets in her hotel room until 5 am.' This was the 'Princess Dis-Grace' that Hitchcock had alluded to and, by the late 1970s, Kelly was publicly admitting what others had believed privately from the start. In an interview with the *Sunday Mirror*, she confessed, 'I gave up films too early. I was on the brink of beginning to understand my profession when I gave it up. That's why I regret I did not stick at it

for five more years. I believe I might then have really made a career as Grace Kelly.'

Kelly was still receiving offers to return to the screen, including that of the starring role in *The Turning Point*, the story of a promising ballerina who gives up her career for marriage and family; it was dismissed out of hand. But if her new-found freedom did not quite extend to a return to film stardom, it did allow her to indulge her love of performing and she made a number of personal appearances to read poetry, including at the Edinburgh Festival and later during a tour of the US.

The legitimate theatre offered Kelly a more credible escape route from the constraints of her formal role and she founded her own stage company and took over an old playhouse near the Royal Palace in Monaco; launching the project, she spoke of her intention to produce and direct her own productions—possibly some of Uncle George Kelly's long-forgotten works—and even hinted that she might consider a return to the boards herself. There was no more talk of appearing in another Hitchcock film, though the princess maintained her close relationship with her former mentor. Hitchcock was still a major shareholder in Universal and an icon to generations of filmmakers, but for Kelly, he was a link to her past rather than her future; no matter how she looked or what she did, she was always Grace Kelly the movie star whenever she was with him. Hitchcock lived the same illusion: seated with her in his office, talking over the old days or dreaming up new cinematic ventures for both of them, Hitchcock could turn the clock back two decades. He was James Stewart again, or Cary Grant, or even Ray Milland. And the most beautiful woman in the world was playing opposite him.

Kelly was back in Los Angeles in February 1978, and she visited Hitchcock at Universal. The director's initial burst of energy after her previous visit had dissipated, and the script for *The Short Night* was no further forward. Hitch was still talking about it in terms of a 'work in progress', but working on the project appeared to have become an end in itself. His attention wandered during their conversation and he talked increasingly about friends who had passed on. He had arthritis in his legs and was in constant pain; he also had a liver complaint and suffered from dizzy spells. Looking after Alma was exhausting him, and he was depressed at his inability to facilitate another film.

Conscious of the deterioration in his health, Lew Wasserman nevertheless assured Hitch that Universal was totally behind *The Short Night*. With Wasserman's blessing, Hitch parted company with Ernest Lehman; the two had reached an impasse over the rape, paralleling the situation with Evan Hunter on *Marnie*, and work on the screenplay had effectively stopped. Whatever demon was driving Hitchcock had evidently not been exorcised by the excesses of *Frenzy*—he was adamant that a graphic assault was to feature in *The Short Night*. Hitch told Wasserman to find him a 'younger man'. No-one at Universal believed in *The Short Night*, or wanted it to be made; privately, Hitchcock's production office was viewed as 'Wasserman's folly'—one dinosaur indulging another—and talk was less of what to do with the production and more of how the studio would use the space when it could finally pull down Hitchcock's anachronistic bungalow.

At the end of 1978, a relatively-unknown TV writer named David Freeman was hired to work on the script. By then, Hitchcock had given up on the idea that he could shoot the film on location; Alma's condition had worsened and Freeman was instructed to rework *The Short Night* so that it could be filmed entirely on one of the studio's sound stages.

Freeman not only reinstated the rape, he created an explicit love scene which he said had 'compulsive, life-changing, soul-altering sex—all to be made more explicit than any scenes in his previous films'. Hitchcock was excited by the prospect: 'After the orgasm, the man must take an ivory comb and comb her pubic hair,' he instructed the writer. According to Freeman, Hitchcock dictated this addendum in such a way that it seemed not to be a scene from the film but more of a glimpse into 'a private vision, playful and from the heart, a true home movie..'

Hitch would sometimes ask for a typist to take notes; invariably, the same pretty girl was sent in to him and he would flirt outrageously with her—what Freeman considered was the harmless teasings of an old man. But on one occasion, Hitch requested her help when he was in his office alone. According to Donald Spoto, Hitch made 'ugly, intimate demands', and the girl ended up so distraught that she could not return to work. David Freeman, who was closer to Hitch in these last days than anyone else, commented, 'I imagine it was something along the lines of Hitch posing her and gazing at her while she unbuttoned herself'; he also felt that the incident was made to seem sleazier than it was in truth and spoke of a 'pathetic innocence'—though some in Hollywood were not as understanding, and the expression 'dirty old man' went the rounds. The typist left Universal soon after, accompanied by rumours that Wasserman had paid her to keep quiet.

In March 1979, Alfred Hitchcock was honoured by the American Film Institute with their Life Achievement Award. He was told by his doctor that he was not well enough to attend but he went anyway: he was not about to miss what might be the last time that he would be feted by Hollywood. Hitch was too weak to perform live, so his speech was taped earlier in the day and intercut with shots of him at the event—where he looked tired and in obvious discomfort. Ingrid Bergman and François Truffaut were his hosts for the occasion, and Anthony Perkins, Sean Connery, Rod Taylor, Vera Miles, 'Tippi' Hedren and the rest thronged the auditorium. Hitchcock sat flanked by Bergman, Wasserman, Cary Grant and James Stewart. Only Grace Kelly was missing. Among those who paid tribute to him were Orson Welles, William Wyler, Bette Davis and James Cagney. Jocular to the last, Hitchcock compared it to appearing at his own wake.

Freeman completed his script of *The Short Night* in May, but Hitchcock's spirit was broken. The director told Lew Wasserman that he no longer had the energy to continue and was abandoning the project. Wasserman nevertheless assured Hitch that it would only be a postponement, not a cancellation, and that the film would stay on the studio's books till he was ready to resume work on it. Both men knew that it would never happen. Hitchcock's life of structure and routine finally crumbled; he went into the office sporadically, watched a movie on his own, dictated some letters and drank. The dream was finally at an end.

Old friends continued to drop by to see him, including Ingrid Bergman, who visited Hitchcock in August 1979. Hitch had adored Bergman and would undoubtedly have made many more films with her had she not left Hollywood; he frequently cited her as the best actress he had worked with. Bergman, who was stricken with terminal cancer, found herself confronted by a broken man, sobbing that he had reached the end of his working life. After offering him what comfort she could, the two said their goodbyes, with Bergman promising to visit again soon. It was not to be, and she would die on August 30, 1982, aged 67.

In the 1980 New Year Honours List, Alfred Hitchcock was awarded a knighthood. It gave Lew Wasserman a final opportunity to pay homage to his old comrade. Wasserman rounded up all the senior executives of Universal, as well as stars like Cary Grant and Janet Leigh, for the formal investiture ceremony on the studio lot. (Hitch was too ill to travel to London.) The honour meant more to this old man of the movies than all of the others that now cluttered his crowded mantelpiece; despite taking up American citizenship in 1955, Hitch still thought of himself as British and he regarded his knighthood as the ultimate accolade.

Soon afterwards, Hitchcock closed his office and dismissed his staff. Typically, he could not bring himself to break the news personally to all those who had served him so loyally for so many years and at first they thought that Universal had fired him so it could use the space. The bungalow had served its purpose, but Wasserman would not allow it to be closed and it remained at Hitchcock's disposal; the director would return to it from time to time, long after the memorabilia of a lifetime had been cleared away, order up a movie to watch, pour himself a drink, and then go quietly home.

Throughout Hitchcock's life, there had been two constants: the movies, and Alma. When it became clear to him that his wife was never going to be well enough for another holiday, or even a trip to their favourite restaurant, he effectively lost her also. She was now confined to bed, and though her condition remained stable, she was a constant source of worry for him. 'I couldn't imagine being alive without Alma,' he told Charlotte Chandler. 'I wouldn't want to be. It never occurred to me that I would survive Alma.'

By April 1980, Hitch had stopped his trips to the studio and taken to his bed. He refused sustenance and swore at anyone who tried to provide it. His doctor told Patrick McGilligan that Hitch had a number of age-related ailments but that his 'constitution was strong and he was not dying'. Hitch, however, had no interest in living on. He felt that life had given up on him, so he would now give up on life.

Asked at the launch of *Family Plot* what he would like to see on his tombstone, Alfred Hitchcock had deadpanned, 'You see what can happen if you aren't a good boy.' On April 29, 1980, at the age of 80, the 'naughty boy' died peacefully at his home in Bellagio Road.

Postscript

Women had a significant influence on the life and work of Alfred Hitchcock. In his formative years, it was his mother Emma who shaped and guided his development. During his career in Britain and America, a number of women occupied crucial roles —Joan Harrison and Ingrid Bergman stand out as being particularly important at various periods of time. However, there were two women who featured centrally in Hitchcock's life, though they belonged to different generations and there could not have been a greater contrast in their backgrounds, looks and personalities. Many women liked Hitch as a person, stayed loyal to him as an employer, and admired his abilities as a film director, but Alma Reville and Grace Kelly could both be said to have understood him as a man.

Alma Reville Hitchcock spent her last years in the carefully-cossetted confines of Bellagio Road. According to Patrick McGilligan, she was for the most part unaware that her husband had passed on and would tell visitors, 'He's at the studio. Don't worry, he'll be home soon.' At the American Film Institute dinner in 1979, Hitchcock had paid tribute to the woman who had been at his side for most of his life and who was 'wife, mother, writer, editor and cook' to him. Alma's influence on Hitch, personally and professionally, was great and far-reaching; she regarded it as her vocation to look after, nurture and support him, as well to provide him with guidance in his professional ventures. More than that, she tolerated and indulged him. Screenwriter Jay Presson Allen once conceded, 'Hitch was a fantasist. I think he might have had fantasy romances with his leading ladies, and, if so, Alma accepted this. It's kind of normal for a man, and they were, after all, fantasies.' Without Alma's acceptance and tacit approval of his fantasies, without her encouragement and support, Hitchcock would not have had the confidence or courage to make the films that he did, and the cinema would have been denied one of its most remarkable and individual talents. He never ceased to love her for what she had given him. Alma Reville passed away on July 6, 1982.

Grace Kelly was not the first or the last of 'Hitchcock's blondes' but, more than any other, she inspired, enthralled and excited him for over a quarter of a century. Much has been made of the reasons why the actress quit Hollywood at the very height of her fame; those who knew her well, including William Holden and Hitchcock himself, were prone to suggest that it was a calculated move, the next step on her career path. Kelly, it could be argued, was aware of her limitations. When Broadway stubbornly refused to open its stages to her, she had found a niche in Hollywood, but leading actresses had a limited shelf-life and the prospect of ageing in the profession held little appeal. Before she 'retired' from films, she told one interviewer, 'I get up at seven for the make-up, Rita Hayworth at six, Joan Crawford and Bette Davis at five. I don't want to know the time when I'll have to come into the studio even earlier.'

There was never any danger of Hitchcock seeing Grace Kelly in that light. When eventually Ingrid Bergman was accepted back into the movie mainstream, Hitchcock never thought to plan another film for her, despite her public rehabilitation. But Kelly was always Lisa Carol Freeman, and when he could no longer have her in his films, he embarked on a long and ultimately fruitless quest to recreate her image by proxy. In later years, Princess Grace told a television reporter, 'I am very flattered that people think I could still be in pictures.. It would mean a complete reorganisation of my life and it would be a very difficult decision to make.'

But it was a dream that Alfred Hitchcock never completely gave up on.

In March 1982, Grace Kelly was the subject of her own tribute at the Annenberg Institute of Communications. Among the guests were Bob Hope, James Stewart, Frank Sinatra and Stewart Granger, as well as her family, old school friends and ex-lovers—even the doctor who had delivered her. Prince Rainier did not attend; he was 'too busy' with the affairs of state. It was to be the princess's last official public appearance.

Later that year, the Rainiers were ensconced in their lodge of Roc Angel in the hills above Monaco on their annual vacation and, on the morning of September 13, Kelly took the wheel of her Rover 3500 for an appointment with her seamstress. Her daughter Princess Stephanie accompanied her for the short journey back to the palace, along the same stretch of road that Francie Stevens had driven John Robie in *To Catch a Thief.* On approaching a hairpin bend, Kelly lost control of the car and it careered over the cliff-edge and down a hundred-foot drop, landing on its roof.

Stephanie was badly injured but was able to summon help. Kelly suffered a collapsed lung, broken collar-bone and fractured leg; she was rushed to hospital in a coma and taken into intensive care but, though initial reports of her condition were optimistic, her injuries proved too severe. The following day, her husband and children were permitted to say their goodbyes and her life-support machine was switched off. The opinion of the doctors was that she had suffered a stroke while driving.

Grace Patricia Kelly—Her Serene Highness, Princess Grace of Monaco—was 52 years old.

MURDER CALLING
IN 3D!
THE MOST FAMOUS
ALFRED HITCHCOCK
MOVIE OF ALL TIME!
DIAL M FOR MURDER
ALFRED HITCHCOCK'S "DIAL M FOR MURDER"
RAY MILLAND · GRACE KELLY · ROBERT CUMMINGS
WITH JOHN WILLIAMS · WRITTEN BY FREDERICK KNOTT
MUSIC COMPOSED AND CONDUCTED BY DIMITRI TIOMKIN
DIRECTED BY ALFRED HITCHCOCK
WARNER BROS. PRESENT
ALFRED HITCHCOCK'S
"dial M for Murder"
RAY MILLAND · GRACE KELLY · ROBERT CUMMINGS
WARNERCOLOR
7
54 244

HITCHCOCK'S BLONDE: Filmography

Dial M for Murder

Cast

Ray Milland....................................Tony Wendice
Grace Kelly.......................Margot Mary Wendice
Robert Cummings.........................Mark Halliday
John Williams..............Chief Inspector Hubbard
Anthony Dawson........Charles Alexander Swann
Leo Britt..The storyteller
Patrick Allen............................Detective Pearson
George Leigh..........................Detective Williams
George Alderson............................First detective
Robin Hughes..............................Police Sergeant
Richard Bender/Robert Garvin/Ben Pollock
....Banquet members
Sanders Clark/Guy Doleman/Thayer Roberts
....Detectives
Jack Cunningham......................................Bobby
Robert Dobson.....................Police photographer
Bess Flowers....................Woman departing ship
Sam Harris...........................Man in phone booth
Harold Miller..............Men's club party member
Martin Milner....Policeman outside Wendice flat
Forbes Murray.................Judge at Margot's trial
with Michael Hadlow

Credits

Directed by................................Alfred Hitchcock
Screenplay...................................Frederick Knott
Based on his play
Producer....................................Alfred Hitchcock
Original Music...........................Dimitri Tiomkin
Director of Photography.................Robert Burks
Editor..Rudi Fehr
Art Director.................................Edward Carrere
Set Decorator..................George James Hopkins
Make Up Artists........Gordon Bau/Otis Malcolm
Hairdresser..............................Gertrude Wheeler
Assistant Director................................Mel Dellar
Second Assistant Director..........C Carter Gibson
Props..Herbert Plews
Sound..........Oliver S Garretson/Stanley Martin/
Robert G Wayne
Camera Assistants.................Eddie Leon Albert/
William John Ranaldi
Camera Operator......................Wesley Anderson
Still Photographer.................................Pat Clark
Gaffer..Vic Johnson
Grip..Louis Mashmeyer
Camera Technician....................Leonard J South
Best Boy......................................Claude Swanner
Wardrobe.................Moss Mabry/Jack Delaney/
Lillian House
Script Supervisor............................Rita Michaels

Rear Window

Cast

James Stewart..........................L B 'Jeff' Jefferies
Grace Kelly............................Lisa Carol Fremont
Wendell Corey.................Det Lt Thomas J Doyle
Thelma Ritter..Stella
Raymond Burr..............................Lars Thorwald
Judith Evelyn..........................Miss Lonelyhearts
Ross Bagdasarian...............................Songwriter
Georgine Darcy..................................Miss Torso
Sara Berner............Wife living above Thorwalds
Frank Cady......Husband living above Thorwalds
Jesslyn Fax..............Neighbour with hearing aid
Rand Harper...............................Newlywed man
Irene Winston......................Mrs Anna Thorwald
Havis Davenport.....................Newlywed woman
Marla English/Kathryn Grandstaff
...................................Girls at songwriter's party
Alan Lee..............................Newlyweds' landlord
Anthony Warde/Fred Graham/Edwin Parker/
Don Dunning......................................Detectives
Benny Bartlett/Dick Simmons
....Men with Miss Torso
Harry Landers..........Man with Miss Lonelyheart
Iphigenie Castiglioni................Woman with bird
Ralph Smiley........................Carl, waiter from 21
Len Hendry/Mike Mahoney................Policemen
Jerry Antes.....................Dancer with Miss Torso
Barbara Bailey...Choreographer with Miss Torso
Sue Casey/Jonni Paris.......................Sunbathers
Bess Flowers...................Party guest with poodle
Art Gilmore...............................Radio announcer
Jack Stoney...Ice man
with Nick Borgani, James Cornell

Credits

Directed by...............................Alfred Hitchcock
Screenplay...........................John Michael Hayes
From the short story 'It Had to Be Murder'
by Cornell Woolrich
Producer...................................Alfred Hitchcock
Original Music.............................Franz Waxman
Director of Photography.................Robert Burks
Editor.......................................George Tomasini
Art Directors..........Joseph MacMillan Johnson/
Hal Pereira
Set Decorators................Sam Comer/Ray Moyer
Make Up Supervisor..................Wally Westmore
Production Manager.......................C O Erickson
Assistant Director....................Herbert Coleman
Illustrator.....................................Dorothea Holt
Construction Coordinator...........Gene Lauritzen
Sound Recordists.....John Cope/Harry Lindgren
Sound Recording Mixer................Loren L Ryder
Special Photographic Effects........John P Fulton
Digital Restoration Producer.....Scott Dougherty
Digital Restoration Supervisor.........Jerry Pooler
Special Visual Effects....................Irmin Roberts
Digital Restoration Coordinator....Tiffany Smith
Stunt Detectives.......Fred Graham/Eddie Parker
Stunts..Ted Mapes
Camera Operator.........................William Schurr
Assistant Camera.......................Leonard J South
Costumes...Edith Head
Colourist.......................................Steve Johnson
Technicolor Consultant.............Richard Mueller
Technical Advisor.............................Bob Landry

JAMES STEWART
ALFRED HITCHCOCK'S
REAR WINDOW
Color by
TECHNICOLOR
GRACE KELLY · WENDELL COREY · THELMA RITTER
RAYMOND BURR
ALFRED HITCHCOCK
JOHN MICHAEL HAYES
PARAMOUNT
JAMES STEWART
ALFRED HITCHCOCK'S
REAR WINDOW
GRACE KELLY
WENDELL COREY
THELMA RITTER
RAYMOND BURR
Color by
TECHNICOLOR
ALFRED HITCHCOCK
JOHN MICHAEL HAYES
6
54-337

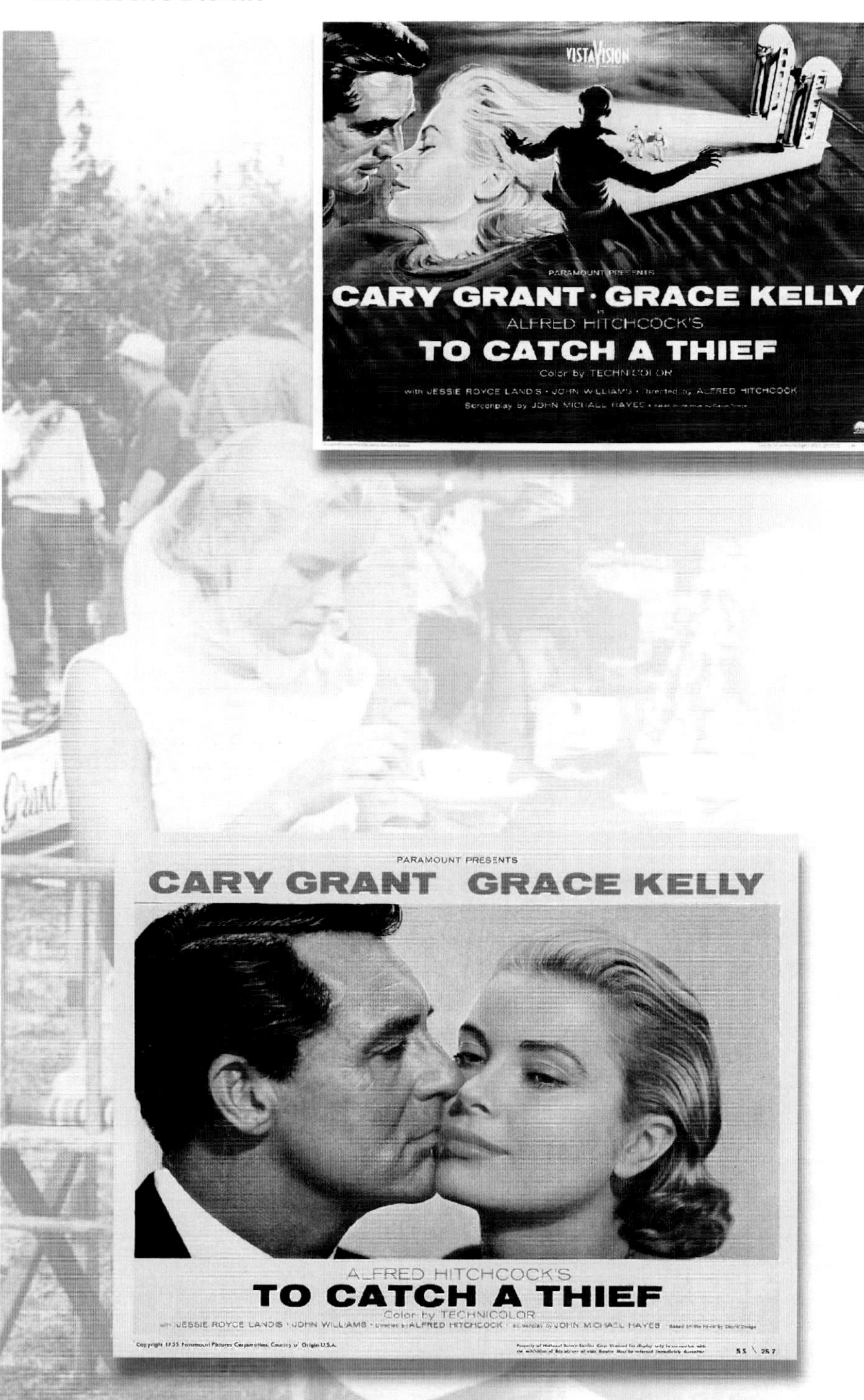
VISTAVISION
PARAMOUNT PRESENTS
CARY GRANT · GRACE KELLY
ALFRED HITCHCOCK'S
TO CATCH A THIEF
Color by TECHNICOLOR
with JESSIE ROYCE LANDIS · JOHN WILLIAMS · Directed by ALFRED HITCHCOCK
Screenplay by JOHN MICHAEL HAYES
PARAMOUNT PRESENTS
CARY GRANT GRACE KELLY
ALFRED HITCHCOCK'S
TO CATCH A THIEF
Color by TECHNICOLOR
with JESSIE ROYCE LANDIS · JOHN WILLIAMS · Directed by ALFRED HITCHCOCK · Screenplay by JOHN MICHAEL HAYES
55 \ 257

To Catch a Thief

Cast

Cary Grant..John Robie
Grace Kelly.................................Frances Stevens
Jessie Royce Landis.......................Jessie Stevens
John Williams................................H H Hughson
Charles Vanel...Bertani
Brigitte Auber..........................Danielle Foussard
Jean Martinelli.....................................Foussard
Georgette Anys....................................Germaine
George Adrian/Guy De Vestel/Bela Kovacs/
Alberto Morin.....................................Detectives
John Alderson/Don Megowan
...................................Detectives at costume ball
René Blancard....................................Insp Lepic
Eugene Borden..............................French waiter
Nina Borget/Jeanne Lafayette/Loulette Sablon
....French women
Margaret Brewster................Cold-cream woman
Lewis Charles...............Man with milk in kitchen
Frank Chelland/Otto F Schulze.................Chefs
William 'Wee Willie' Davis....Big man in kitchen
Dominique Davray.............................Antoinette
Bess Flowers..................Woman at costume ball
Russell Gaige......................................Mr Sanford
Steven Geray..Desk clerk
Michael Hadlow/Leonard Penn
....Monaco policemen
Jean Hébey...................Police Inspector Mercier
Gladys Holland...............Elegant French woman
Eddie Le Baron/Barry Norton..........French men
Roland Lesaffre..Claude
Edward Manouk.............................Kitchen help
Louis Mercier/George Nardelli/George Paris/
Manuel París/Albert Pollet..................Croupiers
Paul Newlan.................................Vegetable man
Adele St Mauer.....Woman with birdcage on bus
Marie Stoddard...............................Mrs Sanford
Aimee Torriani.......................Woman in kitchen
Philip Van Zandt.........................Jewellery clerk
with Martha Bamattre, Donald Lawton,
Cosmo Sardo

Credits

Directed by................................Alfred Hitchcock
Screenplay...........................John Michael Hayes
From the novel by David Dodge
Producer...................................Alfred Hitchcock
Original Music..................................Lyn Murray
Director of Photography.................Robert Burks
Editor.......................................George Tomasini
Art Directors..........Joseph MacMillan Johnson/
Hal Pereira
Set Decorators...........Sam Comer/Arthur Krams
Make Up Supervisor..................Wally Westmore
Make Up Artists.........Bud Bashaw Jr/Harry Ray
Production Manager.......................C O Erickson
Assistant Production Managers
.........................William Davidson/C O Erickson
Assistant Director.....................Daniel McCauley
Second Unit Director...............Herbert Coleman
Illustrator.....................................Dorothea Holt
Sound Recordists.........John Cope/Harold Lewis
Sound Editor...................................Bill Wistrom
Special Photographic Effects.........John P Fulton
Process Photography..................Farciot Edouart
Photographer: Second Unit..........Wallace Kelley
Still Photographer................................Bill Avery
Assistant Camera........George Gall/James Grant
Gaffer..Vic Jones
Second Assistant Camera................Gene Liggett
Camera Operators......................William Schurr/
Leonard J South
Key Grip...................................Darrell Turnmire
Wardrobe..................Ed Fitzharris/Grace Harris
Dialogue Coach............................Elsie Foulstone
Technicolor Consultant.............Richard Mueller
Script Supervisors....................Sylvette Baudrot/
Claire Behnke
Technical Advisor....................Vincent McEveety

HITCHCOCK'S BLONDE:

Bibliography

Anger, Kenneth
Hollywood Babylon II
Arrow Books, London 1986

Auiler, Dan
Hitchcock's Notebooks. An Authorised and Illustrated Look Inside the Creative Mind of Alfred Hitchcock
Avon Books, New York 1999

Balcon, Michael
Michael Balcon Presents.. A Lifetime of Films
Hutchinson & Co., London 1969

Belton, John (ed)
Alfred Hitchcock's Rear Window
Cambridge Film Handbooks. Cambridge, UK 2000

Bruck, Connie
When Hollywood Had a King
Random House, New York 2003

Cassini, Oleg
In My Own Fashion
Simon & Schuster, New York 1987

Chandler, Charlotte
It's Only a Movie. Alfred Hitchcock: A Personal Biography
Simon and Schuster, London 2005

DeRosa, Steven
Writing with Hitchcock; The Collaboration of Alfred Hitchcock and John Michael Hayes
Faber & Faber, London 2001

Englund, Steven
Princess Grace
Orbis Publishing, London 1984

Fallaci, Oriana
The Egotists: 16 Surprising Interviews
Henry Regnery Company, London 1963

Finler, Joel W
Alfred Hitchcock: The Hollywood Years
B T Batsford, London 1992

Fraser-Cavassoni, Natasha
Sam Spiegel: The Biography of a Hollywood Legend
Little, Brown Books, London 2003

Freeman, David
The Last Days of Alfred Hitchcock
The Overlook Press, New York 1999

Gardner, Ava
Ava: My Story
Bantam Books, New York 1992

Hawkins, Peter
Prince Rainier of Monaco: His Authorised and Exclusive Story
William Kimber, London 1966

Lacey, Robert
Grace
G P Puttnam's Sons, New York 1994
Leigh, Janet/Christopher Nickens
Behind the Scenes of Psycho
Pavilion Books Ltd, London 1995
Leigh, Wendy
True Grace
Thomas Dunne Books, New York 2007
McGilligan, Patrick
Alfred Hitchcock: A Life in Darkness and Light
HarpersCollins Publishers Inc., New York 2003
Moral, Tony Lee
Hitchcock and the Making of Marnie
Manchester University Press, Manchester 2002
Porter, Darwin
Brando Unzipped
Blood Moon Books Ltd, Staten Island, New York 2005
Quinn, Judith Balaban
Grace Kelly Princess of Monaco and Six Intimate Friends
George Weidenfeld & Nicolson, London 1989
Rebello, Stephen
Alfred Hitchcock and the Making of Psycho
Marion Boyars Publishers Ltd., London 1992
Spada, James
Grace: The Secret Lives of a Princess
Guild Publishing, London 1987
Spoto, Donald
The Dark Side of Genius: The Life of Alfred Hitchcock
Plexus, London 1988
Taylor, John Russell
Hitch: The Authorised Biography of Alfred Hitchcock
Faber and Faber Ltd., London 1978.
Thomas, Bob
Golden Boy: The Untold Story of William Holden
St Martin's Press, New York 1983
Truffaut, François
Hitchcock
Simon & Schuster Paperbacks, New York 1984
Walker, Alexander
It's Only a Movie, Ingrid
Headline, London 1989
Wayne, Jane Ellen
Grace Kelly's Men
St Martin's Press, New York 1991
Ava's Men
Robson Books, London 1990

Newspapers, Magazines and Periodicals:

American Weekly/Chicago Sun-Times/Cinefantasique/Cosmopolitan/Confidential/ Daily Express/Daily Sketch/Films and Filming/Hello/Hollywood Reporter/Ladies Home Journal/Le Monde/Life/Look/Los Angeles Daily News/Los Angeles Mirror-News/Los Angeles Times/McCalls/Monthly Film Bulletin/New York Journal American/New York Post/New York Times/Newsweek/Photoplay/Picturegoer/Playboy/Publishers Weekly/ Redbook/Saturday Evening Post/Sight and Sound/Star/Sunday Express/Time/Variety

Other Sources:

American Film Institute/British Film Library/BBC Written Archive/www.imdbpro.com/ www.hitchcockwiki.com